CONJURING THE REAL

CONJURING THE REAL

The Role of Architecture in Eighteenth-
and Nineteenth-Century Fiction

Edited by Rumiko Handa and James Potter

Foreword by Iain Borden

UNIVERSITY OF NEBRASKA PRESS, LINCOLN AND LONDON

© 2011 by the Board of Regents
of the University of Nebraska

"Performing History on the
Victorian Stage" was originally
published as part of chapter 4 in
Richard W. Schoch's *Shakespeare's
Victorian Stage: Performing
History in the Theatre of Charles
Kean* (Cambridge: Cambridge
University Press, 1998), 114–39.

All rights reserved
Manufactured in the United
States of America

Publication of this volume was
assisted by grants from the
University of Nebraska–Lincoln
College of Architecture and
the University of Nebraska–
Lincoln Research Council.

Library of Congress
Cataloging-in-Publication Data
Conjuring the real: the role of
architecture in eighteenth- and
nineteenth-century fiction / edited
by Rumiko Handa and James Potter;
foreword by Iain Borden.
p. cm.   Includes bibliographical
references. ISBN 978-0-8032-1743-0
(paperback: alkaline paper)
1. Symbolism in architecture.
2. Architecture in literature.
3. Architecture in art. I. Handa,
Rumiko, 1955– II. Potter,
James J. III. Borden, Iain.
NA2500.C5955 2011
700'.457—dc22   2011001200

Set in Ehrhardt and display in
Fell by Bob Reitz. The Fell Types
are digitally reproduced by Igino
Marini. www.iginomarini.com.
Designed by Nathan Putens.

Contents

List of Illustrations   *vi*

Foreword
IAIN BORDEN   *ix*

Introduction
RUMIKO HANDA   *1*

1 "All That Life Can Afford"? Perspectives on the Screening of Historic Literary London
   IAN CHRISTIE   *21*

2 Architecture in Historical Fiction: A Historical and Comparative Study
   MICHAEL ALEXANDER   *67*

3 Norman Abbey as Romantic Mise-en-Scène: St. Georges de Boscherville in Historical Representation
   STEPHEN BANN   *87*

4 Performing History on the Victorian Stage
   RICHARD SCHOCH   *119*

5 Shops and Subjects
   ANDREW BALLANTYNE   *153*

6 Pride and Prejudice: Establishing Historical Connections among the Arts
   JOSH SILVERS AND TOBY D. OLSEN   *191*

Contributors   *215*

Illustrations

1. The dining hall, Hogwarts School of Witchcraft and Wizardry 3
2. Moria, the land of the Dwarves 4
3. Lothlórien, the land of the Elves 4
4. Inigo Jones's Plan of Stonehenge 10
5. John Britton's "Conisbrough Castle" 13
6. Church House as Steerforth's house in *David Copperfield* 33
7. Junge's set design for *A Matter of Life and Death* 42
8. Korda's set design for *Things to Come* 44
9. Bryan's set design for the climax of *Oliver Twist* 47
10. Box's set design for Westminster Hall in *A Man for All Seasons* 52
11. Doré's "Ludgate Hill: A Block in the Street" 54
12. Box's set design for *Oliver!* 55
13. Langlois' "Abbaye de St. Georges de Boscherville" 90

14 Leprince's "Église de l'abbaye de St. Georges de Boscherville" *94*

15 Fragonard's "Intérieur de l'église de l'abbaye de St. Georges de Boscherville" *96*

16 Deville's "Façade de l'église" *100*

17 Deville's "Salle capitulaire" *104*

18 Leloir's "Saint Georges de Boscherville" *107*

19 Maillard's "Spécimen de l'architecture Saxonne et de l'architecture Normande" *110*

20 Historical Interlude from Kean's production of *Henry V* *141*

21 Bulla, "Nevsky Prospekt" *160*

22 Bulla, "Religious procession on Nevsky Prospekt" *162*

23 Cattermole, "The Shop," in Dickens's *The Old Curiosity Shop* *166*

24 Cattermole, "Little Nell Asleep," in Dickens's *The Old Curiosity Shop* *169*

25 The corner of Rue de la Michodière and Rue Neuve-Saint-Augustin *176*

26 Vallotton, "Le bon marché" *178*

27 Belton House as Rosings in
    Pride and Prejudice (1995) *196*

28 Belton House's interior in
    Pride and Prejudice (1995) *197*

29 Burghley House as Rosings in *Pride
    and Prejudice* (2005) *198*

30 Burghley House's interior in
    Pride and Prejudice (2005) *199*

31 Lyme Park as Pemberley in
    Pride and Prejudice (1995) *203*

32 Sudbury Hall's interior as Pemberley
    in *Pride and Prejudice* (1995) *206*

33 Chatsworth House as Pemberley in
    Pride and Prejudice (2005) *209*

Foreword

Architecture is often thought of as the product of the work of architects and other professionals who work with built environments. Architects, it is thought, make architecture, and therefore they are considered the appropriate focus for any study of the subject. Who architects are, and what they do, becomes the definition of "architecture." Similarly, as architects are primarily the designers of buildings and other urban projects, they and these material objects are conflated into the term "architecture" — and architecture thus becomes "architects and the buildings they design."

With some notable exceptions, it is therefore this broad understanding of architecture that has come to dominate architectural and urban history for the last two hundred or so years. In particular, architectural historians and other interested parties have turned their attention to well-known individuals and buildings, writing monographs of the most influential architects and detailed studies of grand projects and major constructions. Even when they have considered less well-known architects and buildings, the same underlying logic often still holds.

As a result of this, the history of architecture becomes the history of the *production* of architecture, an understanding of architecture that, while undoubtedly erudite, sophisticated, and suggestive, also has a central weakness: it is a history of architecture which stops at the moment when the building has been built. In other words, the whole history of architecture as a living entity — as something that has an afterlife, long after the construction crews have left and the architects have moved on to other projects — is largely absent.

However, for the past decade or so, a new strand of architectural history has been emerging, one that refutes such a position and sees architecture as a dynamic entity that continues to have a life and importance long after the material object has been constructed. In particular, this new kind of architectural history sees the building as having a social, political, cultural, and environmental relevance that stretches far beyond the relatively short time of the building's original conception and construction, and extends into decades or even centuries of prolonged existence. In addition, this new history sees that architecture has its ultimate meanings not in the world of the architect or of other built-environment professions, but in the ways in which the public (or publics) experiences, perceives, and understands it. In short, it is not the architect or somehow the building itself that determines meaning, but the audience or users of the building.

This is where things get really interesting. For if the meaning of architecture is now displaced in part away from the realm of the architect, client, and construction company, away from the material substance of bricks, mortar, concrete, glass, and timber, and instead is moved into the realm of experiencing subjects and what they might think of a building, then how can an architectural history begin to recover that world of perceptions? What are the thoughts, ideas, associations, pleasures, events, uses, and misuses of architecture that are constantly being recreated by those who encounter architecture?

It is into this rich yet somewhat murky realm that *Conjuring the Real* treads. Moreover, it does so in a manner that, I think, offers some highly insightful suggestions as to how this realm might be illuminated, charted, and explored. First, it considers the question of how architecture is represented in ways that are often quite separate from the world of professional design and construction. How are buildings and architects depicted in works of art, in film, in novels? What forms do they take, and how are they described? Such enquiries help us realize that architecture is not always a matter of plan, section, and elevation, but also an affair of impression, psychology, reaction, smell, listening, emotion, and bodily movement. Second, the essays here often explore the minds of the creators of these other — or perhaps it would be better to say "supplementary" — architectures. In showing how architecture is represented in painting, movies, and novels, for example, the question is necessarily raised as to who might also enter the creative process of imagining what architecture is and might be. The architect here is displaced from being the sole owner or controller of architectural meaning and is joined by other, equally imaginative instigators of architectural resonance and implication. Third, and most radically of all, the book also then raises the question — sometimes implicitly and sometimes explicitly — of what the reader or viewer of these supplementary architectures might think of these creations. Who else encounters architecture, how do they do this, and what is their understanding of it?

This is a profound and highly significant redefinition of architecture, or rather of the process by which architecture is continually being redefined and reproduced. For, as *Conjuring the Real* discloses, architecture, when considered in the manner demonstrated in these essays, is no longer in one place and is no longer confined to any single object. Nor is it confined to the mind of any single person or group of persons. Nor is it confined to the geography of a particular site, city, or country, or restricted to a tight period of design and construction. Instead, architecture is dispersed, displaced, and decentered from the architect and building and is instead provisionally recomposed and reconstructed every time someone — whoever, wherever, and whenever that person might be — sees, reads, thinks, listens to, imagines, or otherwise encounters architecture.

This process of reconstruction is necessarily propositional — one that is almost magical in its properties. I say "magical" because it contains precisely those elements of partial viewing and partial understanding, of anticipation, resolution, and delight, that all come together through a particular kind of performance — that is, in the magician's conjuring of the act of magic. Here, a very specific kind of reality is brought into existence, not just by the magician, but through a deliberate series of moments, the audience, and also the way that the audience perceives what is unfolding before them. Except here, in the (re)creation of architecture, of course, the magician can be the architect, or the filmmaker/artist/writer, or the audience/reader — and most usually, in architecture, it is a combination of several or all of these. *Conjuring the Real* provides illuminating insight on how this process occurs in architecture. It discloses architecture as a real thing, certainly, but the reality in which it resides is never fixed or stable; instead, it is always being brought into being by a wondrous, uncertain, and provisional act.

IAIN BORDEN

Conjuring the Real

Introduction

RUMIKO HANDA

In recent years we have seen a number of blockbuster films that use historically significant buildings as filming locations. Buildings that can fill the large screen with their concrete substance are key ingredients when it comes to bringing a former era or fictional world closer to contemporary viewers.

Chatsworth House appears in the 2005 film *Pride and Prejudice* as Pemberley, the fictional residence of Mr. Darcy in Derbyshire. The film's use of this stately residence is hardly surprising: Jane Austen (1775–1817) is thought to have drawn on it as the model for Pemberley after she visited the building in 1811, just two years before publication of the book.[1]

Chatsworth — whose history began in the mid-sixteenth century when Sir William Cavendish (1508–57) and his third wife, Beth of Hardwick, purchased the property — had become one of the most important specimens of country house architecture and landscape. Among its notable designers were William Talman at the end of the seventeenth century and James Paine and Capability Brown in the mid-eighteenth century. William Cavendish (1748–1811), fifth Duke of Devonshire, and his wife Georgiana (1757–1806) lived mainly in London, but on their occasional visits the house was filled with friends and relations, and otherwise the house was open to the public with a monthly dinner for any visitors. According to John Summerson, Chatsworth's south façade (1696) in particular marked the inauguration of baroque style in English private houses, with its rusticated bottom floor, the giant orders on the upper two stories, and the heavy entablature and balustrade with no pediment.[2] The film's ending scene placed this façade and the Canal Pond (1702) in a perspective view with Keira Knightley's Elizabeth Bennet and Matthew Macfadyen's Mr. Darcy in the foreground. Such visually captivating scenes successfully engaged the contemporary audience in imagining the world of Georgian England as Austen may have seen it.

Oxford University and other historical buildings were the locations for Hogwarts School of Witchcraft and Wizardry in the films based on the Harry Potter series. The filmmakers created a larger-than-life replica of the Christ Church College's great hall of the sixteenth century, whose hammerbeam roof structure radiates a sense of awe against the magical starry sky (see fig. 1). Other scenes at Hogwarts were shot at Duke Humfrey's Library, the oldest section of Bodleian Library, which dates as far back as the 1480s and vividly conveys to viewers the young wizards' daunting quest as the actors move through the dark interior finished with oak panels and shelves and full of leather-bound manuscripts and printed books.

Even when no specific building is used, some film sets refer to a particular architectural style. In these cases the designers often exaggerate certain formal attributes of the style, relying on its expressive qualities to exude certain meanings and nuances. In the Lord of the Rings series some interior scenes of Moria reflect the heavy masonry construction and the pointed arches of Gothic style (see fig. 2), creating the sense of aged civilization in the Dwarves' dwelling, while much of Lothlórien is based on the slender organic curves of the art nouveau style, conferring a lofty and serene character to the Elves' land (see fig. 3).

Fig. 1. The dining hall at Hogwarts School of Witchcraft and Wizardry, *Harry Potter and the Sorcerer's Stone*, directed by Chris Columbus (2001).

In the examples just mentioned, buildings give an immediate presence to the historical or fictional world, which otherwise is unknown or unfamiliar to the audience. The portrayal of a building's concrete and specific substance makes the world come alive, although the building itself is a mere segment of the world that it represents. This book will trace the genealogy of this representational role of architecture, going back through the history of film and then further in literature, art, and theater, and identify its pedigree in the nineteenth century, where authors, artists, and stage managers used thorough depictions of buildings to effectively feed the audience's historical imagination.

In chapter 1, "'All That Life Can Afford'? Perspectives on the Screening of Historic Literary London," Ian Christie traces the history of literary adaptation in British films, covering the period from 1896 (*2 a.m., or the Husband's Return*) to 2005 (*Oliver Twist*). Stigmatized as "heritage cinema," films that use period costumes and settings are best known through the work of Merchant and Ivory and have been

Fig. 2. Moria, the land of the Dwarves, *The Lord of the Rings: The Fellowship of the Ring*, directed by Peter Jackson (2001).

Fig. 3. Lothlórien, the land of the Elves, *The Lord of the Rings: The Fellowship of the Ring*, directed by Peter Jackson (2001).

seen as lacking truly cinematic qualities or a sense of relevance to the time of their production, despite the films' international reputation. Christie argues that the antiliterary and antitheatrical prejudices and misunderstandings of cinema criticism have long prevented it from acknowledging the effects of spatial and architectural imagination in British films, which in fact have had an important role in creating the contemporary image of Britain and of London for the world. Christie draws attention to several production designers since the end of the 1920s. Alfred Junge and Vincent Korda brought Continental influence to British cinema in the 1920 and 1930s. During the 1940s and 1950s,

John Bryan, who had worked for Korda, and Carmen Dillon, who had trained as an architect, left lasting influences in art direction. Together with their pupil John Box, these pioneer British designers created an "English school" of design for the screen, which in turn supported the flowering of literary adaptation as British cinema's distinctive genre.

Films are not the only medium in which buildings provide an imaginary creation with a sense of actual existence. Going back a little further in history, we also find nineteenth-century literary authors, theater producers, and painters incorporating depictions of buildings into their works in order to bring the (imaginary) past back to the present.

HISTORICAL IMAGINATION

In the Western world, the period from the mid-eighteenth to the nineteenth century widely is acknowledged for its historical consciousness. Modern historiography was born, novels set in a specific historical time period were written, revivals of Shakespearean historical plays were produced, and historical paintings were made. Buildings and architects played a part in this widespread cultural phenomenon. Historical buildings became tourist destinations and were frequented by antiquarians, literary authors, and painters, both amateur and professional. Ruinous ones were especially popular because their missing roofs and decayed stones, as well as the growing mosses and ivies on them, clearly indicated the passage of time. Medieval buildings, which had been neglected or detested by eyes trained in classicism, began to bear new national significance. Architectural draftsmen were hired by publishers to travel to these buildings and publish their reports in books and magazines. Architects designed artificial ruins or buildings in past styles.

What is interesting about the nineteenth-century historical consciousness is that serious studies of historical events and fictional representations of the past were not necessarily mutually exclusive. Instead, historical research was motivated by a romantic longing for the past, and historical knowledge was incorporated into the imagined past.³

Writing *Ivanhoe*, a novel set in the context of the animosity between the Saxons and Normans during Richard I's reign (1189–99), Sir Walter Scott drew extensively on scholarly works as well as literary sources.⁴ He referred to several historiographical studies: Robert Henry, *The History of Great Britain*; Sharon Turner, *The History of the Anglo-Saxons from the Earliest Period to the Norman Conquest*; Joseph Strutt, *Sports and Pastimes of the People of England*; and David Hume, *The History of England*. His literary references included Geoffrey Chaucer's *Canterbury Tales*; Shakespeare's *King John* and *A Merchant of Venice*; and Joseph Ritson's *Robin Hood: A Collection of All the Ancient Poems, Songs, and Ballads*.

Charles Kean (1811–68), a leading actor of the mid-Victorian era and the successful manager of the Princess's Theatre in London between 1850–59, had a carefully premeditated portrait made that depicted him as a serious historian, as Richard Schoch has pointed out in his earlier study.⁵ Richard II's portrait by the king's contemporary was only one of many historical sources Kean used in preparing for his title role in the Shakespearean production.

Paul Delaroche, an important French historical painter, made use of both primary and secondary sources. As Stephen Bann has discussed, *Princes in the Tower*, one of Delaroche's most important paintings on famous subjects from English history, drew a scene from Shakespeare's history play *Richard III*.⁶ Having traveled to London, he had a maquette constructed for the painting, reportedly had costumes and furnishings made there in the late Gothic style, and possibly met those who were working on historical paintings, including James Northcote, who had produced a painting of the same scene. Delaroche also was familiar with the antiquarian collections of Alexandre du Summerand in Paris or of antiquarians in London, which allowed him to depict several objects—the door lock, the golden medallions, and the illuminated book—with historical accuracy. For Delaroche, however, the historical painting not only allowed antiquarian investigation but also told a narrative story, as Stephen Bann has demonstrated. It is only in relation to the latter role of the historical painting that we understand the significance of Delaroche's composition and a number of details. In *Princes in the Tower*, there is a door to the left of the tableau, and the light outside the room permeates through underneath. The shadows among the light as well as the small dog facing the door indicate the person(s) just outside the door and the impending murder of the princes. The Tudor rose carved in the bedstead, which at first glance seems anachronistic, forecasts the dynastic changes, and the golden medallions add religious implications to the scene.

In the field of architectural design, the mixture of scientific studies of historical buildings and romantic idealization of long-gone societies is evident in the work of Augustus Wilby Northmore Pugin (1812–52), who was well versed in medieval architecture. His father, Auguste Charles (1768/9–1832), worked as an architectural draftsman and contributed drawings to *Architectural Antiquities of Great Britain*, by John Britton (1807–27). The father's own publication, the two-volume *Specimens of Gothic Architecture* (1821 and 1823) provided builders and architects with measured drawings of Gothic details, taking advantage of the sharper and more distinct lines made possible by steel plate engravings. Augustus Pugin inherited his father's passion and engaged himself in sketches and observations of medieval buildings. When he published his most famous book in 1836, *Contrasts, or, A Parallel between the Noble Edifices of the Fourteenth and Fifteenth Centuries, and Similar Buildings of the Present Day; Shewing the Present Decay of Taste: Accompanied by Appropriate Text*, his thesis was not only about physical architecture but also about spiritual life. For Pugin, criticism of contemporary secular society in comparison to the idealism of the medieval society went hand in hand with accurate measurements of buildings.

FICTIONAL PAST AND IDEOLOGY

Interest in the past was not confined to the concrete facts but included how the past activated an historical imagination guided by the author's ideology. We might say that historical imagination was a search for the ideal state of man that was imagined as having taken place in the past. Just as Pugin's fictional past was guided by his ecclesiastical ideology, Sir Walter Scott built his fictional past around the enmity between Saxons and Normans. Scott's protagonist, Wilfrid of Ivanhoe, belongs to one of the remaining Saxon noble families but is out of his father's favor because he courts the Lady Rowena, a Norman, and because of his allegiance to King Richard I, a Plantagenet. A contemporary event had led Scott to consider the Saxon–Norman relationship of the twelfth century: in 1805, a little more than a decade earlier than Scott's writing (1819), the British Navy, led by Lord Admiral Horatio Nelson, defeated Napoleon's forces in the Battle of Trafalgar, bringing British nationalist spirit to its height.

In the second chapter, "Architecture in Historical Fiction: A Historical and Comparative Study," Michael Alexander identifies Scott as the author who established the genre of historical novels. Alexander uses a definition of the historical novel as "an imaginative story set in the past; a fiction that nevertheless offers a form of historical truth" for the purpose of locating the nineteenth-century historical novels in relation to what they are not: the historical narratives of David Hume (*History of England*) and Edward Gibbon (*Rise and Fall of Roman Empire*) whose works supplied the information about and the point of view on the past; or the Gothic fantasy of Horace Walpole (*Castle of Otranto*, 1764), which does not purport to inform the reader of the past. In order to qualify as a historical novel, the past depicted needs to be sufficiently distant from the author: Alexander applies the "sixty-year rule" from the birth of the author, drawing the specific number also from Scott, whose *Waverley*, a historical novel written in 1805, is set at the time of the Jacobite rising of 1745, and carries the subtitle, *'Tis Sixty Years Since*. To Alexander, the genre of historical novels thus defined began with Scott and lasted until about fifty years after his death, and includes works of American (James Fenimore Cooper), English (William Makepeace Thackeray), and European (Leo Tolstoy) authors, with some occasional contemporary pieces such as Charles Frazier's *Cold Mountain*. Depictions of buildings vary in literary works, ranging from appearances merely as place names (many instances in Charles Dickens's works) to more detailed descriptions used to help visualize the setting, as we find in Scott's historical novels. Architecture sometimes sets up a certain mood or even carries a symbolic meaning relevant to the theme of the literary piece: in Scott's *Ivanhoe*, the Saxons live in wooden buildings while the Normans inhabit lofty masonry castles.

Benjamin Disraeli (1804–81) set his novel *Sybil, or the Two Nations* (1845) in the fictional Marney Abbey, which he modeled after Fountains Abbey. The ruins of the medieval architecture provide a tranquil setting for the encounter of two individuals who represent the "two nations": the rich and the poor.[7] Sybil, the daughter of Walter Gerald, a member of the Chartist movement, represents the terrible conditions of the working class. In contrast, Egremont, a younger brother of Lord Marney, takes advantage of the working class. The abbey appears in the story repeatedly, referring readers to the idealized past before the division of the society: the ideal for the future.[8]

EMPHASIS SHIFT: FROM OBJECT TO SUBJECT'S
ENGAGEMENT IN THE OBJECT

The characteristics of the eighteenth- and nineteenth-century engagement with the past, as compared with earlier interests in the past, often are explained by the notions of the sublime and the picturesque, terms as elusive as romanticism. A quick comparison of the two different responses to the same built object from the distant past may clarify the shift in the nature of appreciation that occurred in the middle of the eighteenth century. The built object is Stonehenge, prehistoric megaliths on Salisbury Plain, the site development of which we now know goes as far back as 8,000 BC.

When, in the early seventeenth century, King James I (reigned 1603–25) summoned the court architect, Inigo Jones (1573–1652), to the nearby Wilton House, Jones's task was to explain the monument as it belonged to its original culture, that is, to identify who built it, how, and why. Jones saw Stonehenge as a Roman temple and assigned

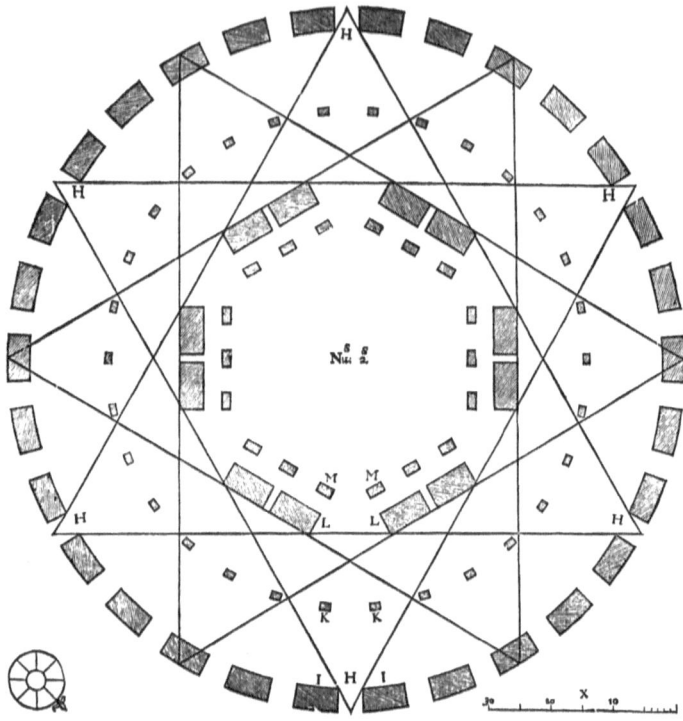

Fig. 4. Inigo Jones, Plan of Stonehenge, *The most notable antiquity of Great Britain, vulgarly called Stone-Heng on Salisbvry plain restored by Inigo Jones* ... (London, 1655).

to it the classical architectural principles of geometry and order (see fig. 4). This erroneous interpretation was a result of Jones's assumption that the monument had been a product of a great civilization, and to Jones, the Roman civilization was the greatest of all that had existed in Britain. Jones's appreciation of Stonehenge was based on his admiration of the culture that built the monument and of its original and perfect state — the complete circles, squares, and equilateral triangles that Jones "found" in the megaliths. Stonehenge was valued *despite* its ruinous state of decay and fragmentation, not *because* of it.

In comparison, for Edmund Burke (1729/30?–1797), an eighteenth-century Anglo-Irish statesman and author who attempted to define the relationships between human emotions and the nature of objects that triggered them, it was the loss of origin that made the megaliths venerable:

> The great stones, it has been supposed, were originally monuments of illustrious men, or the memorials of considerable actions; or they were landmarks for deciding the bounds of fixed property. In time, the memory of the persons or facts, which these stones were erected to perpetuate, wore away; but the reverence which custom, and probably certain periodical ceremonies, had preserved for those places, was not so soon obliterated. The monuments themselves then came to be venerated, and not the less, because the reason for venerating them was no longer known.[9]

More precisely, the newly arisen appreciation was not about the works themselves but about their effect on the viewer's experience. The central question was "Why and how does this object move me?" rather than "Who built this object and when?" The emphasis had shifted from the physical properties of the objects to the viewer's engagement with them.

Ian Ousby, a scholar of English literature, succinctly characterized this shift of interests in historical buildings by asking the question, "In the phrase 'Gothic ruin,' does emphasis fall on the adjective or the noun?: Do people want to admire a Gothic abbey as best they can, even though it survives only in a damaged state? Or do they seek to admire the ruin it has become, with all the accidental features time has added to it?"[10]

Earlier, the Gothic style of these buildings was puzzling and perhaps even offensive to eyes trained in the orderly proportions of classicism, and the style carried the strong connotation of Catholicism. In the eighteenth and nineteenth centuries, people were becoming more and more aware of and interested in their emotional reactions and more accepting of ruins as they found them. For example, Johann Wolfgang von Goethe (1749–1832) was puzzled at first by his emotional reactions to the unfinished Cologne Cathedral and later came to accept the aesthetic qualities that defied the norms and principles of the classicism in which he had been trained: "A significant ruin has a venerable quality, and we sense and actually see in it the conflict between a noble work of man, and time that with silent force spares nothing. Here, on the other hand, we are confronted with an edifice which is unfinished and prodigious, and precisely its incompleteness reminds us of man's insufficiency when he attempts the colossal."[11]

Literary authors often were drawn to architectural ruins to contemplate the past glory of the men who once kept the building alive and the inability of humankind to control the progression of time and nature, which eventually turn the building to the ruinous state. The incompleteness of the ruins worked as synecdoche, not only reminding the viewer of the perfect and pristine state of the original building, but also, and more important, demonstrating the infinity of time and the power of nature, which inevitably governs all mortals and their creations. The ruins, then, were ultimately a clear reminder of one's position in the universe.

The effects of the passage of time, for these authors, create not only a desire to reconstruct the past but also a sense of reverence and veneration. In Sir Walter Scott's historical novel *Kenilworth*, the narrator examines the ruins of the castle. His imagination first goes to the merry entertainments for Queen Elizabeth I and Robert Dudley, but from there, he quickly turns to contemplate the transitory nature of human existence:

> We cannot but add, that of this lordly palace, where princes feasted and heroes fought, now in the bloody earnest of storm and siege, and now in the games of chivalry, where beauty dealt the prize which valour won, all is now desolate. The bed of the lake is but a rushy swamp; and the massive ruins of the castle only serve to show what their splendour once was, and to impress on the musing visitor the transitory value of human possessions, and the happiness of those who enjoy a humble lot in virtuous contentment.[12]

The emphasis on ruins' ability to capture the imagination of viewers also can be seen in the drawings of ruins that were produced in the

Fig. 5. John Britton, "Conisbrough Castle," *The Architectural Antiquities of Great Britain* (London: M. A. Nattali, 1835).

same time period. Most often, as John Britton's drawing of Conisbrough Castle (see fig. 5) shows, such pictures include contemporary visitors in the foreground, positioned some distance away from the ruins themselves. These viewers are usually leisurely observers occupying themselves in no particular activities, sitting on the ground or standing in a reposing position. The viewers in front of the picture are then drawn to associate themselves with the visitors within, relating themselves to the free, imaginative activities in which the latter must be engaged.

SEEING THE HISTORY

Textual and visual depictions of historical buildings helped create the sense of a particular time period. The public's newfound desire for the visualization of history is evident in many publications that depicted historical buildings and other topics. John Boydell's and Robert Bowyer's ideas to illustrate Shakespeare's oeuvre and David Hume's *History of Great Britain* materialized, respectively, as the Shakespeare Gallery and the History Gallery in London's Pall Mall during the last decades of the eighteenth century. Engravings made from the paintings were published in the beginning of the nineteenth century.

Antiquarian, architectural, or archaeological societies, whose purpose was to survey historical artifacts, were established in practically all localities. Topographical studies of buildings were made available to the public through numerous publications, and these served as the basis for the design of pseudohistorical buildings and stage sceneries. William Capon (1757–1827) learned theatrical scene-painting in London under Michael Novosielski, and after assisting Novosielski in building and designing theaters and designing small theaters on his own, went on to work for actor-manager John Kemble at Drury Lane Theatre and later at Covent Garden Theatre. He produced stage sceneries of medieval buildings, including the Old Palace of Westminster in the fifteenth century and a Tudor hall in the period of Henry VII, based on studies of historic English architecture. In 1800 John Britton, a self-taught antiquary, began topographical surveys of the country. In his fifty-year career, Britton was responsible for more than one hundred volumes, including *Architectural Antiquities of Great Britain*.

One of the most popular history books of its time was Augustin Thierry's *Histoire de la Conquête de l'Angleterre par les Normands*. Normandy was an important location because of the early history of the contentious relationship between England and France, which resurfaced because of the Napoleonic Wars. The book's first edition, in 1825, was a simple textual publication, but a lavishly illustrated version was published soon after, and in 1839 the fifth edition was accompanied by an atlas that supplemented the textual narrative with maps and other visual features. One of the copper plate engravings included in the atlas was the facade of St. Georges de Boscherville, a Norman Abbey above the Seine near Rouen. The building was considered a particularly perfect specimen of the Anglo-Norman style. In chapter 3, "Norman Abbey as Romantic Mise-en-Scène: St. Georges de Boscherville in Historical Representation," Stephen Bann analyzes and compares this and other published portrayals of medieval buildings during the 1820s and 1830s, the high epoch of French romanticism. The study reveals the succession in which illustrations of architectural monuments gained great popularity as artists, antiquaries, and subsequently the public shifted their understanding of Gothic from a barbarous oddity to a style of national significance. As the readership grew wider, the lithography capable of depicting subtle effects of light was replaced by inexpensive wood-block engraving. Bann examines the process of myth, message, and coding taking place as the role of illustrations shifted from the representation of mythical historical imagination to didacticism, and then to exemplifying other buildings of the same type.

SHAKESPEARE GIVEN HISTORICAL BACKGROUND

If the printed portrayals of medieval buildings help with the visualization of the past, the theater was an even more powerful agent for allowing the mass audience to realize the past. In chapter 4, "Performing History on the Victorian Stage," Richard Schoch demonstrates how Charles Kean, actor and manager of Princess's Theatre, succeeded in presenting historically conscious productions of Shakespeare's English chronicle plays. Kean adhered to the textual and visual depictions found in historians' works, creating stage sceneries that depicted buildings and architectural remains with historical accuracy. He enacted historical events that had not been included in Shakespeare's original plays, supplied historiographical essays in playbills, and published special, historiographically minded editions of Shakespeare commemorating his theater productions. Through a "synecdochic process," fragmentary representations on stage stood for the fully restored history, thereby making the medieval past come alive in the present. The power of antiquarian dramaturgy appealed to multiple layers of society, all of whom found their genealogical origin in the Middle Ages and "learned how to be English."

NOVELS AND THEIR PHYSICAL SETTINGS

Once the reading public was accustomed to having visual images accompany historical topics and architecture, they naturally came to expect the same in literary works, which may or may not have been meant to portray the past. Many literary publications were accompanied by illustrations that supplied visual representations of the story's characters in physical settings. George Cruikshank (1792–1878), George Cattermole (1800–1868), John Leech (1817–64), Hablot Knight Browne (1815–82), and others supplied illustrations for Charles Dickens, one of the most popular authors of the time, although not all of Dickens's works are historical. Browne, known by the pseudonym "Phiz," which he created to go along with Dickens's early pen name "Boz," was a good friend of Dickens and traveled with him in search of materials to depict in their works. He produced hundreds of drawings for ten of Dickens's major novels. Among those Browne illustrated are stories set in the past, *Barnaby Rudge* (1841) and *A Tale of Two Cities* (1859). Cruikshank and Browne also illustrated for William Harrison Ainsworth (1805–82), another popular author, whose historical novels include: *Rockwood* (1834), *Jack Sheppard* (1839), *The Tower of London* (1840), and *Old St. Paul's* (1841). *Rockwood* is a story of the legendary ride of highwayman Dick Turpin from London to York, an event that became accepted as historical fact after the novel. *Jack Sheppard* was so popular that nine different theatrical versions appeared on the London stage in the same year the novel was published. Cattermole worked for John Britton as an architectural draughtsman, and his drawings of cathedrals and other buildings are included in *Cathedral Antiquities of England* (1821–28) and *Architectural Antiquities of Great Britain*. Cattermole became the foremost historical painter in watercolors in Britain, having exhibited his works at the Royal Academy, the British Institution, and the Society of Painters in Water Colours, the last of which he became a member of in 1833. Before his collaboration with Charles Dickens, Cattermole also supplied illustrations for numerous books of history and historical fiction, including later editions of Walter Scott's Waverley novels.

In the fifth chapter, "Shops and Subjects," Andrew Ballantyne analyzes and compares two literary pieces whose titles contain the names of shops, *The Old Curiosity Shop* (1841) by Charles Dickens and *Au Bonheur des Dames* (1883) by Emile Zola. Although not historical fiction in the strict sense, each work features the shop building to which the title of the book refers, and to which the proprietor of the shop is closely related—the grandfather of Dickens's heroine and the young attractive widower whom Zola's heroine is to marry. The physical settings and conditions of these buildings reflect the human characters and natures of these individuals, and we learn something about the quality of life for certain groups of people.

The book's sixth and last chapter, developed from a student essay in the elective course mentioned in the next section, is a discussion of Jane Austen's *Pride and Prejudice* and how layers of society in Austen's time are reflected in the depictions of buildings in the novel as well as in the buildings selected to portray them in recent films.

ARCHITECTURE IN THE HUMANITIES

This book is the result of the lecture series "The Role of Architecture in Eighteenth- and Nineteenth-Century Historical Fiction," which was held in fall 2007 at the University of Nebraska–Lincoln.[13] Concurrently with the lecture series, we offered an elective course in which students analyzed portrayals of architecture within a selected piece of literature and its film adaptations. Novels the students examined in this course are Austen's *Pride and Prejudice*, Daniel Defoe's *Moll Flanders* (1722), Nathaniel Hawthorne's *The House of the Seven Gables* (1851), Charles Dickens's *Tale of Two Cities* (1859), and Gaston Leroux's *The Phantom of the Opera* (1909–10). The lecture series was part of an ongoing project titled "Architecture in the Humanities," which uses a multimedia relational database to demonstrate various ways in which architecture is incorporated into works of literature, film, theater, and art. The database (http://aith.unl.edu) is open-source on campus and is available free of charge to registered users who have signed a copyright agreement with the university. By offering concrete instances in which a certain piece of architecture is interpreted within creative works, and by covering a wide range of chronology and geography, the database is intended to fill certain gaps that exist in the field.

The first gap the database addresses is regarding the agent of architectural interpretation. Ever-increasing specialization has been the general tendency of modern society in general and advanced scholarship in particular, and architectural interpretation is no exception. We seldom question the notion that architectural interpretation is the realm of professional architects and critics. We read architectural criticism in newspapers and magazines that are written for and by specialists and more often than not dismiss the views of amateurs, as we have done with Prince Charles's account of contemporary architectural designs. Jürgen Habermas, a German philosopher and sociologist, expressed concerns about the distance between the experts and the realities of everyday life, one of the unintended consequences of specialization, and has called for the "re-appropriation of the experts' culture from the standpoint of the life-world."[14] In our database, the ways architectural pieces are incorporated into literature, film, theater, and art are considered important instances of architectural interpretation. The authors, directors, and painters are Habermas's "everyday experts," attentive to the human condition and capable of demonstrating their observations. They have reflected on their emotional reactions to buildings and other physical environments and articulated them in their works. Studying these works may provide us with a way to reconnect to the "life-world."

The database is also intended to address a second gap, created by the time that passes between the building's origin and its interpretation. Books in architectural history might refer to related works in other fields, but the selections often are based on the zeitgeist that these works share with the building. When the works discussed are centuries apart, they usually are cases of revival. By comparison, our database offers both synchronic and diachronic interpretations of architecture. After all, generations of multiple interpretations sustain architecture as "a living heritage" (to use Rudolf Wittkower's phrase) and make architecture an integral part of the humanities.

We offer this book to members of the general public who are interested in historical films, novels, plays, paintings, and architecture. Also, the book will provide the teachers of postsecondary education with interdisciplinary materials. Those who already are incorporating our database into their classes will find exemplary discussions in our book. It is hoped that the reader will find in the chapters that follow the significance and relevance of relational thinking that goes beyond the traditional boundaries of disciplines.

NOTES

1. Austen is said to have taken the name of Mr. Darcy's younger sister from the sixth duke's mother and his sister, who were both Georgiana. The fifth duchess (1757–1806) was an active political hostess to the Whig party. Mr. (Fitzwilliam) Darcy's name came from two prominent Whig party noblemen of the time, Robert D'Arcy (1718–88), fourth Earl of Holderness, and William Wentworth Fitzwilliam (1748–1833), second Earl Fitzwilliam of Great Britain and fourth Earl Fitzwilliam of Ireland. Lyme Hall in Cheshire stood in for the exterior of Pemberley in the 1995 BBC production. The building's south facade resembles the west front of Chatsworth, with the rusticated ground story carrying the giant order on top and the three bays in the center holding the pediment. The number of bays is different: Chatsworth has nine and Lyme Hall fifteen.

2. Designed by William Talman, a pupil of Sir Christopher Wren and the comptroller of the king's works (1689–1702).

3. Hayden White, *Metahistory: The Historical Imagination in Nineteenth-Century*

Europe (Baltimore: Johns Hopkins University Press, 1973), ix. See also Stephen Bann, *Romanticism and the Rise of History* (New York: Twayne, 1995).

4. The Walter Scott Digital Archive, Edinburgh University Library, "Walter Scott, Ivanhoe," http://www.walterscott.lib.ed.ac.uk/works/novels/ivanhoe.html (accessed August 4, 2008).

5. Richard Schoch, *Shakespeare's Victorian Stage: Performing History in the Theatre of Charles Kean* (Cambridge: Cambridge University Press, 1998), 22.

6. Stephen Bann, *Paul Delaroche: History Painted* (Princeton: Princeton University Press, 1997), 94–102.

7. Andrew Ballantyne, "Two Nations, Twice: National Identity in The Wild Irish Girl and Sybil," in *Cultural Identities and the Aesthetics of Britishness*, ed. Dana Arnold (Manchester: Manchester University Press, 2004), 87–98.

8. Melvin George Wiebe, ed., *Benjamin Disraeli Letters: 1842–1847* (Toronto: University of Toronto Press, 1982).

9. Edmund Burke, *An Essay Towards an Abridgement of the English History in Three Books* (London: Luke Hansard and Sons, 1811), book 1, chapter 2.

10. Ian Ousby, *The Englishman's England: Taste, Travel, and the Rise of Tourism* (Cambridge: Cambridge University Press, 1990), 116.

11. Johann Wolfgang von Goethe, "On Gothic Architecture (1823)," in *Essays on Art and Literature*, ed. John Gearey (New York: Suhrkamp, 1986), 10–14, quote on 12.

12. Sir Walter Scott, *Kenilworth, a Romance, by the Author of "Waverley," "Ivanhoe,"* etc. (Edinburgh: Archibald Constable and Co., and John Ballantyne; London: Hurst, Robinson, 1821), chap. 25, 291.

13. The series was sponsored by the University of Nebraska–Lincoln College of Architecture, Research Council, Honors Program, Architecture Program, Convocations Committee, College of Arts and Sciences, Graduate Studies, Undergraduate Studies, College of Fine and Performing Arts, University Libraries, Department of English, Department of Modern Languages and Literatures, Department of History, and the Graham Foundation for Advanced Studies in the Fine Arts.

14. Jürgen Habermas, "Modernity—An Incomplete Project," in *The Anti-Aesthetic: Essays on Postmodern Culture*, ed. Hal Foster (Seattle: Bay Press, 1983), 3–15, quote from 9. Originally delivered as a talk at the award reception of the Theodor W. Adorno Prize in Frankfurt, September 1980.

1 "All That Life Can Afford"?
Perspectives on the Screening of Historic Literary London

IAN CHRISTIE

> No sir, when a man is tired of London, he is tired of
> life; for there is in London all that life can afford.
> SAMUEL JOHNSON

British cinema has often been characterized as a cinema of literary adaptation, with the implication that this tendency has diverted it from being "truly cinematic." The suggestion is that if it were more like American cinema, committed to character-driven action, or, like French cinema, a vehicle for personal expression, it would be truer to the medium's potential, and so more successful internationally. Despite these longstanding charges, the fact remains that many British films have maintained an international reputation precisely because of their "literary" qualities, even if they are not actually adaptations—as in the cases of *The Third Man* (1949) or *Lawrence of Arabia* (1962)—but works that bear the imprint of novelistic or theatrical invention.[1] In the 1980s, a further generalized criticism was introduced with the concept of "heritage cinema," applied to historical fiction "fascinated by the private property, the culture and values of a particular class"—that class being the landowning English aristocracy.[2] Henceforth, many popular films and television series based on classic literature would be stigmatized as ideologically suspect, reducing "the nation itself . . . to the soft pastoral landscape of Southern England untainted by . . . modernity."[3]

So we find, for instance, that the films of the producer-director partnership of Ismail Merchant and James Ivory were for long regarded with a kind of automatic disdain by many British film scholars. Films such as *A Room with a View* (1985), *Howards End* (1992), *The Remains of the Day* (1993), and *The Golden Bowl* (2000) were dismissed as "literary" and too reliant on period costume and setting to be considered truly cinematic — or relevant to the times in which they appeared.[4] Yet all of these can also be seen as intelligent and purposeful adaptations of novels that are very much about themes of continuing relevance, especially the prejudices enshrined in the English class system and its relationship to the realities of the modern world, as well as issues of "deviant" sexuality within a puritanical culture.[5] Nor should Ivory's ability to depict luxury and gracious living be taken for granted, as Martin Scorsese observed in the context of his own recreation of New York's "gilded age" in *The Age of Innocence*.[6]

What was ultimately at stake in the "heritage film" debate was perhaps more the collective prejudices of a postwar generation reacting against the portrayal of an "Englishness" to which they felt instinctively antipathetic than a measured critical response to this upsurge of historical fiction. And it was a social historian, Raphael Samuel, who would provide a broader perspective on the "heritage industry" to which these films related, discussing their role as a "theatre of memory" for the 1980s and 1990s, in which historical time itself is being restructured for a contemporary public.[7]

The rather confused and self-lacerating criticisms of English literary adaptation and "heritage" cinema would not be worth resurrecting if they did not point to a number of underlying prejudices and misunderstandings that I shall argue have long obscured the role of spatial and architectural imagination in cinema more generally — as well as reinforcing a domestic prejudice against some of the most widely admired British films.[8] Quite apart from their critical reputation, these are also works that have created the contemporary image of Britain, circulating around the world and playing an increasingly important part in defining how the nation's capital is perceived.[9] Before turning to some of these, and to their relatively unsung designers, it is necessary to consider the deep roots of an antiliterary and antitheatrical ideology in cinema criticism, and how this has been challenged by a revisionist film history inspired by the study of early cinema. What may appear a detour will show how reexamining the origins of film practice and history can reinvigorate our understanding of the imaginative power of cinema and its wider cultural significance.

"FABRICATED NATURE" — THE CASE AGAINST DÉCOR

The clearest expressions of an emerging opposition to theatricality were voiced, significantly, at important moments of transition in cinema. During the 1920s, it had become conventional to pay tribute to the angular painted Expressionist settings of *The Cabinet of Dr Caligari* (1919), not owing to any immediate visible influence these had, but because they "set working the brains of people both in and out of the film industry"; and because they showed how every aspect of a film's design could be "pointed to the one purpose, the expression of a world seen through the eyes of a madman."[10] However, by the early 1930s, after the introduction of synchronized sound with "the Talkies" promoted a near-universal naturalistic style, *Caligari* came to stand for quite the opposite. When the distinguished art historian Erwin Panofsky published a pioneering paper on the aesthetics of cinema in 1934, he not only revealed the breadth of his knowledge of the medium and so conferred considerable status on it, but his conclusion took *Caligari* as an example of precisely what cinema should *not* do: "an attempt at subjugating the world to artistic prestylization," as in the expressionist settings of *The Cabinet of Dr Caligari*, could be no more than an exciting experiment: "To prestylize reality prior to tackling it amounts to dodging the problem. The problem is to manipulate and shoot unstylized reality is such a way that it has style."[11]

Nearly twenty years later, André Bazin took for granted the "failure" of films such as *Caligari* and *The Nibelungen* because of their reliance on a "fabricated nature and artificial world."[12] As the spiritual father of French cinema's "New Wave" [*nouvelle vague*], and a powerful continuing influence on film aesthetics, Bazin's insistent "realism" led him to distinguish these two examples from other films of the same period, which might otherwise "seem to belong to the same aesthetic family," *Nosferatu* (1922) and *The Passion of Jeanne d'Arc* (1929), claiming that these latter remained fresh because of their use of natural settings and "documentary" treatment of the human face.

Bazin was writing after the impact of Italian neorealism, which had created a strong presumption in favor of location shooting, often with nonactors, to convey the texture of "real life." Yet his aesthetic cannot be reduced to a simple contrast between studio and location "reality," since it also embraced a deep respect for the elaborate mise-en-scène of Hollywood films such as *Citizen Kane* (1941) and *The Best Years of Our Lives* (1946), both of which were wholly studio productions. For Bazin, the deep-focus composition of extended sequence-shots in both of these films restored a sense of "the ambiguity of reality" that he also found in the neorealist films of Rossellini and De Sica.[13] The contrast that concerned him was between "manipulation" of the spectator, which might be produced by stylized sets or rapid cutting between images, and the freedom to interpret, which might equally be given by either elaborate studio settings or *plein air* locations. However subtle, or even contradictory, we might judge Bazin's position, the fact of his association with the widely admired New Wave filmmakers, who would instinctively shoot on location, undoubtedly lent prestige to the idea of "filming reality" as this developed during the 1960s.

But even before Panofsky's and Bazin's arguments against "stylization" gained wide currency, earlier historians of cinema had registered a prejudice against one of the first uses of historically accurate decor in the 1908 French Film d'Art production, *The Assassination of the Duc de Guise*.[14] Written by a distinguished member of the Academie Française and acted by members of the Comedie Française, this impressive recreation of sixteenth-century French history created a sensation on its appearance, and led to an international "art film" movement. However, in the later annals of cinema history, it would be recorded as "an everlasting monument to bombast and stupidity" — the verdict of Maurice Bardèche and Robert Brasillach in their influential 1930s *History of the Film*.[15] Few could have seen the 1908 film in the 1930s, or indeed until the 1980s, and certainly not in a good quality print shown at the correct speed and accompanied by the music specially composed by Camille Saint-Saens. Bardèche and Brasillach's attack could therefore stand unchallenged.[16] Yet seen today, under these conditions, it emerges as a remarkable anticipation of cinema's ability to create vivid historical drama, transcending the resources of the stage. And central to this achievement is the combination of decor, costume, and set-dressing that creates a stylized yet believable context for the film's melodramatic action.

The influence of the *film d'art* spread widely through Pathé's international network of branches. Comparable styles of production that relied on period reconstruction developed in other countries, especially in Italy, as its first generation of producers capitalized on their long tradition of historical spectacle. Yet despite the obvious importance of sets, decor, and costume in the growth of cinema as an immersive experience for mass audiences, aesthetic theories of film continued to stress what were considered "specific" aspects of the medium. The earliest of these, developed in France in the early 1920s, revolved around the concept of *photogénie*, a new aesthetic term that referred to the transformative power of filming objects and the human figure, especially in close-up.[17] Another theory challenged the primacy of the filmic image by insisting on the power of the juncture between images, created by the purposeful editing strategies of "montage."[18] Although both *photogénie* and montage lost much of their appeal after the adoption of synchronized sound, traces can still be found in the theory of "narrative grammar" that was widely adopted as the basis for explaining "the art of film" after World War Two.[19] According to this view, the director builds upon insights first articulated by the Soviet pioneers — one of whom, Vsevolod Pudovkin, had declared that "the foundation of film art is editing"[20] — and the practice demonstrated in D. W. Griffith's canonical films, *The Birth of a Nation* and *Intolerance*. Editing continued to be regarded as central to the process of creating meaning, or demonstrating "art" in what would otherwise be mere recording.

What such accounts of film art routinely ignore and certainly undervalue is the *spatial* construction of the "material" that is photographed and edited. Perhaps paradoxically, it was not until the arrival of a more self-consciously theorized approach to cinema, often described as "semiotic," in the 1970s that a framework appeared which could pay due attention to this aspect of cinema. Although preoccupied with the problem of "narration," semiotic theorists recognized the importance of the "pro-filmic" in the overall process of filmic narration: "The pro-filmic concerns the elements placed in front of the camera to be filmed: actors, lighting, set design, etc. These elements, rather than being seen simply as raw material, can be understood as narrative discourse by the fact that they have been chosen and selected to communicate narrative meanings."[21]

With the concept of set design now assigned narrative significance, the way was open for its theorization, which was undertaken by Charles and Mirella Affron in their ground-breaking study of "art direction and film narrative."[22] After noting the near-total absence of comment on art direction in the popular literature of cinema during the 1930s and 1940s, the Affrons proposed a theoretical model that recognizes five levels of set "intensity," graduated from "transparency" to "opacity": "From denotation, in which the set functions as a conventional signpost of genre, ambience, and character; to punctuation, where the set has a specially emphatic narrative function; to embellishment, where the verisimilitudinous set calls attention to itself within the narrative; to artifice, where the set is a fantastic or theatrical image that commands the centre of narrative attention."[23]

The fifth level in this scheme is termed "set as narrative," which refers to a relatively small number of films where "the field of reading is composed of a single locale" — as in, for example, Hitchcock's *Rope* and *Rear Window*, but also the village street of *How Green Was My Valley*.

Despite the obvious heuristic value of the Affrons' model, it cannot be said that the study of art direction has made rapid progress during the decade since their book appeared. Such relatively few works on production designers as have appeared are essentially tributes to leading figures in the profession.[24] My project here attempts to combine something of the Affrons' analytical approach with an overview of British filmmaking and the persistence within it of the literary-historical genre, in order to shed light on the distinctive contribution of some British production designers, notably John Bryan and John Box.

BRITISH CINEMA AND THE "NEW FILM HISTORY"

The semiotic theorization of film not only provided an opening for the fuller understanding of film practice but led to a revaluation of early cinema during the 1980s.[25] And it has been from this new study of what had previously been considered "primitive" that much evidence has emerged which enables us to trace the progress of design for film. Instead of considering the first films as mere recording of "pre-arranged... pieces of dramatic action," scholars of early cinema have firmly turned away from the teleological model of cinema's progress towards contemporary sophistication, seeing instead the persistence or recurrence of much older tropes, and also placing cinema in a wider field of media and entertainment — in contrast to the tradition of seeking "specificity" at all costs.[26]

From this perspective, it has become clear that moving picture entertainment was much less of a break with previous forms of representation or new beginning in the mid-1890s than had often been implied by film historians. Many of its conventions and subjects were in fact carried over from the variety stage and from other contemporary practices, such as the posing of "life models," first for stereoscope pictures, then for lantern slides, and eventually, postcards. Indeed, during its heyday in the later nineteenth century the Magic Lantern brought into being a vast repertoire of literary, theatrical, and even opera slide-sets, anticipating by some five decades the range of subjects that cinema would tackle. We should therefore not be surprised that early producers were quick to see the potential of representing already-popular subjects. The issue was not whether the new medium of film was "adequate" to portraying, say, a full-scale novel or opera — which it plainly was not in terms of duration, with individual films lasting only a minute or two — but rather that the new device could demonstrate its novel powers by reworking acknowledged cultural icons. This process has been termed "remediation" by Jay Bolter and Richard Grusin, who identify it as a key feature of how new recording media have repeatedly sought validation, in a process that has now carried into the digital era.[27] But it can also be explained in terms of "intertextuality," a term imported into critical theory from the work of the Russian philologist Mikhail Bakhtin, who argued that all literature draws on not only other literary works but also deep "strata of the popular language."[28]

In Britain, brief scenes from current stage successes were filmed from as early as 1896. One of these, *2 a.m., or the Husband's Return*, taken from a London theater production and featuring the original actors, appeared in Robert Paul's Animatographe film program at the Alhambra Theatre of Varieties in August of that year. This single scene of a drunken husband reeling around before being drawn into bed by his wife is notably longer than most other films of the period, with lighting and furniture as they would appear on stage — unlike the close-up that appears out of spatial context in Edison's celebrated film *The May Irwin Kiss* (1896), also based on a popular play.[29] Three years later, the British Biograph company would film scenes from Beerbohm Tree's production of Shakespeare's *King John*, advertising this exclusive as "taken with all the scenery and effects of the original production," which strongly suggests these theatrical features were considered an attraction.[30] When Paul undertook a Dickens adaptation in 1901, *Scrooge, or Marley's Ghost*, this unprecedented six-minute condensation of *A Christmas Carol* in thirteen scenes closely followed a stage adaptation of Dickens's novel that had long been popular. Like all Dickens's work, the original story had appeared with illustrations, establishing a visual tradition from the outset that this latest "remediation" would extend, with the benefit of filmed supernatural effects.[31] Another Paul film, *The Hair's Breadth Escape of Jack Shepard* (1900), which is lost but known from a catalogue illustration, suggests that this pioneer studio was incorporating the kind of dramatic effect already familiar on stage in "sensation melodrama," using a painted cyclorama of rooftops for a scene from the life of the notorious outlaw.

Taking account of such examples of "remediating" theater as film has shifted the early history of cinema away from the concern to demonstrate its novelty and specificity that was once deemed so important, toward a wider, more inclusive notion, sometimes termed "intermediality." In this, newer forms and media are seen to interact with older, established forms by means of emulation and hybridization, to produce what Bakhtin called "the differentiated unity of [an] epoch's entire culture."[32] Rather than supplanting popular theater or the novel, film imitates and extends these, eventually creating its own cultural space.

Even before the first *film d'art* productions of 1908, Pathé, as the largest production company in the world, was developing its studio to make possible a higher rate of production. A key feature of this was the standing set, with a staircase and landing, and rooms that could be dressed for different scenes.[33] From as early as 1901, these features reappear in numerous Pathé films, though carefully redressed to differentiate them within the same film, and to match with the genuine Parisian exteriors often required for chase comedies. When production began somewhat belatedly in Italy in 1907, producers soon realized that one of their distinctive assets was the ability to recreate the ancient world in lavish detail and on an impressive scale. Studios developed rapidly in Turin and Rome; and within five years, Italian epics such as *The Fall of Troy* (1911), *The Last Days of Pompeii* (1912), *Quo Vadis?* (1913), and, climactically, *Cabiria* (1914) had become worldwide attractions, attracting vast audiences and earning significantly more than any previous films.[34] Their palpable aura of "quality" also undoubtedly helped to raise the social status of film exhibition, attracting middle-class audiences to the major new "picture palaces" being built throughout Europe and the United States. While the influence of the Italian spectaculars on American cinema's founding father D. W. Griffith is well known, having encouraged him to conceive his landmark *Birth of a Nation* (1914) on a similar epic scale, another testimony from the same era demonstrates how these films transformed the image of cinema, for many, from a vulgar diversion to a medium capable of cultural expression. The future playwright Eugene O'Neill, then at Harvard, wrote in a letter:

> I went to see *Cabiria* ... last night and returned with a much fairer opinion of the artistic value of the movies. The picture is simply stupendous. The acting is excellent — far above any I have ever seen done by an American company — and the scenery is wonderful. Hannibal's army crossing the Alps, the destruction of the Roman fleet at Syracuse by the reflecting mirrors of Archimedes, the temple of Moloch at Carthage, the desert expedition of the King of Cirta, the siege of Carthage by Scipio — all of these are done with the grimmest realism and are blood-stirring in their gripping action.[35]

O'Neill was not alone in his admiration for the Italian achievement. But this posed problems for domestic producers in many countries, and none more so than Britain.

Here, the pioneer producers had largely failed to adapt to rapidly rising audience expectations, remaining attached to shorter films and lacking large studios to create large-scale spectacle. According to British cinema's first historian, Rachael Low, discussing the period 1910–15: "Even the biggest efforts of Barker, the London Film Company and Hepworth were dwarfed by the towering stature of Italian films like *Quo Vadis* or *The Last Days of Pompeii*."[36]

Writing in the late 1940s, as British cinema entered another period of crisis, Low may well have felt a sense of déjà vu when contemplating the period immediately before the First World War, when British producers saw their share of the domestic market plummet. However, her account of the earlier period also undervalues the efforts of some

British producers — and the significance of the subjects they felt could compete with Italian, American, and Danish imports. Will Barker had started in film production with short, rapidly made "topicals" based on current events, but realized the value of striking a more cultural and patriotic note. His *Henry VIII* (1911) capitalized on the fame of Sir Herbert Beerbohm Tree and his theater company, and was widely regarded as the first British film to offer serious competition to imported historical spectaculars. In a double irony, Barker's promotional strategy for this major production included burning all copies of the film after six weeks of screenings, in a spectacular effort to drive up its value. By all accounts the strategy succeeded in attracting attention and audiences, although since nothing of the film survives, it unfortunately cannot be compared with Alexander Korda's return to the same subject for his debut British production in 1933. At any rate, Barker continued with the same strategy and in 1913 coproduced, with G. B. Samuelson, *Sixty Years a Queen*, a dramatized chronicle of the reign of Queen Victoria.

Only fragments of this ambitious film survive, but research has shown that it drew heavily on the tradition of "illustrated news" that developed during Victoria's reign, and was highly successful in attracting a public avid for British historical subjects.[37] In 1915, Barker followed it with a much more spectacular story, *Jane Shore*, set during the fifteenth-century Wars of the Roses, about the mistress of Edward IV, who outlived him to become a celebrated courtesan. *Jane Shore* involved a large cast and spectacular action, and had two designers credited, indicating how vital this role had become in the era of historical fiction. Low's account of this rare surviving example of a British film of the period is preoccupied with doubt as to how properly "filmic" it is, constantly noting issues of camera placement and editing, very much according to the canons of "film appreciation" laid down in Ernest Lindgren's contemporary book. One passage in particular is fascinating for its avoidance of any direct discussion of the film's actual design: "It is possible . . . that the very size of the sets made possible a greater variety of angle from which they could be taken than the little two or three-walled rooms, the whole of which could clearly be shown from one camera position; while at the same time the size of the sets and the crowds made emphasis of detail a more pressing problem."[38]

Set design here is seen, perversely, in terms of how it facilitates camera angles and cutting, rather than for its contribution to the film's historicity, drama, or atmosphere. The main arena for British filmmakers in the silent era, however, was their treatment of the second most important of all British authors: Charles Dickens. While Shakespeare reigned supreme, he was also an international author, and many Shakespeare adaptations were made outside Britain before the First World War.[39] But Dickens remained very much an English specialty, and by 1912, he had become an important asset in the struggle against imported historical fiction. Cecil Hepworth's company produced three Dickens adaptations in rapid succession, all directed by Thomas Bentley, a former actor who had specialized in Dickens on stage. After *Oliver Twist* (1912), Bentley moved on to *David Copperfield* (1913) and finished this group with *The Old Curiosity Shop* (1914). All were popular, but the last, according to Low, "received such praise as had hitherto been reserved for foreign epics."[40] In the absence of any surviving material, we can only guess at what was done to create the atmosphere of Dickens's "repository for old and curious things," but *David Copperfield* has been preserved, and shows a strong emphasis on "real" locations, ranging from the seafront at Yarmouth and the cliffs near Dover, to David meeting Dan'l on St. Martins in the Field in Trafalgar Square, and Steerforth's house in Highgate. For this last, the filmmakers used Church House in Pond Square, Highgate Village, which survives almost unchanged to the present day (see fig. 6).

Dickens, of course, has long been celebrated for his emotional stories and sharply realized characters. But his novels also rely on a density of description and evocation, as well as a quite precise topography of London and its surroundings, which seems to have made his work highly suggestive for British filmmakers. In a famous essay, written while he was working on *Ivan the Terrible*, Sergei Eisenstein traced

Fig. 6. From Thomas Bentley, *David Copperfield* (1913). For Steerforth's house Church House, Highgate, was used, which survives almost unchanged to the present day.

the influence of Dickens on Griffith, suggesting that the origins of the close-up and parallel action lie in these familiar novels, as Griffith himself acknowledged.[41] However, what is most "cinematic" about Dickens, Eisenstein suggests, is his "creation of an extraordinary plasticity" and the "optical quality" of his observation. The challenge for British filmmakers in the early teens was not only how to compete with the quality and scale of spectacle on offer from foreign producers, but also how to realize the cinematic potential of their greatest modern author.

The climax of this first period of engagement with historic literature was probably Hepworth's ambitious 1915 production of *Barnaby Rudge*, Dickens's novel set amid the anti-Catholic Gordon Riots of the late eighteenth century. The fact that this has not survived, like so many lost British films from the silent era, has undoubtedly diminished its reputation, although at the time of its release, the quality of set construction and design was an important talking point in the trade press:

It is a wonderful piece of stage architecture, complete in every detail, and the illusion of solid realism, when viewed from the proper aspect, is quite perfect. The paved sidewalks, the cobbled roadway, the doors with their link-holders and extinguishers, the glazed windows with their neat white curtains—every tiny point has been remembered . . . Behind the streets, moreover, there is a magnificent reconstruction of Newgate Prison—an immensely lofty structure, grey, drab, and forbidding, with a sinister gallows before its outer wall. The whole of this marvellous city, we understand, was designed by Mr. Warwick Buckland, and it is certain that he merits the very warmest congratulations [on] a remarkable piece of work.[42]

If *Barnaby Rudge*, with its 1,500 extras (or "supers," as they were known at the time), and *Jane Shore* were the most spectacular British historical productions of this period, other producers were also active in bringing classic literature to the screen. The Ideal Film Renting Company launched a series of more modestly budgeted films aimed at discriminating audiences in 1916, which included versions of Oliver Goldsmith's *The Vicar of Wakefield* and Oscar Wilde's *Lady Windermere's Fan*. Ideal's energetic publicity campaigns, aimed at exhibitors and also at key opinion-shapers, stressed the idea of giving discriminating cinema customers the chance to see famous stage actors in films that bring out "the great idea of the drama," with scenery and acting subordinated to this aim. A trade press story of 1917 is clearly contrived to support this policy, with a vicar reporting his admiration for *The Vicar of Wakefield*: "I believe I am expressing the mind of many of my brother clergy when I say that if such pieces, accompanied by such acting, were more frequent, we should hear little of those well-founded complaints of the kinema, with its puerilities and inanities and worse."[43]

The same correspondent concluded that "taste is much higher than managers would have us believe," obviously supporting Ideal's claim that their modestly budgeted "quality" films could attract a new, discriminating audience to the cinema as well as satisfying existing spectators.

The question inevitably arises: how can the apparent success on different levels of Barker's, Samuelson's, Hepworth's, and Ideal's strategies, not to mention those of other companies such as London Films, Turner, and Trans-Atlantic, be reconciled with conventional accounts of British cinema's abject failure during the teens and twenties? To a great extent the answer lies in the larger economics of the international film business, which saw an important shift of power during the First World War, giving American producers and their international agents effective control of the world trade.[44] Certainly British producers had lost ground in their domestic market, and found decreasing export opportunities because of the cartel operated by American producers operating under Edison's Motion Picture Patent Company up to 1915. But against these very real business difficulties, the fact remains that British filmmakers made considerable headway in producing feature subjects throughout the teens that reflected national culture, drawing on a wide range of authors, both classic and modern, for their stories. Equally important, they had laid the foundations of a coherent approach to visual design in film, starting with the pioneer efforts of the painter Sir Hubert Herkomer, who took up filmmaking in 1913,[45] and continuing with the work of Mumford and Ambrose on *Jane Shore*, and Buckland on *Barnaby Rudge*.

Similar developments were taking place across the Atlantic during the same period—although less in the monumental films of D. W Griffith, *Birth of a Nation* (1915) and its successor *Intolerance* (1916), which have long been regarded as the fount of American cinema's critical and commercial success. However rich these were in spectacle and scale, they did not directly influence domestic filmmaking as much as the scenography of the European *film d'art*. This influence came through Adolphe Zukor's success in 1912 with *Queen Elizabeth*, starring Sarah Bernhardt. The great actress had achieved extraordinary international fame through her tours but was understandably wary of appearing on screen in her late fifties, despite the attractions of capitalizing on her reputation.⁴⁶ However, the failure of her Paris stage production *Queen Elizabeth* [La Reine Elizabeth] in 1912, encouraged her to recoup the losses by undertaking a filmed version, which was shot in London by the aptly named Histrionic Film Company and cofinanced by the American exhibitor Zukor. Such was Bernhardt's celebrity that Zukor was able to tour this somewhat old-fashioned tableau-based film around the United States with enormous commercial success, which laid the foundations for his Famous Players company, which would merge with that of another ambitious producer, Jesse Lasky, in 1916, and later become Paramount, one of Hollywood's most successful studios. One of Lasky's employees was a well-connected young figure from the New York theater world, Cecil B. DeMille, who had travelled to California in 1913 to make a Western in "a place called Hollywood."⁴⁷ DeMille would become Paramount's most successful director during the late teens, due in part to his collaboration with the pioneer art director Wilfred Buckland between 1914 and 1919.

DeMille came from a New York theatrical background, having worked with the master of spectacular melodrama, David Belasco, and he would soon infuse his filmmaking with a powerful integration of dramatic elements, paying particular attention to the role of controlled lighting in relation to cinematography and set design—an effect that became known as "Lasky lighting" but was apparently much influenced by Buckland.⁴⁸ But what Zukor brought to the partnership was a shrewd sense of the need for filmmakers to make motion pictures "as artistic, as high-class, and as notable things in [their] line of entertainment as such men as . . . Charles and Daniel Frohman were doing in high-class Broadway theatres."⁴⁹ The choice of subjects that had established cultural appeal, which usually meant a literary and theatrical pedigree, was vital; and among DeMille's great successes of the period were *Carmen* (1915) and *Joan the Woman* (1917), both starring the Metropolitan Opera diva Geraldine Farrar, and both ingeniously adapted to make use of cinema's potential for new ways of staging the classics. *Carmen* benefited from *plein air* Californian landscapes in the scenes that lead up to its denouement, staged outside a superbly realized bullfight arena, while DeMille's account of Joan of Arc, prompted by America's recent entry into the Great War and with a contemporary framing story set in the trenches, showed a growing confidence in handling historical subjects in ways that communicated with cinema's vast and diverse audience.

THE STRUGGLE FOR ENGLAND'S SELF-IMAGE

America's military role was not its only contribution to reshaping Europe after the war. Indeed, the disruption of international trade caused by the war had already brought about favorable conditions for a reshaping of the film business, along with many other industries formerly controlled by London. With two important centers of film distribution, London and Paris, preoccupied by the war, the way was open for American companies to "cash in on Europe's war."[50] Kristin Thompson has identified the period from mid-1915 to early 1916 as the time when "the American move to hegemony occurred," with a significant proportion of American exported film footage thereafter going directly to markets other than Britain.[51] Britain would continue to be American's largest external customer for film, with close links maintained by such figures as Charles Chaplin — London-born, yet launched as an international movie star by the dynamism of American producers — but increasingly, American producers found they could supply the world's exhibitors directly, and on their own terms.

In this climate, British producers found themselves at a multiple disadvantage. Not only had the war drained Britain's economy and shattered its workforce, but British cinemas, like most others around the world, were now overwhelmingly committed to showing American films. Patriotism became an important theme in the trade advertising of British producers such as Ideal, who were trying to reinvigorate British "quality" production in the later teens.[52] The strategy favored by both Ideal and a new company, Stoll, which also had major theater holdings, was to promote adaptations of popular contemporary "British authors," relying on the familiarity of these names to help boost films that might otherwise be seen to lack the glamour of Hollywood.

Despite such well-conceived strategies, the Hollywood studios had achieved dominance over the British distribution and exhibition market, which made it increasingly difficult even to release domestic productions. While Ideal, Stoll, and the long-established Hepworth company all struggled, an expatriate Englishman returned to inject some American showmanship into the depressed domestic business — a pattern that would recur over subsequent decades. J. Stuart Blackton had left Britain in his youth when his family emigrated, and his sketching talent led to early jobs in newspapers and on the vaudeville stage, as a "lightning sketch artist." After appearing in three early Edison films, he set up the American Vitagraph Company in 1900, which later pioneered an American form of *film d'art* with a series of historical and literary subjects.[53] One of their biblical films, *The Life of Moses* (1909), was released reel by reel as a kind of serial, and had a notable success among Jewish immigrant audiences.[54] As new companies entered the business, Vitagraph lost ground and its founders parted company, with Blackton joining Famous Players briefly as an independent producer.

According to his daughter, it was a dinner in New York with Sir Thomas Lipton, the famous tea tycoon, and the whiskey magnate Lord Dewar that persuaded Blackton to consider returning to England, as Lipton put it, "to show our film chaps how to do a proper job."[55] Whatever the precise motive, Blackton set up what was then a major production in British terms, which shrewdly combined a number of striking features. *The Glorious Adventure* (1922) was set during the Great Fire of London, in 1666, and wove its fictional story of society ladies thrown together with criminals from Newgate prison around historical events and characters of this major event, which appears not to have been treated before or for another seventy years.[56] As a showman, Blackton also believed in the need for novelty, and *The Glorious Adventure* demonstrated the latest color process, Prizmacolor, as well as boasting a notable society beauty, Lady Diana Manners, as its star. Launched with a great fanfare at Covent Garden Opera House in January 1922, Blackton's film was soon at the center of controversy:

boosted by Blackton's lavish advertising, yet suspect as a publicity stunt among many in the British film trade. Modern critics and historians had to wait to see it until 1993, when the film was restored and shown at the London Film Festival, where it largely failed to impress, except as an early example of the earthy appeal that Victor McLaglen would demonstrate in his later Hollywood career. To complain, however, about a lack of "modern" qualities is to ignore much that might have impressed audiences of 1922, who were seeing the first-ever "color feature," set in a Restoration London also conceived for the screen for the first time. *The Glorious Adventure* did not reveal Blackton as a gifted director, but it staked out a territory for British production that would be mined intensively and sometimes brilliantly in future decades. Blackton meanwhile went on to make two further historical films in England, *The Gypsy Cavalier* (1922) and *The Virgin Queen* (1923). The former starred the French boxing champion Georges Carpentier and the latter Lady Diana again, now appearing as Queen Elizabeth. *The Virgin Queen* was entirely filmed at Beaulieu Castle and Abbey, with the whole cast and crew based there for two months, and whatever its dramatic qualities, it would mark an important milestone in the use of authentic historical locations.[57] Unfortunately, like the majority of British silent-era films, both it and *The Gypsy Cavalier* are lost, and their success or otherwise can only be conjectured.

THE LONG SHADOW OF *CALIGARI*: CONTINENTAL
INFLUENCES ON BRITISH CINEMA

Most design in cinema before the 1920s was essentially anonymous, organized by craft scenery specialists who would have received their training in the theater.[58] But change was under way in the American and German film industries. Wilfred Buckland is generally credited as cinema's first "art director"; and in Germany, the designers of *The Cabinet of Dr Caligari*, Walter Riemann, Walter Röhrig, and Hermann Warm, were soon known by name. Production in Britain would benefit from these foreign developments toward the end of the 1920s, when Andrew Mazzei came to Gaumont-British, having previously worked at Famous Players-Lasky; Alfred Junge arrived from Germany at British International Pictures; and Vincent Korda joined his brother Alex at London Films.

Alfred Junge and the Architectural Imagination

Junge is often regarded as the father of serious art direction in British studios, which is perhaps more a reflection of the esteem in which German production personnel were held than the literal truth. British International Pictures (BIP) was established in the late 1920s as the production arm of John Maxwell's expanding film empire, which also included a cinema chain and distribution company. Part of the intention was to take advantage of Continental talent and prestige, so BIP made an approach to the German director E. A. Dupont, who had scored a major international success with *Variety* [Varieté] (1925). Largely set in the world of fairgrounds and circus, *Variety* had impressed many by its intensely filmic qualities, in which atmospheric settings and elaborate chiaroscuro lighting effects played an important part. Arriving at BIP's Elstree Studios, Dupont brought with him a group of German technicians who would leave a lasting impression on British filmmaking. Chief among these was Junge (1886–1964), who had originally trained in the theater and opera house, starting as a scenic artist, before joining the Ufa Studio in 1920 and gaining experience during German cinema's most intensively creative period.

Having worked on *Variety* with Oskar Werndorff (who would also come to Britain), Junge became Dupont's sole designer for two of the three lavish films he made for BIP during 1928–29. The first of these, *Moulin Rouge* (1928), involved recreating the stage of the famous Parisian music hall with its exotic sets, but comparatively little evocation of London. But for *Piccadilly* (1929), set in both the West End and the multicultural dock area of Limehouse, Junge created some of the most remarkable settings that had yet been seen in British cinema. His nightclub is a blazing horseshoe-shaped arena where glamorous reputations are made; and when Anna May Wong steps up from the scullery to take over from the club's former star, she is displayed to glittering, seductive effect. Yet when the club's manager, played by Jefferson Thomas, accompanies her to "our Piccadilly" in a rowdy Limehouse pub, the atmosphere is even more electrifying, with a crowded saloon bar, seen in a single extended tracking shot, followed by a jostling dance floor, on which racial tension explodes. For all the impact of these sequences, there is no attempt to impress with excessive decorative detail elsewhere: the coroner's courtroom in which the story ends is bare, allowing the actors to carry the climax of the drama.

Of course — and it will be a recurrent problem throughout the remainder of this essay — we cannot be certain whether either the dramatic atmosphere of Limehouse or the sparseness of the court were due solely to Junge's design decisions. They may have been decreed by the director, or by the film's budget, and they certainly involved the collaboration of the cinematographer and other members of the art department. But from what we know of Junge's later career, especially his collaboration on eight films with Michael Powell, we may be reasonably sure that his was at least a guiding hand in *Piccadilly*. After the Dupont films, Junge worked in Germany and France briefly, before returning to England and taking up permanent residence from 1932. He first became supervising art director for Gaumont-British, under the leadership of Michael Balcon, then from 1938 occupied a similar role at MGM's British studio, working on the major productions *The Citadel* (King Vidor, 1938) and *Goodbye Mr. Chips* (Sam Wood, 1939).

In these roles, and in the many important films he oversaw at Gaumont-British, Junge was in effect the pioneer of modern studio design procedure in British cinema, during the crucial period when old silent-era practices were, of necessity, being replaced by the demands of shooting for sound. Quality, solidity, and organization were the Junge hallmarks, although these virtues could also prove restricting — as Michael Powell increasingly believed after World War Two, when he felt he had to breathe life into such Junge constructions as the heavenly amphitheater of *A Matter of Life and Death* (1946) (see fig. 7). The partnership finally sundered on *The Red Shoes* (1948),

Fig. 7. Alfred Junge, set design for *A Matter of Life and Death* (1946). This set was typical of his meticulous approach to period design.

when Powell's desire for a more expressive, less architecturally based design came to the fore and led him to appoint the painter and former ballet designer Hein Heckroth.

Vincent Korda: A Painter among Producers

Another major Continental influence on British art direction arrived when Alexander Korda brought his brother Vincent to join London Films in 1932. Alexander Korda had already enjoyed a precocious early film career in his native Hungary, followed by successful periods in Vienna and Berlin, a humiliating three years in Hollywood, and "recovery" in Paris, before coming to England. With this wealth of international experience, Korda set about creating a new image for film production, deliberately aiming to raise its social and artistic status. He quickly made connections with English high society, which helped his negotiations with financiers, and his political connections — with

Winston Churchill, among others — would stand him in good stead during the war and later years. But what Korda wanted, above all, was to create "one big solid success to establish himself and open up the sources of finance he needed."[59] The subject should be "'national'... but sufficiently well known to have international appeal"; and drawing on Korda's previous experience with "private lives," he settled on *The Private Life of Henry VIII* (1933). To realize this he needed trusted associates, including his younger brother Vincent, who had been painting in Paris before he was imperiously summoned to London to serve as set designer on this knowing account of England's most famous monarch, played with knowing panache by Charles Laughton.

Stories of Vincent Korda's disheveled appearance and casualness are legion, suggesting a polar opposite to the highly organized disciplinarian Alfred Junge, although the two did in fact collaborate on the design of Alexander Korda's major French film, *Marius* (1931), which was also Vincent's debut in film design. Yet Vincent quickly became Alexander's most important associate, as London Films built on the vast success of *Henry VIII* with a series of calculatedly risqué exotic period pieces, starting with *The Rise of Catherine the Great* (1934) and *The Private Life of Don Juan* (1934), in which the gracefully aging Douglas Fairbanks made his final appearance. The film that is probably Vincent Korda's masterpiece as a designer followed. In *Rembrandt* (1936), starring Laughton again, the two Kordas created a more intimate study of the vicissitudes of age and desire than their earlier successes, which predictably had little popular appeal, despite its impeccable sets and deeply felt performances.

If *Rembrandt* clearly appealed to the painter in Vincent, his brother's other major project of 1934–35 made extraordinary demands on his ability to synthesize Modernist design. Conceived as a massive prestige project, *Things to Come* (see fig. 8) was based on H. G. Wells's didactic novel, in which history is projected forward from 1930 to warn against the danger of another devastating war that will kill millions and virtually destroy civilization.[60] Quite apart from the dramaturgical problems of turning Wells's tract into a workable script, the

Fig. 8. Vincent Korda, set design for *Things to Come* (1936). He synthesized the work of Modernist designers into an impressive, yet workable, vision of the future of "Everytown."

challenge for Vincent was to assimilate the work of the prestigious Modernists that Alex had engaged—including Fernand Léger and Laszlo Moholy-Nagy—and produce a coherent futuristic design for the film. *Things to Come* was hardly more of a commercial success than *Rembrandt*, considering its high cost and practical problems, but the production of two such visually sophisticated works within the same year of release established London Films and Vincent Korda as forces to be reckoned with—equally talented as any in Hollywood. Appropriately, the Kordas moved to Hollywood soon after the outbreak of war, initially to complete their Arabian Nights fantasy *The Thief of Bagdad* (1940), but then to continue to produce high-quality propaganda for American entry into the war, in such films as *That Hamilton Woman* (Alexander Korda, 1941) and *To Be or Not to Be* (Ernst Lubitsch, 1942).

Vincent Korda had shown remarkable versatility during his first decade as a production designer, without perhaps revealing any distinctive personal style.[61] His postwar work would reveal a distinct progression from the chocolate-box confection of *An Ideal Husband* (1947), swamped by the prevailing aesthetic of Technicolor,[62] to the taut drama of two collaborations with Graham Greene as writer and Carol Reed as director, *The Fallen Idol* (1948) and *The Third Man* (1949). In these latter, he would demonstrate a mastery of settings that are realist yet lend themselves to expressionistic interpretation, especially in the nocturnal Vienna, filmed on location, and studio-built sewers of *The Third Man*. And it was arguably these films, together with Powell and Pressburger's three Technicolor masterpieces and David Lean's two Dickens adaptations, *Great Expectations* and *Oliver Twist,* that gave a new status to British production during the years of postwar economic hardship.[63] And fundamental to Lean's Dickens films was the contribution of their designer, John Bryan.

John Bryan and Theatrical Realism

Much of Vincent Korda's best-known work was for "exotic" films, such as *The Drum* (1938) and especially *The Thief of Bagdad* (1940), where he was able to unify a potentially fragmented potpourri of *Arabian Nights* motifs into a convincing, fabulous whole. One of his art department staff on *Things to Come* was John Bryan, who would go on to design the most famous of all sound-era Dickens adaptations, combining Korda's graphic expressivity with an atmospheric sense of architecture. This was no doubt due to his early experience working in a theatrical scenic artists' studio, which led to jobbing film work in the early 1930s before he joined Korda's staff at Denham. His opportunity to shape a whole film came with two George Bernard Shaw adaptations, first *Pygmalion* (1938), a production on which David Lean was editor, then on the troubled *Major Barbara* (1941), where Korda stepped aside, leaving Bryan in sole charge of designing this prestige production.[64]

Ronald Neame, who would later become a producer as would

Bryan, was cameraman on *Major Barbara* and has recalled Bryan's qualities as a designer:

> John Bryan quickly became the best designer I have ever met . . . He was the cameraman's dream boy, and the director's too. When one proposed a set to him, he would move to a sixteen by twelve drawing pad and with a few deft strokes in charcoal he would give you exactly what you had in mind. The moment John began his sketches the film came to life . . .
>
> His sets, when built, were always what one wanted. But he was a perfectionist and had no compunction about making changes if he felt they were needed, no matter what the cost . . . or aggravation he caused the construction department.[65]

Bryan gained more experience designing Victorian London for the screen with the melodramatic *Fanny by Gaslight* (Asquith, 1944), but it was the two Dickens films he worked on for Lean that allowed his talents and personal style to emerge fully. For the autobiographical *Great Expectations* (1946), the unit was based at Rochester, closely linked with Dickens's own childhood, and Lean was determined to give the film a distinctive visual style. His solution was to use long lenses, thereby flattening the image, to which Bryan responded by using forced perspective, with foreground objects larger than life and furniture specially built in perspective, effectively reviving the tradition begun by *Caligari* and its Weimar successors, and for the same reason: to convey an intense subjective view of the characters' world. The effect is first seen in the churchyard, when Magwich startles Pip — and the audience — by appearing from behind a tombstone. The scene was built in the studio, with a church only ten feet high and a cloud painted on glass, but its atmosphere and drama are unquestionable.[66] Bold stylization continues throughout the film, after Pip comes to London and begins his gilded life, with Bryan making astute use of real locations. London, it should be remembered, often represented by the dome of St. Paul's, had become a potent and frequently portrayed symbol of British resilience during the war.[67] So with the

Fig. 9. David Lean shooting the climax of *Oliver Twist* (1948) on John Bryan's set, inspired by Gustave Doré's London engravings.

image of St. Paul's, as well as elaborate studio sets, drawn in part from Cruikshank's original illustrations, *Great Expectations* became both a celebration of victorious "Englishness" in the immediate aftermath of the war, and also a contribution to the climate of neoromanticism then prevalent in English culture.[68]

After the immense success of *Great Expectations*, for which Bryan won the Academy Award, Lean wanted to change direction but found himself obsessed by Dickens's other, much darker, account of childhood, *Oliver Twist*, and so many of the same team found themselves plunged into creating the Victorian underworld. Lean encouraged Bryan to continue using forced perspective, especially to refresh scenes that were already visual clichés, such as Oliver asking for more food in the workhouse. Overall, *Oliver Twist* is literally darker, much of it taking place in squalid settings that had little natural or artificial light (see fig. 9). Chiaroscuro effects, with light seeping through dirty windows, give the film an atmosphere that has since established a new benchmark for picturing the Victorian city, a classic in its own terms, and one that fitted well with the prevailing vogue for film noir.

Bryan also made use of Gustave Doré's famous engravings of London scenes and characters, basing much of the world of Bill Sikes and Fagin on these crowded images with their fantastic Piranesian tracery of arches and bridges and arches.[69] During the 1950s, Bryan would turn toward production, no doubt frustrated by the limited opportunities offered within the British film industry at this time, but one of his last films as production designer was *The Magic Box* (1951), a biography of the controversial British cinema pioneer William Friese Greene, to which all branches of the industry contributed as part of the Festival of Britain.[70] Despite the dubious basis of its claims for Friese Greene, working on the film allowed Bryan to recreate the late Victorian world of photographers and passionate inventors in superb detail, along with London and its supposed earliest filmed images.[71] Among his later productions, *The Horse's Mouth* (1958) offered a rare view of Bohemian London, seen through the eyes of the disreputable Gulley Jimson, an artist comically ruthless in pursuit of his vision.

Neame directed this neglected comic masterpiece, and Alec Guinness, who also scripted the film, played Jimson.

Carmen Dillon: A Versatile Professional

The closest counterpart to John Bryan in British cinema during the 1940s was also its only female art director until recent times. Carmen Dillon (1908–95) had trained as an architect before starting to work in cinema in the 1930s, during the production boom that followed the introduction of the British "quota."[72] An art director from 1937, she worked on many of Anthony Asquith's wartime films, before being nominated for an Academy Award for her contribution to Laurence Olivier's highly original *Henry the Fifth* (1943). The film that Olivier directed and starred in was partly inspired by Eisenstein's stirring evocation of medieval Russia in *Alexander Nevsky* (1938), and was originally conceived by an ex-BBC producer, Dallas Bower.[73] But its greatest innovation was to recreate the Globe Theatre for its opening, before moving into heavily stylized scenes based on medieval illustration, and finally into a vivid naturalistic portrayal of the Battle of Agincourt. Dillon worked under Paul Sheriffs on this landmark Shakespeare adaptation and went on to become production designer on all Olivier's subsequent films, winning the Academy Award in 1948 for *Hamlet*.

While there is no single classic "literary London" film to her credit, her prolific forty-year career saw British cinema pass from a formulaic studio-based style through the bold experiments of the 1940s, back to retrenchment in the 1950s and early 1960s (when she designed for both the populist "Doctor" and "Carry On" comedy film series). Yet amid these often routine projects, she designed in rapid succession one of the few 1950s Dickens adaptations, Ralph Thomas's *A Tale of Two Cities* (1958), with Dirk Bogarde as Sidney Carton, and Basil Dearden's shocking exposé of London racism in the murder mystery *Sapphire* (1959), a harbinger of the new realism of the 1960s. And many of the film designers who would make their mark in the '60s and '70s owed their training to Dillon's inspiring professional example.

John Box: Reinventing Historic London for the 1960s

John Box (1920–2005) considered Carmen Dillon and John Bryan the two formative influences on him as a production designer. Having served in the war as a tank commander, and qualified as an architect, Box started work in the studios during Britain's uncertain postwar years, but was lucky to gain wider experience from working in the art department on a number of American productions based in Britain, such as *Treasure Island* (Byron Haskin, 1950), *The Black Knight* (Tay Garnett, 1954), and *The Inn of the Sixth Happiness* (Mark Robson, 1958). He is certainly best known today for his collaborations with David Lean, especially on *Lawrence of Arabia* (1962) — which he took over when Bryan fell ill — and *Doctor Zhivago* (1965), but I want to focus here on his two 1960s films that involved creating an historical London, *A Man for All Seasons* (1966) and *Oliver!* (1968), which also offer an instructive comparison in scale.

A Man for All Seasons, based on Robert Bolt's 1960 play, focuses on the moral struggle between Thomas More and his king Henry VIII over the latter's determination to ignore the Catholic Church and change English law in order to divorce his wife and marry another. As a loyal Catholic, More cannot accept this and resigns as chancellor, but he is then accused of treason by Henry and, after refusing to give way, executed. The play had enjoyed great success, with Paul Scofield becoming closely associated with the part of More, striking a defiant note of conscience and sacrifice amid the hedonism of "swinging London" in the mid-1960s. Yet when it was acquired for filming by Columbia, the project was given a much lower priority than the studio's other current production, a James Bond extravaganza, *Casino Royale*.[74] As the director Fred Zinnemann explained, *A Man* was "a very modest and, in a box-office sense, totally unpromising project . . . a costume movie [with] very little action, let alone violence, no sex, no overt love story and, most importantly, *no stars* . . . No wonder the budget was tiny."[75]

The fact that the film was being made on a low budget seems to have given all concerned an exceptionally clear focus on the priorities. With most of the script's themes being conveyed by dialogue — the play has always lent itself to being staged in a bare, Brechtian style — the film's makers had to consider how best to negotiate a balance between location and studio shooting, and what use to make of the considerable amount of surviving visual evidence of More's life and Tudor London.

Their solution involved focusing on three main settings, one of which would be realized by the use of different locations constructed in the studio, and the other two constructed in the studio, with only a few brief exterior shots to "place" one of them. More's house, supposedly beside the River Thames in a still rural Chelsea, where he first feels the force of the king's determination and which later becomes his retreat, was created by using the exterior of an historic house in Oxfordshire. For Henry's "informal" visit, part of his campaign to win over More, the filmmakers used a stretch of river on the Beaulieu estate in Hampshire, and lined the muddy water's edge so that the king could stride ashore and leap over the wall, to arrive in More's garden, actually a hundred miles away, before entering the interiors skillfully constructed in Shepperton Studio. The other key location is Hampton Court Palace, where More's predecessor as chancellor, Cardinal Wolsey, wielded his power. This palace still stands, but the production could not afford extensive location shooting, so its façade was represented by a single exterior view, supplemented by John Box's false perspective rendering painted onto flats: "Fortunately, one of the great production designers, John Box, was with us. Using three enormous flats raised in perspective, he built a replica of the palace at Hampton Court for £5000. When comparing photographs of the movie set and the real thing, no one could tell the difference."[76]

Wolsey's chamber was ingeniously made small to emphasize the menacing bulk of Orson Welles, with the walls painted in the same imperious red as his cardinal's robe. The other key setting is Westminster Hall, where More's trumped-up trial for treason takes place before Parliament. Here, director and designer were fully agreed that the setting should be spare as well as imposing — "conceived by us as a kind of bullring"[77] — relieved only by the red robes of the judges

Fig. 10. John Box, set design for *A Man for All Seasons* (1966). Standing in for Westminster Hall, the set was conceived as "a kind of bull-ring."

and the green silk costume of More's opportunistic accuser, Richard Rich (see fig 10).

There is a comparatively extensive iconography of More's life and martyrdom, owing to his high position and subsequent canonization by the Catholic Church, which the filmmakers used as a basis for the More family scenes and the trial. But Zinnemann resisted the temptation to "open out" what is essentially a study of conscience resisting tyrannical power. The film's limited budget no doubt helped maintain this focus, avoiding any irrelevant period detail and ensuring that what visual spectacle there is serves a dramatic purpose. Even More's execution at the Tower of London is shown tightly framed, keeping the drama of conscience wholly at the center of attention. As a film of theological controversy and of early Tudor London, *A Man for All Seasons* is notably austere, yet unquestionably all the more effective for its restraint.

By contrast, John Box's second essay in representing historic London counts as one of the most lavish and exuberant screen celebrations of the Victorian city. *Oliver!* (1960) was a successful musical version of Dickens's novel by Lionel Bart, originally nurtured by Joan Littlewood's East End Theatre Workshop (itself partly inspired by the British discovery of Brecht), which interpolated both lively and sentimental songs into the original story and created major roles for "The Artful Dodger," Fagin, and Nancy. After its great success on stage, the film version was keenly awaited, but its progress to the screen was dogged with problems. John Box, already appointed production designer, was responsible for proposing Carol Reed as a last-minute choice for director, with the result that most of the key production personnel lacked any previous experience making musicals. This may account for a lack of slickness and the frank engagement with darker issues that makes *Oliver!* the equal of some major American musicals, and a major contribution to the long history of Dickens adaptations for stage and screen mentioned earlier.

Unlike *A Man for All Seasons*, *Oliver!* had a substantial budget for the construction of sets at Shepperton. Three of these are particularly interesting in relation to the iconography of Victorian London: the Covent Garden market in which Oliver first experiences London's excitement; the network of wooden walkways that provide entry to Fagin's attic den and to the waterside tavern where those in the underworld gather; and the crescent of luxurious new houses that represent the moneyed world to which Oliver will finally escape. None of these sets depicts an actual city location: all are composites that combine accurate period detail with elements of stylization and fantasy. The market scene into which Oliver emerges from his ride to London in a produce wagon bears some relation to the Covent Garden fruit and vegetable market that has featured in many films as a signifier of "historic London," centered around Inigo Jones's Piazza and church of St. Paul's.[78] But it is also an "expanded" Covent Garden that includes some activity of the meat market of Smithfield, while the main street offers a perspective clearly inspired by Gustave Doré's

Fig. 11. Gustave Doré, "Ludgate Hill: A Block in the Street," from *London: A Pilgrimage* (1872).

engraving "Ludgate Hill: A Block in the Street," with a train crossing overhead (see figs. 11 and 12).[79]

The wooden steps and the recurrent distant dome of St. Paul's also owe much to Doré, and to the earlier *Oliver Twist* designs of Box's mentor John Bryan, but there is evidence of new research on historic London buildings, as Colin Sorenson demonstrated in his pioneering

Fig. 12. John Box, set design for *Oliver!* (1968). His construction of the main London street exterior was inspired by Doré.

study *London on Film*.[80] For the later sequence, built around the song "Who Will Buy?" and set in fashionable London, when Mr. Brownlow has first rescued Oliver from the clutches of Fagin, Box designed and built on the Shepperton backlot a full-scale crescent terrace. Faced in brilliant white, with elaborate ironwork and a central garden, this may be more evocative of Bath, but it also corresponds to the elegant stuccoed crescents that were being built around London in the early nineteenth century.[81] And in dramatic terms, the contrast between the darkest London that Oliver has been incarcerated in and this shining vision of a new London of wealth and benevolence becomes a vital axis of the film, giving substance to both Dickens's and Bart's redemptive fantasy.

Can we draw any general conclusions from these case studies? Rather than attempt to consider them merely in terms of "accuracy," it is more fruitful to place the work of production designers in the wider context of the history of representing London — which has never been merely a matter of topographic precision.[82] Between William Hogarth's well-known prints of the 1750s, including "Gin Lane" and "Beer Street," and Doré's portfolio of 1872, there was a rich tradition of London illustration, greatly supplemented by the engravings published by the *Illustrated London News* from the 1850s onward.[83] Often the aim of such illustration was to convey an impression, or a judgment (as in Hogarth's moralistic print series).[84] Doré was accused by at least one contemporary critic of "inventing rather than copying" in his portrayal of a relentlessly gloomy, teeming metropolis.[85]

From the earliest moment at which they could escape the painted canvas of the studio and take to the streets, filmmakers have been seeking to convey what Samuel Johnson called "the wonderful extent and variety of London." In doing so, they have been constrained by many factors, not least the ever-changing face of the city itself, which, driven by commerce, has left few historic views unaltered and also made it immensely, prohibitively expensive to shoot on location. *Pace* Panofsky and his faith in "unutilized reality," this has meant that, paradoxically, many of the most "authentic" screen representations of London have been created in the studio (albeit often a suburban London studio), using cinema's range of trompe l'oeil effects.

Nor has such authenticity usually been a matter of strict visual correspondence between image and reality, since the viewer's referent is more likely to be other representations of London. In terms of the Affrons' categorization of set functions, London settings are usually both denotative *and* narrative, in that the location of characters within, or movement between, particular districts of the city constitutes a narrative in itself.[86] Thus, no less than any twentieth-century London gangster moving from East to West or contemplating the disappearance of the "old East End,"[87] Thomas More commutes between his home in Chelsea and the centers of state power, Hampton Court, Parliament, and the Tower, while the Oliver of the 1968 film is the first to traverse a richly textured yet deterritorialized "Dickensian" London conceived in color.

The founders of the British school of production design were, perhaps unsurprisingly, both foreigners, central Europeans who made England their temporary home. But Alfred Junge and Vincent Korda brought with them international experience that British studios badly needed at the beginning of the 1930s, and both stayed long enough to train their native pupils and successors. Both believed implicitly in the professional principle that art direction should be "invisible," yet both contributed to the rising prestige of the designer that would lead to their successors becoming highly influential in giving British films a distinctive stylization, a creative intertextual relationship with the literary works that are often their premise.[88] What is more, these relationships and traditions have continued. Most recently, Stuart Craig emerged from the Bryan-Box succession to design very different versions of Victorian London for *The Elephant Man* (David Lynch, 1980) and *Chaplin* (Richard Attenborough, 1992), before creating a paradigmatic version of contemporary London in *Notting Hill* (Roger Michell, 1999) and then embarking on the hugely popular Harry Potter series, rooted in the tradition of English juvenile fantasy fiction and combining British studio practice with the new graphic resources of CGI.[89]

Meanwhile, the process of reimagining an earlier London also continues, with notable contributions from foreign designers. One of the most remarkable in recent years has been a rare vision of the seventeenth-century city, in *Restoration* (1995), Michael Hoffman's film drawn from a novel by Rose Tremain and designed by the Argentinean Eugenio Zanetti. An American critic's response encapsulates the sense of revelation that London films have attempted, and have occasionally achieved, over the past century: "Never before in the movies have I seen such a riotous depiction of period London: The overwhelming excess of the royal court, the teeming traffic on the Thames, the bridges groaning with buildings and people, the streets jammed with life and lowlife, the delight in all the pleasures of the flesh — and then, like two grim wake-up calls, the Black Plague and the Great Fire. It is remarkable that this movie, which re-creates a world, cost only about $18 million, and never seems to cut a corner."[90]

The adaptation of Dickens for the cinema has also continued apace, despite the prevalence of television serial adaptation, which allows for greater textual fidelity to the novels.[91] Alfonso Cuaron successfully transposed *Great Expectations* to an American setting in 1998, with his English designer Tony Burrough finding narrative equivalents to Dickens's Kent and London in modern Florida, Manhattan, and Long Island. And Roman Polanski returned to the roots of the studio tradition with his *Oliver Twist* (2005), made at the Barrandov Studio in Prague, where the distinguished Polish production designer Alan Starski was able to create a more realistically squalid London than either Bryan or Box could have contemplated for this study of survival against the odds. Within a longer perspective, Grahame Smith has shown how "visualization" played a vital part in Dickens's imaginative life and works, and notes that his evocative power was readily compared with the new photographic media of the nineteenth century by his contemporaries.[92] We should therefore not be surprised that the "remediation" of Dickens continues to play an important role in British, and indeed world, cinema.

NOTES

The Samuel Johnson quote in the epigraph is from James Boswell's *London Journal, 1762-73*, ed. A. F. Pottle (William Heinemann, 1950).

1. Although written by the novelist Graham Greene, *The Third Man* was an original screenplay, while *Lawrence of Arabia* was scripted by the playwright Robert Bolt, after earlier attempts to adapt Lawrence's own memoir, *The Seven Pillars of Wisdom*, had failed to reach production.

2. Andrew Higson, "Representing the National Past: Nostalgia and Pastiche in the Heritage Film," in *British Cinema and Thatcherism*, ed. L. Friedman, (London: UCL Press, 1993), 114. For an overview of the "heritage cinema" debate,

see Sheldon Hall, "The Wrong Sort of Cinema: Refashioning the Heritage Film Debate," in *The British Cinema Book*, 2nd ed., ed. Robert Murphy (London: British Film Institute [hereafter BFI], 2001), 191–99.

3. Hall, "Wrong Sort of Cinema"; Higson, "Representing the National Past," 114.

4. A typical dismissive review, though by a literary rather than a film critic, is Alan Hollinghurst's review of *A Room with a View*, in which he describes the novel as Forster's "least interesting" and the Merchant-Ivory film as "a spirited if simple-minded confection" ("Detached about Attachments," *Times Literary Supplement*, April 11, 1986, 375).

5. See, for instance, Claire Monk's argument that *A Room with a View* and *Maurice* are more radical in their portrayal of sexuality and gender than apparently more frank recent films such as *Carrington* and *Orlando* ("Sexuality and the Heritage," *Sight and Sound*, n.s., 5 (October 1995): 33–34.

6. "In the Merchant-Ivory films, where they make use of English settings, one wide shot says it all, and you really get a sense of who these people are" (Quoted in *Scorsese on Scorsese*, 3rd ed., ed. Ian Christie and David Thompson [Faber, 2003], 187).

7. Raphael Samuel, *Theatres of Memory* (Verso, 1994). See also Carolyn Steedman, Obituary of Raphael Samuel, *Radical Philosophy*, March–April 1997, 53–55.

8. On the peculiar history of British critics' animosity toward British cinema, see, for instance: Victor Perkins, "The British Cinema," *Movie*, no. 1, 1962; Ian Christie, *Arrows of Desire: The Films of Michael Powell and Emeric Pressburger*, 2nd ed. (Faber, 1994); Julian Petley, "The Lost Continent," in *All Our Yesterdays*, ed. Charles Barr (London: BFI, 1986), 31–46; Alan Lovell, "British Cinema: The Known Cinema?" in Murphy, *The British Cinema Book*, 200–205 (see note 2 earlier).

9. See, for instance, the UK Film Council report *Stately Attraction: How Film and Television Programmes Promote Tourism in the UK*, 2007, summarized in *The Guardian*, August 27, 2007.

10. On the "brains of people both in and out of the film industry," see Paul Rotha, the author of the first influential survey of world cinema after the pioneer period, in *The Film Till Now* (London: Jonathan Cape, 1930), 47. The "eyes of the madman" quote is from C. A. Lejeune, *Cinema* (London: Alexander Maclehose, 1931), 113.

11. Panofsky's paper "Style and Medium in the Motion Picture," first given as a talk at Princeton University, was intended to help raise interest in the proposed film department of the Museum of Modern Art in New York and published in Princeton's *Bulletin of the Department of Art and Archaeology* in 1934. A revised

version appeared in *Critique* vol. 1, no. 3 (1947), but the piece's wider influence was owing to its inclusion in the pioneering collection edited by Daniel Talbot, *Film: An Anthology* (Berkeley: University of California Press, 1966), 15–32.

12. André Bazin, "Theatre and Cinema," in *What Is Cinema?* ed. and trans. Hugh Gray (Berkeley: University of California Press, 1967), 109.

13. Bazin, "The Evolution of the Language of Cinema," in *What Is Cinema?*, 37.

14. Although the "Film d'Art" production company proved commercially unsuccessful and was absorbed by Pathé, this style of "historical" production was widely imitated through Pathé's international network of affiliates.

15. Bardèche and Brasillach's book was first published in France as *Histoire du cinema* in 1935, but it reached a wider public when it was translated into English by Iris Barry, first head of the film department at MoMA, and was published as *History of the Film* in 1938.

16. Echoes of the verdict that Film d'art represented a "wrong turn" in cinema's early development can be found in many popular histories before David Robinson's *World Cinema: A Short History* (London: Eyre Methuen, 1973), which set the record straight.

17. On *photogénie*, see Jean Epstein, various articles translated in *Afterimage* 10 (1981): 9–16, also Richard Abel, *French Film Theory and Criticism, 1907–1939*, vol. 1 (Princeton: Princeton University Press, 1988), 107–11.

18. See, for instance, Sergei Eisenstein, "Bela Forgets the Scissors," a polemical article written as a riposte to the Hungarian critic Bela Balazs, who had praised the imagery of Eisenstein's *Battleship Potemkin*. The film's power, according to Eisenstein, followed from its use of editing, or montage. The article is translated in Richard Taylor, ed., *Sergei Eisenstein: Selected Works*, vol. 1: *Writings, 1922–34* (London: BFI, 1988), 77–81.

19. See, for example, Ernest Lindgren, *The Art of the Film* (Allen and Unwin, 1948). Lindgren's guide to "film appreciation" appeared among a large number of postwar publications that constituted the earliest library of writings on film as art. The work of the "art director" is mentioned only briefly in the introductory chapter, while "editing" is the subject of two out of ten chapters.

20. The opening sentence of Pudovkin's influential book *Film Technique* (1928) is quoted as canonical in Lindgren, *Art of the Film*, 47.

21. Robert Stam, Robert Burgoyne, and Sandy Flitterman-Lewis, *New Vocabularies in Film Semiotics* (Routledge, 1992), 142.

22. Charles Affron and Mirella Jona Affron, *Sets in Motion: Art Direction and Film Narrative* (Rutgers University Press, 1995).

23. Affron and Affron, *Sets in Motion*, 36–37. The fifth level of the scheme, referred to in the next paragraph, is discussed on 39.

24. Examples include: Catherine A. Surowiec, *Accent on Design: Four European Art Directors* (London: BFI, 1992), which deals with Heckroth, Junge, Korda, and Lazare Meerson; Christopher Frayling, *Ken Adam and the Art of Production Design* (Faber, 2005); Peter Ettedgui, *Production Design and Art Direction* (Switzerland: Crans-Prés-Céligny, 1999). On terminology: it should be noted that although the lead designer on a film is now called "production designer," this role was known as "art director" until the 1950s. Today, the art director is usually the immediate subordinate of the production designer; and the field of work is ambiguously referred to as "production design" and "art direction."

25. This revaluation is often dated to the 1978 FIAF international film archives congress at Brighton, which considered the surviving films of the first decade of cinema and led to influential publications by, among others, Noel Burch, Tom Gunning, André Gaudreault, and Stephen Bottomore. For an overview and examples of these writings, see Thomas Elsaesser and Adam Barker, eds., *Early Cinema: Space, Frame, Narrative* (BFI, 1990).

26. On the view of early films as merely recording "pre-arranged" dramatic action, see Lindgren, *Art of the Film*, 47 Regarding the teleological model of cinematic progression, and in fairness to earlier scholars, please note that both Terry Ramsaye, in *A Million and One Nights* (1926), and Ernest Lindgren placed cinema in a larger context, especially that of literature.

27. Jay Bolter and Richard Grusin, *Remediation: Understanding New Media* (MIT Press, 2000).

28. Mikhail Bakhtin, *Speech Genres and Other Late Essays* (University of Texas Press, 1986), 5.

29. On *The May Irwin Kiss*, see Charles Musser, Film Notes, Disc One, notes accompanying the DVD set *Edison: The Invention of the Movies*, at http://www.kino.com/edison/pdfs/FilmNotes_DVD1.pdf (accessed August 23, 2008).

30. Richard Brown and Barry Anthony, *A Victorian Film Enterprise: The History of the British Mutoscope and Biograph Company, 1897–1915* (Flicks, 1999), 272.

31. Dickens's *A Christmas Carol in Prose, Being a Ghost Story of Christmas* (usually known as *A Christmas Carol*), was first published in December 1843, with illustrations by John Leech.

32. Bakhtin, *Speech Genres*, 5.

33. On the international evolution of early scenography, see my entry for "set design" in Richard Abel, *Encyclopedia of Early Cinema* (Routledge, 2005), 584–87.

34. Italian films' high earnings were partly due to the new business terms for "exclusive" release that they helped initiate around 1911–13. Distributors and exhibitors would compete when offering terms for these major attractions.

35. Letter from O'Neill to Beatrice Ashe, October 7, 1914, quoted in Richard Hayes, "'The Scope of the Movies': Three Films and Their Influence on Eugene O'Neill," *The Eugene O'Neill Review* 25 (Spring/Fall 2001), http://www.eoneill.com/library/review/index.htm (accessed August 23, 2008).

36. Rachael Low, *History of the British Film*, vol. 2: *1906–1914* (George Allen & Unwin, 1948), 134.

37. The *Illustrated London News* was founded by Herbert Ingram in 1842 and is widely regarded as the first illustrated periodical in the world. Judith Cowan has established how closely Barker and Samuelson followed ILN treatment of key events in Victoria's reign ("Creating the British Feature Film Industry: W. G. Barker and G. B. Samuelson, 1909–1916," PhD thesis, Birkbeck College, University of London, 2008).

38. Low, *History of the British Film*, 2:219.

39. On the range of early Shakespeare films, see Luke McKernan and Olwen Terris, eds., *Walking Shadows*: Shakespeare *in the National Film and Television Archive* (London: BFI, 1994).

40. Low, *History of the British Film*, 2:190.

41. Sergei Eisenstein, "Dickens, Griffith and the Film Today" (1944), published in *Film Form: Essays in Film Theory*, ed. and trans. Jay Leyda (Harcourt, Brace and World, 1949), 195–255.

42. *The Bioscope*, September 24, 1914, 1160; quoted in Low, *History of the British Film*, vol. 3: *1914–1918*, 54–55. Warwick Buckland appears to have been unconnected with Wilfred Buckland, DeMille's art director, and to have served as an all-round member of Hepworth's studio staff.

43. *The Kinematograph and Lantern Weekly*, March 1, 1917, 23.

44. See Kristin Thompson, *Exporting Entertainment: America in the World Film Market, 1907–1934* (London: BFI, 1986).

45. Sir Hubert Herkomer RA, one of England's most distinguished painters, announced in 1913 that he was giving up painting to embark on a new career as a filmmaker, believing that "the cinematograph is going to be the greatest educational force of the time." Unfortunately, he died less than a year later, leaving only a handful of completed films, none of which survive. See Lynda Nead, "Paintings, Films and Fast Cars: A Case Study of Hubert von Herkomer," *Art History* 25, no. 2 (2002): 240–55; and Ian Christie, "Before the Avant-Gardes: Artists and Film, 1910–1914," in *The Tenth Muse*, ed. Leonardo Quaresima and Laura Vichi (Udine, 2001), 369–70.

46. On Bernhardt's early film career, see Richard Abel, *The Ciné Goes to Town: French Cinema, 1896–1914* (Berkeley: University of California Press, 1998), 313–16.

47. DeMille famously cabled to his financiers in New York that he had reached "a place called Hollywood" where he proposed to begin filming his first production, *The Squaw Man*, in 1913. On DeMille's early career, see John Kobal, *L'Eretità DeMille* (The DeMille Heritage), ed. Paola Cherchi Usai and Lorenzo Codelli (Edizione Biblioteca dell'immagine, 1991).

48. According to accounts of Buckland's relationship with DeMille, it was the former who insisted on integration and followed Belasco's precepts. See Leon Barsacq, *Caligari's Cabinet and Other Grand Illusions: A History of Film Design*, trans. and rev. Elliott Stein (New American Library, 1976), 200.

49. Adolph Zukor, "Famous Players in Famous Plays," *Motion Picture World*, July 11, 1914, 186, quoted in Sumiko Higashi, *Cecil B. DeMille and American Culture: The Silent Era* (Berkeley: University of California Press, 1994), 8.

50. "Cashing in on Europe's War, 1916–18" is the title of a chapter in Kristin Thompson's invaluable study, *Exporting Entertainment* (see note 45). The frontispiece to the book is a 1917 trade paper cartoon captioned "Zukor annexes Australia."

51. K. Thompson, *Exporting Entertainment*, 63–64.

52. "Patriotism and Business" is the heading of an Ideal trade advertisement that insists these should not be confused, while arguing that its films successfully combine them (*Kinematograph and Lantern Weekly*, March 22, 1917).

53. See Roberta Pearson and William Uricchio, *The Vitagraph Quality Film* (Princeton University Press, 1983).

54. See Miriam Hansen, *Babel to Babylon* (Harvard University Press, 1991), 113.

55. Marion Blackton Trimble's "Personal Biography by His Daughter" is certainly not always reliable, but her account of this dinner in 1920, which arose from shared interests in yachting, strikes a convincing note. See Marion Blackton Trimble, *J. Stuart Blackton* (Scarecrow Press, 1985), 102–4.

56. *Restoration* (1995), adapted from a novel by Rose Tremain and directed by Michael Hoffman, is set in the reign of Charles II and includes both the Plague and the Great Fire. Significantly, it won Eugenio Zanetti the Academy Award for production design.

57. Marion Blackton Trimble's account of the filming, in which she participated (*J. Stuart Blackton*, 124–44), is unfortunately entirely anecdotal.

58. Some art directors were emerging in the late teens, however, as is apparent from occasional articles in the trade press. See, for instance, a report on a talk by E. P. Kinsella, which included a contribution by "Hayward Young ... the first artist in this country to become an Art Director in the film studio," in "Kinsella on 'Art in Production,'" *Kinematograph and Lantern Weekly*, December 12, 1918, 59.

59. This and the subsequent quotation are from his nephew's memoir: Michael Korda, *Charmed Lives: A Family Romance* (Penguin, 1979), 99.

60. After World War I, Wells had campaigned for an international organization, which led to the League of Nations, and wrote *An Outline of History* (1919–20) to spread popular awareness of the lessons of history. *The Shape of Things to Come* (1933), set in 1930, uses the conceit of a "dream diary," based on the theories of J. W. Dunne, in which the hero foresees the following century.

61. In his *Designing for Moving Pictures*, the art director Edward Carrick wrote of Vincent Korda, "There is no distinctive personal touch about [his] sketches or finished sets," adding that, "I think he is apt to look on films too much as a commercial product," *Designing for Moving Pictures* (Studio Publications, [n.d.]), 39.

62. During the 1930s and much of the 1940s, the Technicolor company stipulated that a representative from the firm had to be involved in each production using the process. This was usually Natalie Kalmus, wife of the founder Herbert Kalmus, and she notoriously insisted on the maximum range and saturation of color, to the irritation of many filmmakers and cameramen.

63. The Powell-Pressburger films that impressed many outside Britain were *A Matter of Life and Death* (1946), *Black Narcissus* (1947), and *The Red Shoes* (1948). On these and the course of British cinema history in the postwar period, see Ian Christie, *Arrows of Desire: The Films of Michael Powell and Emeric Pressburger*, 2nd ed. (Faber, 1994). See also Sarah Street, *British National Cinema* (Routledge, 1997).

64. The history of film adaptations of George Bernard Shaw's plays, in which the playwright took a close interest, is almost a chapter of British film history in its own right. For Shaw's views, see Bernard F. Dukore, ed., *Bernard Shaw on Cinema* (Carbondale: Southern Illinois University Press, 1997).

65. Ronald Neame, quoted in Kevin Brownlow, *David Lean* (Richard Cohen Books, 1996), 138–39.

66. Brownlow, *David Lean*, 208–10.

67. See for instance the recurrent image of St. Paul's in Humphrey Jennings's wartime documentaries *Listen to Britain* and *Fires Were Started*, and in many newsreels of the period.

68. Among the neoromantics could be included the painters Graham Sutherland, John Piper, and Cecil Collins, along with poets, musicians, and filmmakers. See David Mellor, ed., *Paradise Lost: The Neo-romantic Imagination in Britain, 1935–1955* (London: Lund Humphries, 1987).

69. Gustave Doré and Blanchard Jerrold, *London: A Pilgrimage* (London: Grant and Co., 1872).

70. *The Magic Box* was based on a biography of Friese Greene (1855–1921) that supported his claim to have devised practical moving pictures by 1899, before Edison or the Lumières. Although Greene's claims would later be disproved, the film, which vividly evokes the late nineteenth-century pioneer photographic ethos, lives on through Bryan's rich color décor, Jack Cardiff's cinematography, and an all-star cast led by Robert Donat.

71. *The Magic Box*'s recreation of the alleged first showing of Greene's Hyde Park film, to a bewildered policeman, is justly celebrated — even if wholly fictitious.

72. The 1927 Cinematograph Film Act obliged British exhibitors and distributors to meet a rising minimum quota of domestic productions throughout the 1930s; this encouraged many new companies to start making low-budget "quota films."

73. Bower had produced *Alexander Nevsky* as a radio play in 1941. See Ian Christie, "Censorship, Culture and Codpieces: Eisenstein's Influence in England during the 1930s and '40s," in *Eisenstein at 100: A Reconsideration*, ed. Al Lavalley and Barry P. Scherr (Rutgers University Press, 2001), 113–16.

74. This Bond title was the only one not owned by the Saltzman-Broccoli partnership that had launched the Bond series with *Dr No*. It had become a Peter Sellers "vanity project," with multiple actors playing Bond and up to six directors, described by Roger Ebert as "a definitive example of what can happen when everybody working on a film goes simultaneously berserk" (http://rogerebert.suntimes.com, accessed July 13, 2010).

75. Fred Zinnemann, *An Autobiography* (Bloomsbury, 1992), 199.

76. Zinnemann, *Autobiography*, 199.

77. Zinnemann, *Autobiography*, 201.

78. Films that feature the Covent Garden market include *Pygmalion* (Anthony Asquith, 1938), *The Red Shoes* (Powell and Pressburger, 1948), *My Fair Lady* (George Cukor, 1964), and *Frenzy* (Alfred Hitchcock, 1972). In Dickens's novel, Oliver arrives in Barnet and proceeds to Islington and Saffron Hill.

79. Doré and Jerrold, *London: A Pilgrimage*, pl. 115.

80. Other Doré prints that likely had an influence on the *Oliver!* set include no. 4, "The Tide of Business in the City," no. 23, "A River-Side Street," and especially no. 130, "St. Pauls from the Brewery Bridge," all in *London: A Pilgrimage*. In *London on Film*, Sorenson juxtaposes a photograph from the Society for Photographing Relics of Old London, "Old Houses in Fore Street," with part of Box's backstreet set (*London on Film: 100 Years of Filmmaking in London* [Museum of London, 1996], 104–5).

81. Pelham Crescent, SW7, for instance, was built in 1827–30. Another model might be Percy Circus, WC1.

82. There is a wider continuing debate on film's "challenge to our idea of history," as the subtitle reads for Robert Rosenstone, *Visions of the Past* (Cambridge: Harvard University Press, 1995). See also writings by Natalie Zemon Davis, Hayden White, and Raphael Samuel.

83. On eighteenth-century imagery, see Sheila O'Connell, *London 1753* (British Museum Press, 2003), catalogue of an exhibition in the Print Room of the British Museum. On mid-Victorian London illustration, see Lynda Nead, *Victorian Babylon: People, Streets and Images in Nineteenth-Century London* (New Haven: Yale, 2000), especially part 1, "Mapping and Movement."

84. Roy Porter observes, however, that Hogarth's print series *A Rake's Progress* and *A Harlot's Progress* are "allegories but also literal journeys through the capital" (Porter, "The Wonderful Extent and Variety of London," in O'Connell, *London 1753*, 17).

85. *The Art Journal*, 1872.

86. Affron and Affron, *Sets in Motion*, 40–41.

87. As in such modern gangster classics as *Performance* (Roeg/Cammell, 1970) and *The Long Good Friday* (Mackenzie, 1980).

88. Developing Bakhtin's concept of "intertextuality," whereby various texts are seen in shifting relations to each other, without a presumed hierarchy of chronology or status, may provide a firmer basis than "adaptation" for considering the translation from verbal to audiovisual text. On specifically filmic applications of intertextuality, see Mikhail Iampolski, *The Memory of Tiresias: Intertextuality and Film* (Berkeley: University of California Press, 1998).

89. Computer generated images (CGI) have come to play a significant part in many films during the last ten years, replacing what was once achieved by "glass" or matte shots, whereby painted imagery was introduced into the photographic image. However, many contemporary films use a combination of built structures and CGI to create a more substantial effect.

90. Roger Ebert, review of *Restoration*, *Chicago Sun-Times*, January 26, 1996.

91. Television serial adaptation offers the opportunity to retain more narrative. The BBC's *Our Mutual Friend* in 1998, for instance, ran for 360 minutes, while its 2005 *Bleak House* extended to 480 minutes.

92. Grahame Smith, *Dickens and the Dream of Cinema* (Manchester University Press, 2003).

2 Architecture in Historical Fiction
A Historical and Comparative Study

MICHAEL ALEXANDER

"Historical fiction" usually is understood to mean the new kind of prose fiction developed two centuries ago by Walter Scott, now known as the historical novel. Scott established the genre, so much so that a discussion of historical fiction would lack perspective without some consideration of Scott's own output, which is both copious (twenty-five novels and romances) and various. "Historical fiction" may be defined as an imaginative story set in the past: a fiction that nevertheless offers a form of historical truth. The "past" in which the true historical novel is set belongs to a period before the birth of the author and sometimes is characterized by the "sixty-year rule," which is understood to mean that the readers of such a text cannot have experienced any of the events it depicts. In such fiction, imaginary as well as historical persons may appear as characters, yet the story is offered as something worthy of historical credit, not as a fantasy. The history drawn on by the author is traditional and legendary as well as factual, but a general impression of historical trustworthiness is intended. These senses all are included in the term "historical fiction" as used by literary critics and literary historians.

In modern usage, "fiction" and "the novel" are almost interchangeable. In Scott's day, however, readers of fiction distinguished between the novel and the romance, the latter a term that indicated a less probable kind of fiction. Scott's own fictional practice ranges from what can be believed readily by the historically minded to that to which only lovers of legend can give imaginative assent. His historical novels, such as *Waverley*, *Old Mortality*, and *The Heart of Midlothian*, are generally far more realistic than the series of later romances which he began with *Ivanhoe*, a title to which he pointedly gave the subtitle, *A Romance*. To state the distinction firmly, the historical *novel* is set in an historical period, employs events, persons, and manners of that period, and offers itself as credible. The *romance*, a kind of story more ancient than the novel, more like a legend, folktale, or fairy tale, is set in the past but does not offer itself seriously as historical; the historical romance that Scott developed is less realistic than the historical novel both in the events portrayed and in the manner of their portrayal. The characters in *Ivanhoe: A Romance*, for example, are simple types. Some are based on historical figures, such as King Richard I of England and his brother Prince John, though Scott presents them as hero and villain. A second hero of *Ivanhoe* is Robin Hood, a hero familiar from many ballad romances, which had achieved a new popularity in print in Scott's childhood. Besides the nominal hero, Ivanhoe himself, the cast of Scott's romance includes such Gothic caricatures as Ulrica, a Scandinavian witch, and the chief villain, Sir Brian de Bois-Guilbert, a cruel Templar knight, secret atheist, and foiled rapist.

The writing of history has become an academic profession since Scott's day. The English word "history" originally comprehended both "story" and "history," as it still does in French and Italian. Moreover, if we look back beyond the year 1800, in which historical novels began to appear, even a brief survey of literary history discloses that narratives with some claim to historical truth existed in forms quite unlike the historical novel as developed by Scott. At the beginnings of Western literature, the Homeric epics are historical fictions, telling traditional stories about real events and persons of the past. Homer influenced the first Greek historian, Herodotus. Likewise, a sincere Christian can regard parts of the Bible as historical fiction, since parts of the Old Testament fit our working definition of an imaginative story that nevertheless offers an historical truth — the adventures of David before he became king, for example. The Scriptures also include details of a more factual kind, such as the building specifications for the Temple of Solomon. Greek historians believed that there was a siege of Troy, but it is not literally true that Achilles, as Homer relates in detail in the *Iliad*, had a new shield made for him by the god Hephaistos. We can say that ancient narratives wove together strands of what are now distinguished into history, legend, myth, and allegorical fable. Yet even the most historically accurate narratives are shaped to some extent by the patterns and needs of storytelling. The nonfactual nature of historical fiction that purports to offer historical truth has to be borne in mind when we look at the role of architecture within such writing.

The historical novel established by Scott had spectacular international success, and the fashion lasted for fifty years after his death in 1832. To indicate its scope, we have only to name some practitioners: James Fenimore Cooper in the United States, William Makepeace Thackeray and George Eliot in England, and Stendhal, Alessandro Manzoni, and Leo Tolstoy in Europe. The tide of historical fiction reached its highest point in the 1860s with Tolstoy's *War and Peace*. It had begun to ebb before the death of Robert Louis Stevenson in 1894, though it never has ebbed in the popular market. Serious novelists still sometimes use it, as did William Golding and Tomasi di Lampedusa, and every year sees a number of would-be serious historical novels, often based on the more sensational parts of modern history. Charles Frazier's *Cold Mountain* is a successful modern instance of an epic romance, a modern odyssey that is also a historical novel. Fictionalized biographies of Tudor figures are popular in England.

The invitation extended to me by the editors of this volume was to address the role of architecture in historical fiction, and specifically "between 1700 and 1900." With regard to the genre of historical novels as developed by Walter Scott, nothing that scholars would call historical fiction — certainly nothing that is read today — was written before 1800, when Maria Edgeworth published *Castle Rackrent*. It is not generally recognized that Walter Scott's own historical fiction was at first in verse, and only later in prose. He borrowed and developed his verse forms and his narrative techniques from the ballad romances surviving from the Middle Ages. These had been collected and republished by editors in Scotland and England in the late eighteenth century and found a large audience. Scott's historical verse romances, beginning with *The Lay of the Last Minstrel* in 1805, were wildly popular. *The Lady of the Lake* earned its modern minstrel £10,000. These verse romances also enjoyed a critical esteem that lasted for decades; Thomas Hardy held that Scott's verse romance *Marmion* should be spoken of in the same breath as Homer. Walter Scott set his verse romances in Scotland on the eve of the Reformation and followed them with a series of historical novels set in Scotland after the Reformation. These begin with *Waverley*, a novel that addresses the most dramatic event to occur in Scottish history since the Union of Parliaments in 1707: the Jacobite rising of 1745, led by the Young Pretender, Bonnie Prince Charlie. *Waverley* draws attention to its historical scope by the apparent precision of its subtitle: *or 'Tis 60 Years Since*. When *Waverley* was published, in 1815, the year of British victory at Waterloo, it not sixty but seventy years since 1745. Scott later explained that he had begun (and abandoned) the writing of it in 1805.

Critics consider these novels of Scottish history to be Scott's major achievement. Just as he gave up writing historical romances in verse to write historical novels in prose, he now gave up historical novels in order to write historical romances in prose. These are set mostly in pre-Reformation times and not in Scotland but in England, in the parts of Europe nearest to Britain, and in the Palestine of the Crusades. They begin with *Ivanhoe: A Romance*, which uses stories and characters found in old ballad romances about Robin Hood and others about Richard the Lionheart. Scott's fiction is conceived theatrically: localities and costumes are described elaborately, and scenes are shaped in ways that are familiar to us from the stage. *Ivanhoe* took the stage by storm. Published in Edinburgh in 1819, it appeared on five London stages in 1820. Illustrated editions soon appeared. Scott's historical fictions transferred easily into costume drama and opera, and later into the more visual media of painting and then film. *Ivanhoe* has been the most influential historical romance, and not only for other writers, but also for the popular media, especially the cinema, and not just for films like *Robin Hood, Prince of Thieves* or *Braveheart*. The subtitle of *Waverley* is *'Tis Sixty Years Since*. The subtitle of *Ivanhoe* is *A Romance*, not *'Tis Six Hundred Years Since*; the precise dates of *Waverly*'s subtitle are not needed for *Ivanhoe* because romance does not claim historical credibility.

As part of their theatrical conception, Scott's novels contain descriptions of a considerable number of buildings. The architecture of *Ivanhoe* begins with the "low-built" hall of Ivanhoe's father. This Saxon hall is a wooden building belonging to the hospitable descendants of the former rulers of England, the Anglo-Saxons. The "low-built" old hall is a home, not a palace, and as such offers a clear contrast to the two lofty stone-built Norman castles of Torquilstone and Templestowe. The political symbolism embodied by the architecture of these buildings is clear: in the England of those days (the 1190s), the Saxons were kept too low, and their Norman rulers bore themselves too high. The pages of Scott are full of lofty castles, and his works contribute to the prominence of castles in our ideas of the Middle Ages. The Church too was a prominent feature of medieval life, and yet there are no churches in *Ivanhoe*. There is a hermit's cell, very low indeed, and in a ruinous condition. This is the abode of Friar Tuck, a glutton, a boozer, and a brawler. The only other member of the clergy mentioned is an abbot, who is fat and lecherous. More marginally religious are the Knights Templar, a chivalric order who protect pilgrims going to Jerusalem and have taken religious vows. The Templar headquarters in *Ivanhoe* is the castle of Templestowe, a building more secular than religious. This brief survey of the buildings and clergy in *Ivanhoe* seems to show that Scott, a Unionist Scot, took a Protestant and Enlightenment view of the Catholic religion of medieval England. Similarly, in *The Lay of the Last Minstrel*, set in Scotland, Melrose Abbey already seems to be half-ruined well before the Reformation. Scott preferred his medieval churches picturesque and ruined.

In reconstructing the past, Scott had before him the example of Shakespeare, and especially of the history plays. Shakespeare had set all but one of his plays in the past or else in a foreign country, not in the England of his own day. (The exception is *The Merry Wives of Windsor*, yet this too revolves around Falstaff, a figure developed from the historical Sir John Oldcastle, executed in 1417.) Scott learned the most from Shakespeare's most novel-like play, *Henry IV*, with its scenes at court, in the tavern, and on the battlefield, and its story of a disguised prince who learns from his people. (This is what happens in *Ivanhoe*, both to Ivanhoe himself and to Richard Coeur-de-Lion.)

A brief comparison of the way Shakespeare and Scott set their scenes in the past illustrates two main points. First, the England of the history plays is not very different from Shakespeare's own England, whereas the past in Scott's novels is offered in clear contrast to the world of the early nineteenth century. Historical consciousness had grown in the eighteenth century, and Edinburgh was especially conscious of its own enlightenment. Secondly, the major differences between the "histories" of Shakespeare and Scott stem from the fact that Shakespeare wrote not for the page but for the stage. The theater of his day had no scenery and relied on words and the imagination of the audience to compensate for what could not be shown. He reserves lengthy description for events occurring offstage. Onstage, a scene is introduced either not at all or with a single line such as: "What is this forest called?" or "Is this a dagger that I see before me?" which gives the audience's imagination a cue. A simple place-name gives a local habitation to a scene — especially if we already know the name. Shakespeare wanted the audience of *Julius Caesar* to know that Caesar was killed publicly, at the center of Rome. Though Caesar was killed in the Curia of the Senate, Shakespeare refers only to the Capitol, which is not described but named, five times: all we have to know is that Caesar is killed in the heart of Rome. "[T]he two hours traffic of the stage" specified in the Prologue to *Romeo and Juliet* left little time for describing architecture or anything else.

An apparent exception occurs in *Macbeth*, when Duncan remarks that:

> This Castle has a pleasant seat. The air
> Nimbly and sweetly recommends itself
> Unto our gentle senses.

Banquo replies:

> This guest of summer
> The temple-haunting martlet, does approve
> By his loved mansionry that the heaven's breath
> Smells wooingly here. No jutty, frieze,
> Buttress, nor coign of vantage but this bird
> Hath made his pendant bed and procreant cradle. (I.vi.1–9)

Shakespeare clearly had noted where and how swallows or house-martins build their nests on castle walls: high up under the projecting battlements. But Lady Macbeth already has told us that Duncan's entrance "under my battlements" will be fatal. The architectural detail, like the mansionry of the temple-haunting martlet, is done lovingly. Yet this fresh description is there not in order to enable us to visualize the castle but for a deeper purpose. The overhang that provides shelter for innocent birds to woo, to build and to breed new life, will also offer concealment to the killing of a kindly lord and guest at the hands of his hosts: a couple with no children. Only incidentally does Shakespeare inform us about the design of castle battlements; rather, he is showing how nature's innocence is not a sign of human innocence.

Scott, by contrast, loves battlements. He devotes paragraphs and sometimes pages to setting a scene in leisurely detail. Scott elaborates a scene slowly, first describing natural settings, then building up his descriptions of buildings, and of costumes, in profuse and material detail. The effect is visual and pictorial, for Scott's settings matter almost as much as the characters, who themselves are presented in a noticeably pictorial way. Scott's first readers knew virtually nothing about medieval social life and wanted to know more. They lapped up his realistic detail.

The first castle to be described in architectural detail in English is that of Sir Bertilak in the fourteenth-century verse romance *Sir Gawain and the Green Knight*. But the first poet to describe architecture with an attention to the building's features was the young John Milton, toward the end of *Il Penseroso*, a poem composed in about 1631, when he was a student at Cambridge. The pensive man prays:

> But let my due feet never fail
> To walk the studious cloister's pale,
> And love the high embowéd roof,
> With antique pillars massy proof,
> And storied windows richly dight
> Casting a dim religious light. (Lines 55–60)

This architecture is historical, for the cloister and the church are "antique" (that is, medieval) with "high embowéd" (that is, vaulted) roof and "storied windows richly dight": stained glass windows portraying stories on sacred subjects. Historical fiction is often "richly dight": elaborately decorated. In the next decade, Puritans were to smash Gothic stained glass and graven images, and Protector Cromwell closed all the cathedrals in England. Shakespeare had written with a Catholic sympathy of the "bare ruined choirs where late the sweet birds sang," a reference to the monastic choirs silenced by Henry VIII, sixty or seventy years before this sonnet was composed. But Milton, before his Protestantism became radical, was the first to describe in loving detail the cloisters, antique pillars, storied windows, and dim religious light of the architecture of the old religion. The past was on the point of becoming romantic, and Milton was not yet Puritan enough to distrust visual images. He never could quite do without verbal images.

In the centuries that followed, attitudes toward medieval architecture show a curious evolution. What iconoclasts had smashed under Henry VIII and Edward VI, and then under Oliver Cromwell, and what the enlightened looked down on between 1650 and 1750, did not disappear from England, which still has 10,000 parish churches from the Middle Ages. These churches, restored in the nineteenth century, were not appreciated by the neoclassical taste of the eighteenth. Tobias Smollett and Edward Gibbon abhorred Gothic. A generation later, J. W. von Goethe, taking his "Italian Journey" now that the Napoleonic Wars were over, reached Assisi. He admired the Temple of Minerva, but he did not bother to look into the Basilica of St. Francis with its frescoes by Giotto and others, for at Assisi an upper church is built on top of the lower church, rendering the structure (to classical taste) irregular and therefore monstrous. A generation later, Nathaniel Hawthorne's Italy, as portrayed in *The Marble Faun*, is more picturesque but not essentially different. Smollett, Gibbon, Goethe, and Hawthorne were anti-Gothic (for a long time "Gothic" was used simply to mean "medieval"; it was not originally an architectural term). They were also anti-Catholic. The most neoclassical of English poets, Alexander Pope, was a Catholic. But in the only part of his writing concerned with events from history, his *Eloisa to Abelard* of 1717, he wrote of a gloomy medieval convent with the horror that was then the fashion. (Pope's taste in architecture, as shown in his verse *Epistle to Lord Burlington*, was Anglo-Palladian.) But in later Augustan England, poets with less exclusively classic tastes were to linger pensively by Gothic country churches and to write poems in the shade of their ivy-mantled towers. Ruins were coming into fashion. Thomas Gray was drawn to gloom, and Horace Walpole rather liked gloom as long as it was comfortable. After 1750 a revival of interest in medieval romances was to lead to the Romantic revival.

The writing of narrative history in a form that would be familiar to modern readers was practiced in English for the first time in the eighteenth century. David Hume and Edward Gibbon were similar in their initial assumptions, but Gibbon added to the ideological simplicity of Hume's *History of England* a far more professional research into documentary sources over an enormously wider field. Other writers investigated coins, busts, and other antiquities — and manuscripts. Scott's historical fiction was informed by the "philosophical" history of Hume, which gave him a superior perspective on the past, and by the research of antiquaries, which furnished his materials, as well as by a new kind of respectful sympathy.

This essay drew attention at its outset to Scott, the historical novel, and the historical romance, and went on to show that historical fiction is a kind of writing more ancient and more various than the historical novel developed by Scott and practiced by Tolstoy. But we now need to make some distinctions. Daniel Defoe's remarkable *Journal of the Plague Year* (1722) does not qualify as a historical novel even though it purports to be a first-person account of London's Plague Year, 1664–65, and is a montage of eyewitness reports. While it is a vivid piece of documentary journalistic re-creation, it has neither the characters nor the larger themes of a novel. It is a plausible chronicle that makes your flesh creep.

But if a "documentary" account of an historical event does not qualify as an historical novel, nor does sheer fantasy. Horace Walpole pretended that his anonymously published *Castle of Otranto* of 1764 was a translation from an old manuscript. But there was no manuscript, and Otranto was a name found on a map. He published his fantasy on Christmas Eve with the subtitle *A Story*; the second edition is subtitled *A Gothic Story*. This Gothic tale is set nominally in the deep south of Catholic Italy in the thirteenth century, an imaginary milieu far from the comfortable villa at Strawberry Hill, Twickenham, in which Walpole had dreamed it up. *The Castle of Otranto* opens with a bridegroom crossing a courtyard. He is crushed to death by a falling helmet: a helmet so enormous that it soon is used as a prison to hold the servant suspected of the killing. This is not medieval history but Gothic fantasy. As for the "local habitation" of this castle, it was only much later that Walpole learned there was indeed a castle at Otranto, a name that Italians stress on the first syllable, not, like the English, on the second. The castle itself looms large in Walpole's story, and fantasy architecture figures even more largely in William Beckford's repulsive *Vathek, An Arabian Tale*.

Architecture is dominant in Gothic fiction, for the Age of Reason placed its nightmares in castles, abbeys, or convents: large, dark, irregular medieval buildings, suggestive to the philosophical mind of feudal tyranny, clerical superstition, and cruel confinement. Enlightenment ignorance of medieval history allowed philosophical writers, as for example David Hume in his *History of England*, to portray the early Middle Ages as entirely dark, with the single exception of Alfred the Great, whom Hume presents as the ideal philosopher-king. Alexander Pope had written of the Dark Ages that "The Monks finished what the Goths begun." The Goths had indeed sacked Rome, but Pope evidently did not know that it was "the Monks" who had preserved in their libraries the classical literature he valued. The Enlightenment found the Gothic style unintelligible and therefore distasteful. The word "medieval," incidentally, is not found in English before 1827, after which it became the term of choice for historians. The application of the word "Gothic," which previously had designated all things medieval, became restricted to architecture — and to the new horror fiction pioneered by Walpole.

Historical fiction, then, is neither pseudo-documentary journalism nor Gothic fantasy, though it may borrow from both. At Walter Scott's birth in 1770, people still knew almost nothing about the Middle Ages, but had begun to want to know something. Scott fulfilled this desire with theatrical treatments of stories from popular history, upholstered with antiquarian learning. At the climax of *Ivanhoe*, Rebecca threatens to throw herself from the battlements of Torquilstone rather than yield to the wicked advances of Brian de Bois-Guilbert, Master of the Temple: "'I will not trust thee, Templar,'" she says, "standing by one of the embrasures, or *machicolles*, as they were then called" (chapter 24). Scott put in these *machicolles* to authenticate, to inform us about machicolation, to furnish the imagination, to make the scene easier to visualize. For modern readers, however, these *machicolles*, and the explanatory clause that follows their introduction, reduce the tension needed at such a moment, making it less easy to care about Rebecca's fate. The greater the detail, the less the imaginative potential. The comparison with the economy of Banquo's description of Macbeth's castle is a punishing one for Scott. This is, however, to compare Shakespeare at his best with a routine passage of Scott, who was never entirely serious when writing about England. It also should be remembered that if the furniture of Scott's tales now seems to us too antiquarian, he writes in a style far more natural than is to be found in the supposedly historical fabrications of Macpherson, Chatterton, Walpole, and Gray. Our historical sense now has developed so far that we find it difficult to believe that anyone ever took these Gothic mummeries seriously. The fabrications of Macpherson and Chatterton, however, were accepted widely as authentic, especially by those unfamiliar with English history.

Scott derived the verse form for *The Lay of the Last Minstrel* from the late-medieval romances and ballads in Percy's popular collection, *Reliques of Ancient English Poetry* of 1765. In doing so, he was following the example of Coleridge in his verse romance *Christabel*. Scott also anchored his romances firmly in medieval locales, Gothic buildings described in detail. In my book, *Medievalism: The Middle Ages in Modern England*, I offer a detailed comparison of *The Lay of the Last Minstrel* with *Christabel*, and of both these verse romances with Keats's "The Eve of St. Agnes."

Briefly, in all three of these historical romances in verse, the action takes place in and around a castle in the wild border country between Scotland and England. The most crucial action takes place in a lady's chamber in a feudal castle: a bower in a tower, inhabited by a pure maiden. In each, the story is influenced greatly by moonlight shining through stained glass. In "The Eve of St. Agnes," everything in Madeline's bower is "richly dight," particularly the window:

> A casement high and triple-arched there was,
> All garlanded with carven imag'ries,
> Of fruits and flowers, and bunches of knot-grass,

And diamonded with panes of quaint device,
Innumerable of stains and splendid dyes,
As are the tiger-moth's deep-damasked wings;
And in the midst, 'mong thousand heraldries,
And twilight saints, and dim emblazonings,
A shielded scutcheon blushed with blood of queens
    and kings. (Stanza 24, lines 208–16)

Keats's moon throws a blood-red light: "Full on the casement shone this wintry moon, / And threw warm gules on Madeline's fair breast. . . ." In Coleridge, the stained glass admits a moonlight that is silvery. In Scott, the moonlight passes through the Red Cross of St. Michael and "casts a bloody" stain on the tomb of the wizard Michael Scott. In all three of these historical verse romances, architectural detail is used for purposes that are not informational but symbolic: symbolic of Gothic enchantment in Coleridge and of Gothic superstition in Scott. Keats also uses architecture symbolically, although not, as Coleridge and Scott had, to portray an historical period but rather to develop a character. The light that is thrown on Madeline's fair breast transforms her, if not into a scarlet woman, into a warm one; the name of her lover is Porphyro (purple). This instance shows that architectural detail, though derived from antiquarian research, is used here for purposes not historical but symbolic.

I dealt summarily with the role of architecture in *Ivanhoe: A Romance*, and I turn now to Scott's novels, which more properly can be described as historical in that they are more credible, more realistic, and more closely concerned with actual historical events. Scott acknowledged that this genre had been pioneered by Maria Edgeworth in *Castle Rackrent*, but it was he who made it as popular as Harry Potter is today. *The Heart of Midlothian*, one of the best of his Scottish novels, takes its title from a medieval building, the Toll-booth, also known as the Heart of Midlothian, which housed the jail of Edinburgh. The Toll-booth (tax office) became the meeting place of Parliament, Town Council, Privy Council, and the High Court.

(Scott was a lawyer.) It housed the prison and the hangman's scaffold. This grim building was demolished in 1817, and Scott's novel appeared in 1818. Scott shows the prison being broken into by a mob, and the hangman hanged. The destruction of a prison or castle became a favorite motif in historical fiction. At the end of *Heart of Midlothian*, the action returns to the prison named in the title, which represents the harshness of capital punishment, the likelihood of wrongful imprisonment in doubtful cases, and the need for authority to show clemency. The prison is important as the site of the novel's action and a symbolic representation of injustice, but the detail of its architecture is immaterial.

Charles Dickens wrote two romances about the past: *Barnaby Rudge*, about the anti-Catholic Gordon Riots of 1780, in which prisons and churches are burned down by mobs, and *A Tale of Two Cities*, in which the Bastille prison is destroyed by a Parisian mob. These two books are not Dickens's best — his imagination was not historical — but they show the impact that Scott's historical fiction had on him. (*A Tale of Two Cities* was inspired also by Thomas Carlyle's *French Revolution*.) In Dickens's romances, architecture, in any stricter sense, plays no part: the prisons are prisons, and their representation is expressionist: they are there to induce claustrophobia, moral revulsion, and subjective horror, not to convey a clear and objective visual picture. Thus, his settings are often broadly symbolic, usually oppressive: the castle, the big house (grand or spooky), the tavern; the city streets, courts, and slum housing; the workhouse, school, or prison; and the home. They give an impression of how such buildings and surroundings affected Dickens himself: they are true, that is, to the subjective impressions of a visionary writer, and are not intended and should not be taken as documentary history.

As historical fiction is set before the author's birth — sixty years ago, not twenty — the genre has to exclude Dickens's autobiographical *David Copperfield*, or such less autobiographical, if Gothically personal, romances as Charlotte Bronte's *Jane Eyre*. Fiction about the author's growing up may *incidentally* provide much of historical interest, as Willa Cather does about the Nebraska of her childhood in *My Ántonia*. Of course, such autobiographical fiction now can seem to us historical, but in a different way. All older literature can seem historical, especially if we don't know much history. But it is not, properly speaking, historical fiction.

What, then, does count as historical fiction? Let's try some more examples. George Eliot's *Romola*, set in Florence at the time of Savonarola, is decidedly an historical novel: it is set in a remote period with full and accurate detail as to clothes, houses, and historical events, and offers a credible picture of the life of the time and of the issues that agitated that time. George Eliot's *Middlemarch, A Study of Provincial Life*, is not an historical novel, for its action begins in 1832, when the author was thirteen, and ends at a time close to the time of the novel's composition. It offers social history of the author's lifetime, but this does not make it an historical novel. The same sixty-year rule excludes Thackeray's *Vanity Fair: A Novel without a Hero*, which begins in Thackeray's youth. His true historical novels begin with *The History of Henry Esmond*, set in the early eighteenth century. Here the passages of Castlewood House are as important as the man who turns out to be its rightful lord, the Henry Esmond who eventually emigrates to Virginia. There are historical novels in which architecture is hardly more than a background setting, as in R. L. Stevenson's *Kidnapped*, or in Hardy's sketchy romance *The Trumpet Major*, even though Hardy was a practiced architectural draftsman and a church restorer. Historical novelists are often tempted to pile on the architectural detail, a mistake made in Harrison Ainsworth's *Old St. Pauls*, Charles Reade's *The Cloister and the Hearth*, and Bulwer Lytton's *The Last Days of Pompeii*. Although Victorians lapped it up, such detail, while good for historical information, is less good for the fiction; excess in authentic detail tends to weaken symbolic power.

My *Medievalism: The Middle Ages in Modern England* looks at Tennyson's "The Lady of Shalott," which features the symbolic use of architecture. The imprisoned lady was a favorite subject of Pre-Raphaelite painting, as in J. E. Millais' *Mariana*, set in the moated grange of Tennyson's poem. I also discuss Benjamin Disraeli's *Sybil; Or, the Two Nations* (1845). This is not an historical novel but a novel that seeks to debunk Whig historiography, a fable in which architecture consistently plays a symbolic role. The announcement of the key doctrine of "the two nations, THE RICH AND THE POOR" is framed by the "vacant and star-lit arch" of the "grey ruins of Marney Abbey" [based on Fountains Abbey, ruined at the Dissolution of the Monasteries]. Then, "from the Lady's chapel" [*sic*] there arose "the evening hymn to the Virgin" [*sic*]. This operatic soloist is Sybil, a religious sister who cares for the poor. All Disraeli's locales are significant: the gilded London club, the grimy industrial town, the mock-medieval Mowbray Castle, sacked at the end by a mob. *Sybil* influenced social thinking in the Hungry Forties. It drew on A. N. W. Pugin's manifesto, *Contrasts* (1836, 1841), which also informed Carlyle's *Past and Present* (1843). In the 1830s and 1840s, the medieval past was presented as superior to the present. So it was that in a single generation, medieval church architecture had come to advertise not the hobby of a gentleman of taste, as in the eighteenth century, but the public absence in industrial England of Christian devotion and of Christian compassion for the poor.

Thus far, we have seen that architecture in historical fiction can be signaled minimally by a significant place-name, as with the Capitol in *Julius Caesar*; and that it can function more meaningfully, as part of the locale or setting, as in *Ivanhoe*, in which the dwellings of the Templar and the Friar, and of Normans and Saxons generally, are given cultural and political meanings. We also have seen that stained glass can cast a light that is religiously dim, or magically silver, a Gothic blood-red, or an erotic *gules*. Historical novels, like other novels, often are set in big houses, whether castles or stately homes. But it is rare for architectural information itself to feature largely, still less for architecture to become the novel's focus. Such a focus, however, is central to Gothic fiction, in which the castle, palace, or prison is often as real as or more real than the characters. The French Revolution affected the role of architecture in fiction, for it lent a new and particular meaning to the destruction of a prison or the removal of a king from his castle or palace: it marks the end of a regime. It is employed in this way in the works of fiction by Disraeli, Dickens, and Charlotte Bronte mentioned above. But of these works, only the two novels by Dickens are historical, and they are more like romances than histories. Even in *The Heart of Midlothian*, or in the Castlewood House of Thackeray's *Henry Esmond*, architecture does not rise symbolically very far above its primary role of setting the scene and creating a mood. It is from the Gothic, fantastic-horrific side of its ancestry that the historical novel derives most of its symbolic power. Unfortunately, the Gothic side of historical fiction is the side which, from a literary point of view, often is crude and unsatisfactory. The attention recently paid to Gothic fiction in some English departments avoids the question of literary quality. Architecture in the true historical novel is not an agent of terror, as it is in the Gothic fiction that squeaked into the cellars of literature with Walpole's *Castle of Otranto* and ascended to the heights of kitsch in Bram Stoker's *Dracula* (1897).

The conclusion of this comparative survey must be that architecture in the historical novel chiefly plays the role of background, creating the setting for the action, though often with symbolic import. A partial exception to this rule may be Tomasi di Lampedusa's *Il Gattopardo*, translated as *The Leopard*, in which the opening scene evokes with historical sympathy as well as irony the old princely way of life in Sicily. This is accomplished through a minutely detailed evocation of the palace's architecture and of the elaborate mythological decoration of the room in which the Rosary is said by the Salina family. Into this rococo saloon, once the Rosary is over, bounds the Prince's hunting dog, Bendico. The novel ends a generation later, not with the destruction of the palace, but with the throwing out of a rug made out of the skin of Bendico, a rug that breaks up and settles into a pile of dust.

Yet even in *The Leopard* architecture is not central. Architecture can, however, have a strong symbolic function in fiction which is neither historical nor Gothic, as in the work of Anthony Trollope and of Evelyn Waugh, both of whom enjoy describing buildings.

Indeed, the country house and its estate is the subject of Jane Austen's *Mansfield Park* and *Northanger Abbey*, novels in which the building named in the title is central to the story and to its significance. But Austen's fiction is contemporary, not historical.

My book *Medievalism* begins with a contrast between two acts of rebuilding, of St. Paul's Cathedral and of the Palace of Westminster, in order to introduce a study of the medieval revival as a whole, which, as a many-sided cultural phenomenon, has largely has been studied by architectural historians neglecting literature, and literary scholars neglecting architecture. By the time of Scott's death in 1832, attention increasingly was being paid to medieval models, not just in churches but in public architecture, religion, social thought, and art. The Palace of Westminster, burnt down in 1834, was rebuilt in what the Select Committee of the Commons prescribed as "the national style . . . Gothic or Elizabethan." The success of Barry's submission certainly owed much to its having been "richly dight" in the Gothic designs that Barry had commissioned from A. N. W. Pugin. Parliament's decision was less architectural than historical and political. The medieval origins of the English kingdom, and the continuity of its institutions, are not historical fictions. The English Church dates from the seventh century, its monarchy from the tenth, its Parliament from the thirteenth. The medieval claim is justified fully by history, even if the Whiggish "Norman Yoke" theory, which often accompanied it, is not. Parliament's decision to build in Gothic, not in the neoclassical styles chosen in Paris, Washington, and Berlin, maintained, if with a difference, the political creed of the Whigs, who held that the Gothic peoples of northern Europe, the Germanic peoples whom Tacitus held up for the admiration of his Roman readers, loved liberty of a republican kind. Among these Gothic tribes were the Anglo-Saxons. James Thomson, in his "Rule, Britannia!" (from the *Masque of Alfred*, 1740, with music by Thomas Arne) asserts that "Britons never will be slaves." Frenchmen, it is implied, lived content under the absolutist rule of their kings, while the supine Latins were happy to be slaves. In 1741, Lord Cobham, a prominent Whig, erected in the gardens of his house at Stowe a "Temple of Liberty." The architect was Gibbs, who designed St. Martin-in-the-Fields, in what later became Trafalgar Square. The name "Temple of Liberty" plays on the name of the Cobham family, Temple. A temple dedicated to Liberty *had* to be Gothic in style. It had statues of the Seven Saxon Worthies and the motto "I am not a Roman." "Roman" points to the Church of Rome, the Roman Empire, and to Continental empires whose Catholic monarchs ruled without due consultation of their free people. Such consultation supposedly had been observed by "Gothic" kings, like the exemplary Alfred, and ought to be observed by the dynasty brought over to England from Hanover. The tradition of Gothic constitutionalism, developed by Parliamentarians in the 1630s, was revived by the Founding Fathers of the United States. It is a paradox that Thomas Jefferson, the designer of the Palladian Monticello, also proposed that the study of Anglo-Saxon should be made compulsory in American schools, since it was the language of constitutional liberty. He also proposed that Hengist and Horsa, the conquerors of Kent in the fifth century, and thus the founders of England, should be shown on the obverse of U.S. coinage.

POSTSCRIPT

Gothic Westminster is a famous symbol of the reinstatement of the medieval in English life. Less familiar is the following passage, which does not come from an historical novel, but shows how far the architectural commonplaces of medieval antiquarianism had sunk into the popular mind by 1837. It comes from chapter 2 of *The Pickwick Papers*, the chapter in which Charles Dickens began to write at his best. Mr. Jingle is a confidence trickster who poses as an expert on everything. He has won the confidence of Mr. Pickwick and joins the members of the Pickwick Club on their coach-trip to the old city of Rochester in Kent. Dickens is making a joke about the innocence of Mr. Pickwick and his young admirers and about the sentiments everyone was supposed to feel about picturesque medieval buildings: sentiments that Dickens, as a Cockney, did not share.

"Magnificent ruin!" said Mr. Augustus Snodgrass, with all the poetic fervour that distinguished him, when they came in sight of the fine old castle. "What a study for an antiquarian!" were the very words which fell from Mr. Pickwick's mouth, as he applied his telescope to his eye. "Ah! fine place," said the stranger, "glorious pile — frowning walls — tottering arches — dark nooks — crumbling staircases — Old cathedral too — earthy smell — pilgrims' feet worn away the old steps — little Saxon doors — confessionals like money-takers' boxes at theatres — queer customers those monks — Popes, and Lord Treasurers, and all sorts of old fellows, with great red faces, and broken noses, turning up every day — buff jerkins too — match-locks — Sarcophagus — fine place — old legends too — strange stories: capital.

Jingle begins pretty well, saying the things a guide was supposed to say, but he can't keep it up. He rattles on, becoming less accurate and more disbelieving about the past about which he began speaking so enthusiastically, ending his medieval fantasy by killing off medieval man with matchlocks and putting him in a Sarcophagus.

3 Norman Abbey as Romantic Mise-en-Scène

St. Georges de Boscherville in Historical Representation

STEPHEN BANN

One of the discoveries that has preoccupied me most in recent years was a travel journal compiled by the English gentleman and future collector of curiosities, John Bargrave, in 1645.[1] This journal was compiled to recount a visit of a few months to the French city of Bourges during the spring and summer of that year, when the imminence of civil war in the writer's home country had made it dangerous for a junior member of a staunchly royalist family. Bargrave was from Canterbury, and his uncle, the dean of Canterbury, had suffered for his strenuous defense of the traditional privileges of cathedral chapters and universities by having his deanery invaded by Roundhead soldiers; being subsequently committed to the Fleet prison by the order of Parliament, he had died in captivity in 1642.[2] The young nephew's journey to Bourges was, as I have argued, a journey of symbolic as well as pragmatic significance. He invested in the French archiepiscopal city (in many ways very comparable to Canterbury in its history) his hopes and fears for the future of his native land, and particularly so in the great cathedral of Bourges dedicated to St. Etienne, whose features he surveyed and described with an exemplary care. This seventeenth-century episode led me to think again about the striking way in which the cathedral becomes a powerful and polyvalent symbol in the wake of another revolutionary upheaval: the French revolution. The great fictional project of the French novelist, Honoré de Balzac, who was also an admirer of the cathedral of Bourges, was compared at the time to the ecclesiastical architecture of the Middle Ages.[3] That other giant of the French Romantic period, Victor Hugo, was so fascinated by the precedent of the medieval cathedral that he used it to epitomize in concrete form the measure of his own literary ambitions. For him, the image of the cathedral marked the transition from a premodern culture in which public messages were transmitted by the emblematic facades of great buildings to a present situation in which an individual creator could confront the challenge of mass communication by means of the written text. "Le livre tuera l'édifice," was his message. The great book would supplant the architectural monument.[4]

This prognosis was indeed amply fulfilled in the course of the nineteenth century, not least by the achievement of John Ruskin, whose *Bible of Amiens* was pondered by the young Marcel Proust while he incubated the vast symbolic structure of *À la recherche du temps perdu*. The latter is the text whose message Julia Kristeva has aptly summed up in the following terms: "If you will be so good as to open up your memories of felt time, *there* will arise the new cathedral."[5] But to leap from Hugo to Proust—from one gigantic literary achievement to another—is inevitably to foreshorten the intricate sequence of literary and visual transactions through which the cathedral—and indeed the type of the great medieval building in general—entered discourse in the postrevolutionary period. *Pace* Hugo, the book did not so summarily supplant the built form. Rather, the monuments of the past were themselves successively translated, and transmitted to the eager Romantic public, in the form of descriptions and images working in conjunction. New techniques of visual reproduction combined complemented critical and historical studies in the process of familiarizing a mass audience with what had previously been relegated as "Gothic" and therefore barbarous. Moreover, this development of greater public awareness was, in my view, a process in which discernible sequences and structures can be observed. Successive mediations in the form of text and reproductive images entailed an accumulation of positive knowledge, as well as involving an enrichment of the imagination.

So I arrive at the main subject of this essay. The great medieval building that will be considered in this light is the Norman Abbey of St. Georges de Boscherville, situated high above the Seine valley in the vicinity of Rouen. My argument will cover a couple of decades in the course of which this now relatively little-known medieval complex became an object of discourse, or, more precisely, an element in several plural and shifting discourses, over the period between 1820 and 1840, which we can acknowledge to be the high epoch of French Romanticism. I will try to demonstrate the significant continuities and discontinuities in the visual representation of the major features of this building, as they lend themselves to interpretation on a number of different levels. In the first instance, it will be a question of relating the successive published portrayals of the abbey, and its immediate surroundings, to a mythic model of historical discontinuity: the overall cycle of death and rebirth that informed much of the public language (and no doubt empowered the private fantasies) of an epoch that was officially placed under the sign of "La Restauration": the return of the Bourbon monarchy to France after Napoleon's defeat at the Battle of Waterloo in 1815. Second, it will be a matter of tracking the progress of a new and more scientific concept of historiography, essentially at variance with this mood of mythic recuperation but, at the same time, feeding off it and relying on its deep-rooted psychological mechanisms. My third (and by no means least) concern is to relate these points to a range of visual examples. Here I am placing in the foreground the exciting technical achievements of this abundantly inventive period in which the technical development of lithography, followed rapidly by the commercialization of radically new modes of wood-block printmaking, were both contributing in their turn to

Fig. 13. Hyacinthe Langlois, "Abbaye de St. Georges de Boscherville fondée sous Guillaume-le-Conqt. vers 1066," 1821, lithograph. Stephen Bann Private Collection.

a revolution in visual culture. The special interest attaching to this particular example, the Abbey of Boscherville, lies in the clarity with which it demonstrates the intimate conjunction — one might almost say the dovetailing — of the new epistemological factors deriving from the Romantic conceptualization of history, and the new techniques of image-making together with the types of publication that supported and promoted them.

We start then with an image (see fig. 13) that appears conventional enough at first sight. From a high point, presumably a hillside, the full breadth of a range of ecclesiastical buildings is placed before our eyes. We see the apse of the church, and its central spire, to the left, and the conventual buildings, evidently more recent in date, stretch in a northerly direction beyond the north transept, very roughly continuing the roofline and picking up the lines of fenestration. It is quite a countrified prospect — there is a vigorous young tree that frames the prospect in true picturesque fashion on the right, and the randomly placed shrubs and bushes give the impression that the surroundings of the abbey have been abandoned, or at least left relatively wild. A semiruined building can be perceived in the right distance, and two detached stones, presumably deriving from a former built structure or maybe a wall, lie in the left foreground. But this is certainly not just a scene of neglect, let alone desolation. A lengthy procession of people clothed in long robes and carrying banners emerges, one presumes from the interior of the church, and is greeted with rapt attention by the various bystanders who gesticulate to each other and, in some cases, fall to their knees in reverence.

Hyacinthe Langlois's lithograph, signed and dated 1821, brings together a number of features that make it a significant starting point for this discussion. It is not simply a lithograph, but the work of one of the very first artists to practice lithography in Rouen, the provincial capital of Normandy. Hyacinthe Langlois (1777–1837) was a former pupil of the great painter Jacques-Louis David (not to be confused, however, with the more well-known pupil Jérôme Langlois). Nominated a professor at the Drawing School of Rouen through the influence of the Duchesse de Berry, he took up residence there in the early Restoration period and appears to have trained the odd pupil for the prestigious competition between young engravers for the Grand Prix de Rome. He himself was certainly highly skilled in the traditional techniques of line engraving. Before he adopted the new medium of lithography, he had employed this technique in the plates for a *Description de la cathédrale de Rouen* in 1816, and a pioneering record of prints of the old houses of Rouen; as a result of the latter, he was credited with being one of the first French artists to "understand and draw Gothic architecture."[6] Henri Beraldi, the leading expert on French nineteenth-century printmaking who delivered this verdict at the end of the century, also threw in one or two less favorable judgments: first, that Langlois' work was "more addressed to the archaeologist than the iconophile," and second, that he has the habit of "sowing his foregrounds with a crowd of Lilliputian figures, a few millimeters high, and quite amusing to look at, as Viollet-le-Duc did later in his architectural drawings and his dictionary."[7] This end-of-century perspective on Langlois is, of course, not one that we are obliged to endorse. From a more balanced viewpoint, he appears as a serious scholar, and a pioneer in the accurate recording of the medieval buildings in Normandy. Indeed, he would later take the view that "Romane" (or Romanesque) was an inappropriate title for the architecture of the province, which had a right to be considered specifically "Norman."[8]

Moreover, it is precisely this collection of "Lilliputian figures" assembled by Langlois in the foreground of his lithograph of St. Georges de Boscherville that provides our entry into the labyrinth of historical representation, as regards the significance of the action that they are performing. Langlois has alerted the reader in his elaborately scripted title to the evocative date of the abbey's foundation — "about 1066" — and the name of its putative founder: William the Conqueror ("Abbaÿe de St. Georges de Boscherville fondée sous Guillaume-le-Conqt.") Such historical pointers frame the present-day scene in the foreground to which the viewer's attention is directed. Nor should we lose sight of the fact that, by contrast with his earlier practice, the well-practiced engraver Langlois has chosen to work in the new and strongly evocative medium of lithography. The implied address to the viewer is not just "archaeological."

The Abbey of St. Georges de Boscherville was indeed founded during the lifetime of William the Conqueror, Duke of Normandy and (from 1066 onwards) King of England. The Atlas to the 1839 edition of Augustin Thierry's *Histoire de la conquête de l'Angleterre par les Normands* (to which we shall return at a later stage) indicates the adjoining village of St. Martin de Boscherville that nestles in the loop of the Seine just to the west of Rouen.[9] We should note the full title of this work, which pursues the history of the Norman Conquest of England "and its consequences up to our own times." In effect, the map of Normandy (engraved by Ambroise Tardieu) represents the place-names as they were at the time of the Conquest. But it also calls to mind the exceptional interest invested in the history of Normandy throughout the period of the Restoration in France. This was a time when the fresh recollection of renewed Anglo-French conflict in the Napoleonic Wars, and an actual occupation of Northern France by British troops after 1815, gave contemporary relevance to this major scene of interchange between the two nations. Thierry's history had first been published in 1825, and was to become, with Prosper de Barante's *Histoire des ducs de Bourgogne* (1824–26), the standard-bearer for the new, voracious research into the Middle Ages.[10] Yet even before Thierry's work appeared, the primacy of Normandy as an exemplary historical site had been underlined in the first volume of the most ambitious and substantial topographic project of the Romantic period in France: Baron Taylor and Charles Nodier's *Voyages pittoresques*. Appearing in successive *livraisons* between 1820 and 1825, the sumptuous collection of original lithographs devoted to Normandy was to remain the fullest — as well as being the first — visual documentation of the monuments of a French province in the whole series. This was of course no accident, but a consequence of Normandy's plentiful medieval architecture as well as its emblematic significance. Nowadays the Abbey of St. Georges de Boscherville would appear to be much less well-known than the great sequence of ruined abbeys along the Seine valley — St. Wandrille, Jumièges, and Fécamp. These abbeys, in particular, have captured the attention of tourists because of their picturesque settings and their ruinous state. But the priority was far from clear in the 1820s. In the *Voyages pittoresques*, Boscherville figured as prominently as any of these buildings, although it differed from them (then as now) in being in an unusually pristine state of preservation. In one of the earliest batches of prints, published for subscribers around 1822, the abbey church was shown from its exterior aspect as well as its interior, with special attention being paid to the adjoining chapter house.

   A lithograph by Xavier Leprince of the west front of Boscherville (see fig. 14) inaugurates the sequence in 1822, and a significant contrast is struck immediately with Langlois' image from the previous year.

Fig. 14. Xavier Leprince, "Église de l'abbaye de St. Georges de Boscherville," 1822, lithograph. Collection Centre Canadien d'Architecture/Canadian Centre for Architecture, Montréal.

This new print is the work of an artist of the younger generation, who was born as late as 1799. But where Langlois relied on the local lithographic press of Periaux, Leprince's work has benefited from the more impressive technical skills of the Parisian editor Gottfried Engelmann (one of the two pioneers of the lithographic process in France) in order to convey the finer detail of the façade's stonework and its intricate architectural moldings. The contrast with the cruder registration of the Rouen-based lithographic studio is plain to see. Leprince has also decided to create a prospect that neatly eliminates the nearby conventual buildings, and we should note that these bulky appendages dating from the eighteenth century do not occur in the plates contributed by his colleagues, either. However, Leprince has probably seen Langlois' print, since he appears to have borrowed the motif of the religious procession, which in his case, spills directly out from the church door into the public space of the foreground. What was still rather indistinct in Langlois is here made much more specific. The main participants in the procession are a number of young women dressed in long white robes. They could well be first communicants, though it has also been suggested to me that this could be a procession marking the feast of Corpus Christi. A dais borne by acolytes, a priest, a beadle, and a person firing a gun in celebratory fashion are also clearly distinguishable. There is an attentive huddle of village folk who kneel devoutly.

This is the message of a medieval church that is witnessing a revival of religious ritual after the revolutionary interruptions — one that subsumes the signs of contemporaneity into the mythical, timeless present of the church festival. It is also implied in the simpler motif of Jean-Philippe Schmidt's complementary close-up of the west door, in which the monks take their stand as if to declare the church open for business once again, and the villagers come and go. Schmidt was, like Leprince, an artist of the younger generation, having been born in 1790, and he was to specialize in lithography from the early 1820s onwards. His most memorable print, according to Beraldi, was an evocation of "the Romantic Muse," which depicted that lady

Fig. 15. Évariste Fragonard, "Intérieur de l'église de l'abbaye de St. Georges de Boscherville," 1822, lithograph. Collection Centre Canadien d'Architecture/ Canadian Centre for Architecture, Montréal.

"by night, on a tomb, in the ruins of a Gothic abbey lit by the torch that is held by the specter of some 'awakened nun.'"[11] Despite these romantic credentials, his technique in this particular lithograph is odd, and suggests that he was originally trained in a more traditional form of printmaking. As a general rule, lithographers worked from their own drawings, whereas the process of engraving required two stages, with the draftsman and the engraver both being credited on the final print. However, Schmidt has here credited the drawing to one Jorand, and has employed for his own attestation of authorship the form *excud* (short for *excudit*), usually adopted by engravers, despite the fact that the finished product is signaled as a lithograph from the presses of Engelmann. What we observe in Schmidt's work is, in effect, a lithographic print that deliberately eschews the soft pencil effects usually associated with the lithographic crayon. Instead, it evokes the precise tonal register previously used by the English printmaker J. S. Cotman, whose series the *Architectural Antiquities of Normandy* (1819–22) was an immediate precursor to the *Voyages pittoresques*.[12] Like Cotman, Schmidt has conveyed the surface values of the stone columns through a dense texture of lines, rather than choosing to exploit the subtle gradations of grey tones on the white paper ground that lithographers generally utilized to create effects of surface and ambient light. One might conclude that, being trained in etching and engraving, he is tackling lithography against the grain.

This important difference between the two techniques is further illustrated if we compare Cotman's etching entitled "Mount St. Michel, The Knight's Hall" from the *Architectural Antiquities of Normandy* with the luminous lithograph of the interior of St. Georges de Boscherville, by Évariste Fragonard (see fig. 15), from the *Voyages pittoresques*. Cotman defines the incidence of raking light in the great Gothic hall with an almost mathematical precision.[13] For Fragonard, by contrast, everything has been rendered soft and suggestive, with the whole nave of the abbey church bathed in a subtle light that emanates from the choir, and engulfs the figures that kneel on the paving or gaze with studied attention. In this case, there is a further visual and parallel to be drawn, not with the printmaking tradition, but with the distinctive and popular series of paintings of church interiors that François-Marius Granet had begun to produce in Rome over the previous decade. These had become familiar in France through the showing of a version of his *Choir of the Capuchin church, Rome* at the 1819 Paris salon.[14] It was this famous rendering of the friars' choir of the church on the Piazza Barberini in Rome that won Granet the Légion d'honneur, provoking a much repeated remark of the Duc de Berry when he presented the award: "Monsieur Granet, someone tells me he has just heard one of your Capuchins sneeze."[15]

The foregoing comments on the different modes of representing church interiors in the period need to be glossed more fully. Granet's paintings, with their intense backlit lighting and their consequent reputation for intense visual realism, were pioneering in the effect that they obtained from what Michael Fried would term an essentially "absorptive" subject matter.[16] Granet's work did not significantly influence the direction of Romantic painting, which, from the 1824 Salon onwards, found its vanguard in the Venetian wealth of color and the ostentatious brushwork of such artists as Eugène Delacroix and Eugène Devéria. But it surely did encourage the cult of topographical lithography surrounding medieval church interiors that was heralded so triumphantly by the *Voyages pittoresques*. And at the same time, it fostered the development of a novel form of visual spectacle that broke away completely from the confines of the salon: Louis-Jacques-Mandé Daguerre's diorama. In the Cromer archive at George Eastman House, Rochester, there is a notebook by Daguerre's collaborator Charles-Marie Bouton that records the rumbustious expedition of a group of young Parisian lithographers to the Seine valley on a sketching expedition, shortly following the publication of the Boscherville series. Their destination was on this occasion not the relatively intact abbey of St. Georges, but the neighboring ruins of St. Wandrille.[17] Daguerre opened the Paris diorama in 1822, and he would literally put his view of the ruins of St. Wandrille on stage in a presentation dating from 1826.

Not yet mentioned here is possibly the most striking of the lithographs devoted to the interior of St. Georges de Boscherville, which serves in fact as a concluding vignette for the *livraison*, and may well have utilized the sketches done for Fragonard's earlier image of the nave and choir. The leading French painter Théodore Géricault, who was a beacon for the younger generation of French Romantic artists, died on February 18, 1824. In his last years, he had turned with great enthusiasm to the exploration of the new techniques of lithography, and his prints remain among the most accomplished ever achieved in the medium. The print that comes at the end of the descriptive text on St. Georges de Boscherville in the *Voyages pittoresques* — no doubt one of the last that he produced — displays the corpse of William the Conqueror laid out in the interior of the abbey, with four candles blazing behind his head, and a picturesque huddle of monks who are praying for the soul of the great Norman warrior. A crown, presumably the crown of England, sits on a cushion in front of him. The motif of a crown with crossed scepters appears already to have been incised on the adjacent paving stone.

It must be admitted straight away that this evocation of a mighty warrior lying in state — by the great Romantic artist whose own deathbed scene would be the subject of a famous painting by Ary Schefer only a few months after the print was published[18] — was based on legend and not on historical fact. To be precise, the medieval history of Normandy by Orderic Vitalis had initiated a lasting confusion between the neighboring churches of St. Georges and St. Gervais. This would, however, be rectified later in the 1820s by the more accurate historical account supplied by the local antiquarian Achille Deville. This will be discussed further, as it also provides a further important link in the chain of visual representations. Géricault's vignette may indeed have been based on a misconception, but from the point of view of the ideological bearing of the *Voyages pittoresques*, it comes right on cue. Charles Nodier's rousing introduction to the entire gigantic enterprise had been completed just after the shocking event that galvanized the French nation in the summer of 1820 — the assassination outside

Fig. 16. Achille Deville, "Façade de l'église," *Essai historique et descriptif sur l'église et l'abbaye de Saint-Georges-de-Bocherville près Rouen*, 1827, lithograph. Collection Centre Canadien d'Architecture/Canadian Centre for Architecture, Montréal.

the Opéra of the nephew of King Louis XVIII and heir presumptive to the French throne (the same patron of the arts who had wittily complimented Granet on his realism): the Duc de Berry. Nodier concludes his introduction with the observation that he has been unexpectedly deprived of the Duc de Berry's enlightened support for the publication: "In sum, a few days earlier, a name guaranteeing the future would have covered us with a protection that was always assured for useful works, for honorable enterprises, and for French ideas. We could have named BERRY! And this history of tombs, it is with his tomb that it commences!"[19]

The vignette that fills out the page displays a medieval knight standing on guard beside a wayside cross, while the spires of a great Gothic church may be glimpsed in the background. This uncredited print exactly underscores the basic premise of the *Voyages pittoresques*, which is that the French nation can be resacralized by the revivification through word and image of its ancient architecture.

Achille Deville, the Norman antiquarian whose exhaustive description of the Abbey of St. Georges de Boscherville was published just five years later in 1827, has a very different objective in mind, and one that uses words and images coherently in its more modest, antiquarian aspirations.[20] Just as Deville endeavors to correct his predecessors' mistakes, so he presents a simpler visual image, less freighted with Restoration and Romantic ideology, of the abbey and its main features. His lithograph of the façade (see fig. 16), taken from his own drawing and published by the same local lithographic studio as the print by Hyacinthe Langlois, provides no visual evidence of revived ritual but inserts instead a single spectator, seemingly a local passerby who has paused there, and rests with his walking stick. The light does not flood the scene from the northwest, creating dramatic effects of light and shade, but apparently arrives from the opposite direction, revealing the west front of the building, pristine and bare. Deville has also shifted the point of view very slightly so that the transepts disappear. Even the spire is just vestigial, but a slice of a Norman half-timbered house intervenes at the right margin to give regional color. Deville's term for describing the church, and a word that perfectly sums up this visual mise-en-scène, is that it is "virginal":

> We are not afraid to say so . . . there are few churches, not only in Normandy, but even in France, which offer an aspect as virginal as that of Saint-Georges. It is free of the ill-assorted vulgarities that dishonor the most beautiful of religious monuments, and from which none of the foremost basilicas in France is perhaps exempt. So it is entirely right that people have applied to it the happy English expression: *it is chaste.*[21]

This reference to St. Georges de Boscherville as being "chaste" in character is in fact borrowed from the earlier description in the *Voyages pittoresques* where Nodier invokes an unspecified English source that I have been unable to locate. But it is Deville who seeks to make his choice of visual descriptions correspond most precisely to this character of unsullied, virginal "chastity." In the series of prints contained in the *Voyages pittoresques*, to take another example, there is a spectacular lithograph by the Baron Atthalin, a pupil of David like Langlois, which shows the chapter house of the monastery swarming with livestock.[22] To the left is a vignette of a stable-boy tending horses that is reminiscent of Géricault's lithographs, and on the right, a charging bull is terrifying a nursing mother and her child. It should be mentioned in parenthesis that the Baron Atthalin rather unusually combined the character of an artist and a soldier. If one looks carefully into the foreground detail of Horace Vernet's *Bataille de Montmirail (1814)* (National Gallery, London), it is possible to detect the dashing figure of the horse-borne cavalry officer Atthalin, who took part in this final battle on French soil of the Napoleonic Wars. In 1822, when Horace Vernet completed the painting of the battle for the duc d'Orléans, he was still a serving officer acting as aide-de-camp to the duke. Atthalin's lithograph, which dates from the same year, no doubt reflects his professional knowledge of livestock, no less than his admiration for Géricault's prints of horses. But there is no fantasy involved here. Although the church itself preserved its "chastity," the adjoining chapter house was indeed still being used as a stable when Atthalin visited it in 1822. It was Achille Deville's own initiative that resulted in this important vestige of the former monastery being bought back by the Seine-Maritime department. In a pioneering move toward state-sponsored conservation, the building was rescued from its equine and bovine tenants.

The difference between Atthalin's treatment of the chapter house and that of Deville in his study of 1827 (see fig. 17) is, for that reason, a very marked one. Atthalin frames the composition in order to exclude the architectural anomaly that, at second storey height, the Gothic chapter house had been amalgamated with the eighteenth-century conventual buildings. Even today, it is easy to see that there were holes in the wall above the Norman arches that would have supported the beams for the roof of the cloister. Atthalin has reproduced these, and no doubt in 1822 there was no surviving structure attached to them as has been put in place at the present day. But Deville has taken the liberty of engaging in a bold and persuasive piece of historical reconstruction. He has chosen the viewpoint looking west from the inside of the chapter house in the direction of the former cloister. A part of the nave of the church is visible at the far left. But he has superimposed on the three Norman arches that we see from the other side in Atthalin's composition the light and elegant Gothic second storey that is actually situated at the opposite end of the chapter house. Any recollection of the turbulent farmyard scene of 1822 depicted by Atthalin is dissipated in Deville's vision of the medieval past: we witness one monk meditating in the shade while his companion emblematically sweeps clean the threshold of the chapter house. Pollution has been well and truly exorcised.

Between the deluxe edition of the *Voyages pittoresques*, charged with a national mission, and the humbler, more regionally based and in many respects more accurate description of Deville, there has therefore been an ongoing process of artistic and historical disclosure.[23] French artists, French antiquaries, and their public have begun to learn to see what they could not see before — what had been veiled to their

Fig. 17. Achille Deville, "Salle capitulaire," *Essai historique et descriptif sur l'église et l'abbaye de Saint-Georges-de-Boscherville près Rouen*, 1827, lithograph. Collection Centre Canadien d'Architecture/Canadian Centre for Architecture, Montréal.

predecessors in the intervening centuries, when the "Gothic" was regarded as, literally speaking, something that resisted observation. The most celebrated description of how a classically educated person came to discover the intrinsic qualities of a great medieval religious building is, of course, Goethe's account of his experience at Strasbourg

Cathedral. In Goethe's case, as he himself frankly put it, medieval architecture represented initially nothing more than the opposite of acceptable taste: "I called Gothic whatever did not fit my system."[24] But the attention paid to St. Georges de Boscherville in France half a century later testifies to a further stage in the casting off of these ancestral prejudices. It brings medieval architecture into focus at a time when the issue is not just how to respond appropriately to the appearance of medieval buildings, but also how to set about the necessary task of restoring them. Here Deville is again most perceptive in the recognition, which could well be correlated with his imaginary rehabilitation of the chapter house of St. Georges de Boscherville: "We are finally beginning to understand that one must renounce Greek and Roman architecture in the restorations to be carried out on buildings in the Gothic style. All honor then to the artists who shake off the yoke of routine, searching for this unity that is so much to be desired in monuments!"[25]

In the event, St. Georges de Boscherville seems to have been adopted as a model not just because of its pristine purity, but because it offered an example of how the lessons taught by architectural features could propagate the analysis and understanding of the elements of the medieval style. Despite his commitment to accuracy, Deville had, in effect, conjured up a view of the chapter house that never existed in reality. But far from turning out as a Frankenstein-style monster composed of ill-assorted parts, this newly visualized chapter house seems to have become a veritable emblem of how stylistic differences could be detected and understood within the context of a historic building. Victor Hugo was surely inspired not by the sight of the building itself, but by Deville's creative rendering of it, when he noted in his *Notre-Dame de Paris* (a work whose very title evoked the textual representation of medieval church architecture): "It is the charming semi-Gothic chapter-house of Boscherville where the Romanesque layer comes half-way up the body."[26]

We should bear in mind here that it was through appraising what the English (then as now) referred to as "Norman" architecture that regional antiquarians like Arcisse de Caumont developed the new concept of a "Romanesque" architecture that preceded the Gothic and was stylistically distinct from it. Hyacinthe Langlois resented the affront to regional pride.[27] However, Hugo is wittily utilizing the new architectural terminology. The chapter house at Boscherville is indeed only "half-Gothic." But though the two levels of the building can be broken down into two architectural styles, its fundamental unity is recuperated through the use of a corporeal metaphor ("The Romanesque layer comes half-way up the body"). Nodier, as we have seen, called the *Voyages pittoresques* a "history of tombs," and Géricault's evocation of the lying in state of William the Conqueror struck a similar commemorative note. But Hugo is putting the knowledge acquired by antiquarians such as Deville to good use by encouraging his fellow countrymen to restore the long neglected national heritage. His clarion call, written in 1825 and published in 1829 — "On the destruction of monuments in France" — had already called upon them to repudiate the "bastard edifices" of a debased classicism, and to bring about the resurrection of the national architecture of the Middle Ages.[28]

In the process of cultural stocktaking that has been described up to now, it has been emphasized that the historical referent is given concrete form by successive visual representations, and specifically by modes of visual registration whose common feature is the modeling of the dynamic effects of light. Granet's paintings may have supplied a prototype. There would have been a comparable effect, I suggest, in the phenomenon of real light filtered periscopically from the daylight above, in the case of the diorama, and in the surprising illusion of light that emanated from the white ground of the paper in the case of the print, though the latter depended also on the subtle suggestion of the crayon marks on the smooth surface of the lithographic stone. And if the surprise of the initial technical effect produced by diorama and lithography must surely have diminished by the end of the 1820s, the distinctive features of medieval church building had by that point begun to lodge themselves in popular consciousness. An

Fig. 18. Andrew Best Leloir, "Saint Georges de Boscherville," *Magasin pittoresque* 2 (1834): 316, wood engraving. Collection Centre Canadien d'Architecture/Canadian Centre for Architecture, Montréal.

inevitable dilution of visual impact must have occurred as popular low-cost publishing ventures replaced these earlier modes of visual representation.

Accordingly, Deville's lithographs may seem modest in their achievement when set beside the pioneering enterprise of the *Voyages pittoresques*. But they are still impressive when set beside the wood-block engravings that enlivened the pages of France's first popular illustrated magazine, the *Magasin pittoresque,* when it commenced publication in 1833. St. Georges de Boscherville makes a prompt appearance here, in an issue dating from the following year, which features what is obviously an original print (see fig. 18) deriving from a drawing *sur le motif.*

The Anglo-French team of engravers going under the trade name of "Andrew Best Leloir," whose stamp identifies the print, must have worked from a drawing prepared on the spot by the artist whose monogram "TF" appears in the right-hand lower corner. The editorial text that accompanies this view of the abbey makes explicit reference to Deville's authoritative study while making no mention of the *Voyages pittoresques*. But if the draftsman working for the engravers shows some knowledge of the details of the sculpture at Boscherville already included in Deville's publication, he has also made the aesthetic decision to revert to Xavier Leprince's oblique view of the abbey façade. This allows both the spire and the south transept to appear to better advantage than in Deville. Moreover, he has decided to include a little patch of wooded hillside, which, though consistent with the actual topography of the landscape behind the abbey, must have required a certain license with perspective. As for the human elements in the foreground, the cruder technique of the engraving makes any precise characterization almost impossible to achieve. But the presence in the foreground of a seated woman in peasant costume suggests that there is no more at stake than a requirement for a touch of local color.

Where the *Voyages pittoresques* had been sold to a few hundred wealthy subscribers, the *Magasin pittoresque* was habitually published in an edition of around 100,000. If the former had been technically avant-garde and romantically revivalist in its ideology, the latter was cut-price, didactic, and broadly populist in its confident assertion of the educational role of the image.[29] The difference in the way in which the two publications represent the façade of the Abbey of St. Georges de Boscherville accords closely with these very disparate social and cultural aims. But I would argue that this should not be regarded simply as a matter of conflicting agendas but rather as the outcome of a cumulative process of habituation, comparable to the learning of a new language by different constituents of the French public in turn. Already in the seventeenth and eighteenth centuries, antiquarians in France and Britain had begun to use visual scenes and diagrams to enhance their presentation of historic sites and buildings. By the second quarter of the nineteenth century, this practice of visualizing architectural monuments had acquired genuinely popular appeal. Throughout this period, however, it proves impossible to eliminate the mythic dimension of historical revivalism — omnipresent in historical novels and salon paintings — from the avowedly scientific aims of contemporary publications on historical topics.

At its date of first publication in 1825, Augustin Thierry's *Histoire de la conquête de l'Angleterre par les Normands* was a textual publication pure and simple, though it could claim to be historiographically innovative in its scheme of incorporating popular poems and other records of the medieval period as historical evidence. As one of the most popular histories of the day, it went into numerous editions, including a revised third edition that Thierry completed in 1830. By the end of the decade, a lavishly illustrated edition was current, and for the fifth edition, which appeared in 1839, an accompanying Atlas was published. Maps, facsimiles of charters, and other visual features supplemented the specially commissioned plates by contemporary artists that were engraved to illustrate significant episodes in the narrative. This development was as much a testimony to the newfound desire of the reading public to "see" their history as it was a tribute to the visual potential of Thierry's lively narrative.

Fig. 19. A. Maillard after a drawing by A. H. Cabasson, "Spécimen de l'architecture Saxonne et de l'architecture Normande," in Augustin Thierry, *Histoire de la conquête de l'Angleterre par les Normands*, 5th ed., Atlas (J. Tessier, 1839), copper engraving. Stephen Bann Private Collection.

It will come as no surprise that this Atlas accompanying Thierry's fifth edition features Boscherville on its map of medieval Normandy. It also includes the Abbey as the only monument to be illustrated with an elevation drawing (see fig. 19). But in Thierry's case, it is not a question of marking the transition from Romanesque to Gothic, as demonstrated by Deville's image of the chapter house. Consistent with Thierry's mission of analyzing the Norman conquest of England, it plays the most prominent role in enabling us to visualize the historical opposition between the Anglo-Saxon and Norman architectural styles. Yet another original view of the abbey's façade has been engraved to illustrate this point. It is comparable to the oblique view that had appeared in the *Magasin pittoresque*. But the young draftsman Alphonse Cabasson (b. 1816) was a native of Rouen who joined Paul Delaroche's studio at the École des Beaux-Arts in

1833, and it seems likely that he took the opportunity of sketching the abbey on a trip to his home town. His drawing, which obscures the south transept from view but compensates by placing an interesting withered tree in the background, was transferred to a copper plate and engraved by A. Maillard, as was still the rule for the publication of maps, music, and architectural plans.

This plate in Thierry's Atlas could thus be said to belong somewhere between the luxurious lithographs of the *Voyages pittoresques* and the wood-block prints of the *Magasin* as regards both pricing and popular accessibility. However, its message is again explicitly didactic. The full page that includes the view of the Abbey of St. Georges de Boscherville—juxtaposed with a number of smaller architectural details from both French and English ecclesiastical buildings—is entitled "Spécimen de l'architecture Saxonne et de l'architecture Normande." Deville's earlier lithographic presentation of salient sculptural details from the abbey is distantly reflected in the illustration of a couple of stone carvings under the abbey façade, whose rendering is however a good deal more crude, the purpose simply being to contribute to a repertoire of generic differences. That the Abbey is the only building reproduced here in a full frontal view is no doubt a measure of the reputation that had accrued to it over the previous twenty years. It had become an exemplary medieval building, and so qualified to appear in this group of reproductions. However, the caption that we read in the Atlas for Thierry's sixth edition affords the building a simple and accurate pedigree, stripped of mythic afflatus: "This charming church is situated a few leagues from Rouen; historical testimony, and notably a charter of William the Conqueror, establish in a positive manner that it was founded in the eleventh century by Raoul de Tancarville."[30]

In choosing for my final illustration (fig. 19) an image from the Atlas accompanying Augustin Thierry's history, I am also revisiting a question I first raised many years ago, in an essay first published in 1970 and included in *The Clothing of Clio*.[31] The original article was written in the heyday of structuralism, and it is perhaps worth considering how this sequence of visual representations of St. Georges de Boscherville fits, or does not fit, the structural development that I posited at that time. Taking a hint from a tantalizing observation in a letter by the historian Jules Michelet, I put forward the hypothesis that three of the most important French historians of the Romantic period—Prosper de Barante, Thierry, and Michelet himself—demonstrated a cyclical pattern as successive exponents of historical discourse.[32] "Cycle" was in fact precisely the term employed by Michelet, and his well-known interest in the cyclical notions of the eighteenth-century Neapolitan philosopher and rhetorician Giambattista Vico clarifies this reference. I suggested that what he was identifying could be equated with three structurally related rhetorical strategies pursued by the three historians, of which he himself represented the last. I also invoked a parallel with Claude Lévi-Strauss's notion of the cycle of "code," "message," and "myth," itself deriving from Roman Jakobson's model of the functions of discourse, which was used in the "Overture" to *Le cru et le cuit* to define successive compositional procedures in musical history: Bach, musician of the code, Beethoven, musician of the message, and Wagner, musician of the myth.[33] My idea was to transfer this structural model to the cycle suggested by Michelet: Barante as historian of the code, Thierry as historian of the message, and Michelet himself as historian of the myth.

The present analysis has, however, taken an opposite direction. It began by emphasizing the mythic investment in St. Georges de Boscherville by Nodier and the artists contributing to the *Voyages pittoresques*. It continued by way of the antiquarian and didactic exegesis of Deville, then tracked the popularization of the image of the abbey in the *Magasin pittoresque*. The final point was the reduction of the image of the building to a "specimen," an example of Norman as opposed to Saxon architecture, in Thierry's Atlas. Thus the sequence proceeded from "myth" to "message," and ultimately to "code." This reverse movement also corresponds, incidentally, to the cyclical model devised by Lévi-Strauss, since he takes his second musical example from the Vienna School of the early twentieth century, when Arnold

Schoenberg (myth) gives place to Alban Berg (message), and finally to Anton von Webern (code).

What should we make of this apparent anomaly in early nineteenth-century historical discourse — namely, that historical texts proper appear to have followed a cyclical process reversing that of historical images? Clearly, the problem exists only to the extent that these two registers are considered in isolation. It will disappear if we regard historical discourse as a domain encompassing both modes of representation. According to this light, the relationship between word and image within the evolving discourse of Romantic historiography might indeed be seen as dialectical. The overwhelming prestige of the visual, as signaled by the publication of the *Voyages pittoresques*, has its contemporary counterpart in the plain narrative of Barante's *Ducs de Bourgogne*, which eschews any illustration by contemporary artists. Only when the histories of Barante, and Thierry, have run through several editions are illustrations of the narrative commissioned for them, and the visual is thus incorporated as a new dimension of the text, which is also essentially subservient to it. We might also bear in mind that, in the same year that Thierry's Atlas was first published, Daguerre unveiled his other visual invention — the photograph — to the artists and the scientists of France. Neither the diorama nor the lithograph could retain for very long their early primacy as vehicles of illusion and propagators of myth.[34] The print image of St. Georges de Boscherville could no longer work as a thrilling evocation. The abbey itself had become a scientific specimen, exemplifying the progress of a positive history.

NOTES

1. See Stephen Bann, "Scaling the Cathedral: Bourges in John Bargrave's Travel Journal for 1645," in *Monuments and Memory, Made and Unmade*, ed. Robert S. Nelson and Margaret Olin (Chicago: University of Chicago Press, 2003), 15–35. The manuscript of the travel journal (Canterbury Cathedral Archive, U11/8 IRBY Deposit) came to my attention several years after the publication of my book on John Bargrave (see note 2).

2. The English Civil War developed as a result of a growing antagonism

between King Charles I and the English Parliament, which erupted into armed conflict in the 1640s, and led eventually to the king's execution. In this process, there was an increasing polarization of the two opposing parties, which was reflected throughout the different regions of the country, and a concerted assault on the established church by the so-called Roundhead or Puritan faction, which dominated the Parliament. For further details of Dean Bargrave's identification with the cathedral, both as a conserver of its architecture and as a defender of traditional rights attaching to religious and educational institutions that were challenged by Parliament, see Stephen Bann, *Under the Sign: John Bargrave as Collector, Traveler, and Witness* (Ann Arbor: University of Michigan Press, 1994), 56–60.

3. See Félix Davin's introduction (1834) to Balzac's *Études philosophiques*, where the writer is characterized as an "architect" who wishes us "to roam across the great intersecting ribs of his cathedral," in Honoré de Balzac, *Oeuvres complètes*, Pléiade edition, (Paris: Gallimard, 1965), 11:209. (Translations from the French are my own.)

4. For a brilliant survey of this development, see Ségolène Le Men, *La cathédrale illustrée de Hugo à Monet — Regard romantique et modernité* (Paris: CNRS Editions, 1998).

5. Julia Kristeva, *Proust and the Sense of Time*, trans. Stephen Bann (London: Faber & Faber, 1993), 7.

6. Henri Beraldi, *Les Graveurs du XIXe siècle* [1885–92] (Laget: Nogent-le-Roi, 1980–81), 9:47.

7. Beraldi, *Les graveurs*, 9:48.

8. See his letter dated Rouen, 3 May 1832, to "Monsieur Alavoine . . . Architecte du gouvernement," in which he stresses this point, in relation to a recent publication: [One thing that I particularly approve of in his work is his little movement of ill humor against the denomination of *Romanesque* being given to the *Norman* architecture of the monuments in *our* province] "Une chose que j'approuve surtout dans son ouvrage c'est son petit mouvement d'humeur contre la dénomination de *Romane* donnée à l'architecture *Normande* de monuments de *notre* province," 2002-A-1121, Frits Lugt Collection, Fondation Custodia, Institut Néerlandais, Paris.

9. Augustin Thierry, *Histoire de la conquête de l'Angleterre par les Normands, de ses causes et de ses suites jusqu'à nos jours, en Angleterre, en Irlande et sur le continent*, 5th ed., Atlas (Paris: Just Tessier, 1839), plate 2.

10. For a discussion of the relation between these two major historical works, see Stephen Bann, *The Clothing of Clio: A Study of the Representation of History*

in *Nineteenth-Century Britain and France* (Cambridge: Cambridge University Press, 1984), 32–53.

11. Beraldi, *Les graveurs*, 12:18. My translation.

12. See Stephen Bann, *Romanticism and the Rise of History* (New York: Twayne, 1995), 112–18, for a discussion of Cotman's prints as historical representation.

13. The Cotman print is illustrated in Bann, *Romanticism and the Rise of History*, 115.

14. See illustration in Bann, *Romanticism and the Rise of History*, 109.

15. See Bann, *Romanticism and the Rise of History*, 107–11.

16. See the discussion of the significance of "cloistering" scenes in Michael Fried, *Manet's Modernism, or, The Face of Painting in the 1860s* (Chicago: University of Chicago Press, 1996), 254.

17. See B781:84:362, ff. 1–30, Print Collection, Cromer Archive, George Eastman House, Rochester, New York.

18. See Leo Ewals, *Ary Schefer 1795–1858 — Gevierd Romanticus* (Zwolle: Waanders Uitgevers with Dordrechts Museum, 1995), 99. The similarity between the features of the dead artist and those of William the Conqueror as conveyed in the lithograph is striking.

19. "Enfin quelques jours plus tôt, un nom garant de l'avenir nous auroit couvert d'une protection toujours assurée aux travaux utiles, aux entreprises honorables, aux idées françoises. Nous aurions pu nommer BERRY! Et cette histoire des tombeaux, c'est au sien qu'elle commence!" Charles Nodier et al., *Voyages pittoresques et romantiques dans l'ancienne France,* vol. 1: *Ancienne Normandie* (Paris, 1820), 15. Translation in the main text is mine.

20. Jean-Achille Deville, *Essai historique et descriptif sur l'église et l'abbaye de Saint-Georges-de-Boscherville près Rouen, ornée de planches lithographiées ou gravées, et de plusieurs vignettes* (Rouen: N. Périaux jeune, 1827). Deville (1789–1875) was the son of a *fermier général* (royal tax collector) under the Ancien Régime, who followed in his father's footsteps and became *receveur général* at Alençon. By the stage of this publication, he had however decided to devote himself to archaeology, and had become the founder of the Musée des Antiquités in Rouen.

21. "Nous ne craignons pas de le dire . . . il est peu d'églises, non-seulement en Normandie, mais même en France, qui offre un aspect aussi vierge que celle de Saint-Georges. Elle est pure de ces grossières disparates qui déshonorent les plus beaux monuments religieux, et dont aucune des premières basiliques de France n'est peut-être exempte. Aussi est-ce à juste titre qu'on lui a appliqué l'heureuse expression anglaise: *it is chaste*, elle est chaste" (Deville, *Essai historique*, 11). Translation in the main text is mine.

22. Nodier et al., *Voyages pittoresques*, 1: plate 110.

23. Deville notes, for example, that his measurements of the church, "taken with great care," are an improvement on the plan printed in the *Voyages pittoresques*, which makes it "a few feet shorter in length" (*Essai historique*, 7, note 1).

24. See Bann, *Romanticism and the Rise of History*, 82–88.

25. Deville, *Essai historique*, 11, note 1.

26. "C'est la charmante salle capitulaire demi-gothique de Bocherville [sic] à laquelle la couche romane vient jusqu'à mi-corps." See Victor Hugo, *Notre Dame de Paris*, in *Oeuvres complètes*, ed. Jean Massin (Paris: Club français du livre, 1970), vol. 4, pt. 2, 96. Translation in main text is mine. Hugo adduces Notre Dame itself as a similar example of a medieval building involving two architectural styles, classing it with St. Georges de Boscherville among "monuments de deux formations."

27. See note 8.

28. See Victor Hugo, "Sur la destruction des monuments de France" (October 1825), in *Oeuvres complètes*, vol. 2, pt. 1, 569–74.

29. The first issue of the *Magasin pittoresque*, which appeared in 1833 "at two *sous* per issue," expressed its policy in the following way: "One will encounter, here and there in the sequence of our issues, the most remarkable of *ancient monuments, monuments of the Middle Ages,* and *modern monuments*. The engravings will faithfully reproduce their character, their overall effect, and often their details" (*Magasin pittoresque*, vol. 1, 1833, 1, my translation).

30. Augustin Thierry, "Architecture," in *Histoire de la Conquête de l'Angleterre par les Normands*, 6th ed., Atlas (Paris: Just Tessier, 1843), n.p.

31. Stephen Bann, "A Cycle in Historical Discourse: Barante, Thierry, Michelet," *Twentieth Century Studies*, special issue on Structuralism, 3 (May 1970): 110–30; the version in *Clothing of Clio*, 32–53, is slightly revised.

32. Michelet wrote in a letter to Sainte-Beuve: "If you examine the historians of this age, you will take into account, I imagine, both *the point at which I found history, and the step which I have made*. Barante, Thierry and I form a kind of cycle. You can only make a fair judgment of each one of us through seeing him in his relationship to the others" (quoted in Bann, *Clothing of Clio*, 33).

33. See Claude Lévi-Strauss, *Le cru et le cuit* (Paris: Plon, 1964), 38.

34. It is interesting to note that photography has itself proved capable, over a long period, of renewing our experience of medieval buildings through technical innovations that recall these earlier developments in lithography. The development of the *Zodiaque* collection of photographically illustrated books on medieval French architecture, acclaimed by André Malraux in 1973,

demonstrates the point. In this case, the resourceful use of the photographic technique of *héliogravure* was a decisive factor. For a fascinating account of this "resacralizing" of French Romanesque architecture, see Cédric Lesec, "*Zodiaque* est une grande chose, maintenant . . . ," *Revue de l'art* 157 (2007, issue 3): 39–46.

4 Performing History on the Victorian Stage

RICHARD SCHOCH

The popular culture of Victorian Britain, as described by a contemporary observer, comprised heterogeneous "exhibitions, galleries, and museums" devoted to "popular education in the young and in the adult."[1] These forms of respectable recreation became the "libraries of those who have no money to expend on books . . . [and] the travel of those that have no time to bestow on travel." Among the "amusements for mind and senses," which "woo the world of London at every turn," the *National Review* counted "lecture-rooms, dioramas, panoramas, cheap concerts, oratorios, public gardens, and innumerable other diversions, suited to every scale of purse and every variety of taste and cultivation."[2] Informative entertainments such as the Diorama in Regent's Park, the Cosmorama in Regent Street, and Wyld's Great Globe in Leicester Square exercised cultural governance over an imperial city whose population at midcentury passed 2,000,000. This thriving popular culture was nothing if not visual. From the *Illustrated London News* to stereoscope photographs, and from the annual Royal Academy exhibitions to *cartes de visite*, the Victorians were insatiable consumers of pictures.

But for Londoners "high or low, rich or poor," enthused *Blackwood's Magazine*, theater was the "supreme delight."[3] The "upper, middle and lower classes" of the nation's capital could take their pick of "theatres for the east, and theatres for the west; theatres for this side of the river, and theatres for that; theatres for performances equestran and aquatic; theatres legitimate and illegitimate."[4] The theater was a central part of Victorian visual culture because its audience was predisposed to look at the stage as if it were a series of living pictures. Pictorial staging entailed not only highly elaborate scenery but also detailed costumes and properties, spectacular effects, and the frequent use of tableaux vivants — a static pose held by the acting ensemble at a climactic moment which made the stage look as if it were a painting.

Never an illicit pleasure, Victorian theatrical pictorialism was intimately tied to the middle-class obsession with rational amusement: the education and instruction of mass audiences through popular culture. History was the ideal subject for the theater to teach through its historically accurate scenery, costumes, and stage properties. While Shakespeare's English and Roman chronicle plays were an obvious place to start, his tragedies, comedies, and romances were all treated as opportunities for historical instruction. The theater's commitment to historical accuracy was the very sign of its modernity. To prefer anachronistic performances of Shakespeare, as Charles Dunphy of the *Morning Post* argued, was to prefer "the semaphore to the electric telegraph" or "the stage-coach to the locomotive."[5] And thus the measure of success for Shakespearian revivals became their ability to surpass the vivacity and precision of history novels, genre paintings, museum collections, and architectural restorations. Archaeological eclecticism flourished throughout the century, and a lively range of historical places, personages, and events was recreated for eager and ever-expanding audiences.

But which past should be restored? Which relic prized above all others? Though largely neglected by Renaissance humanists and Enlightenment philosophers alike, the Middle Ages was the chief historical touchstone for the nationalistic nineteenth century, and the rehabilitated Gothic style occupied a privileged position in a northern European strategy of cultural search and seizure. As Alice Chandler and Lee Patterson have demonstrated, medievalism in Victorian Britain was a complex and often contradictory mix of social, political, and spiritual ideals that were nonetheless united by a shared desire to make a "home" in history.[6] When the Middle Ages finally transcended the Romantic aesthetic of contemplative melancholy—the age of the Gothic ruin—it emerged as the cornerstone of English civil society: the age when English language, law, and literature were born. And thus it is not surprising that ideologues and reformers of all stripes would invoke the medieval past.[7]

While we tend to associate Victorian medievalism with architecture, painting, literature, and arts and crafts—with Pugin, Rossetti, Ruskin, Disraeli, and Morris—theatrical performance was also an active partner in the effort to recover the Middle Ages. Performance was a powerful agent of historical consciousness because it realized the past with a "bold and master hand"[8] greater than that of literature, painting, or even photography. In the words of one Victorian actor-manager, performance "endows the creations of the painter's art with animated reality."[9] As a central part of a vibrant and spectacular popular culture whose audience was equipped to recognize and read historical iconography, the mid-Victorian theater was uniquely poised to ensure the material continuity of the medieval past. In the theater, above all, the past was not dead. It was not even sleeping. It was alive and well and appearing nightly.

In performing the Middle Ages, Victorian theatrical managers turned first to Shakespeare, the great national poet whose English chronicle plays were regarded as history books written in dramatic verse.[10] The most medievalizing productions of Shakespeare in the nineteenth century were those staged by the actor-manager Charles Kean at the Princess's Theatre in London: *King John* (1852), *Macbeth* (1853), *Henry VIII* (1855), *Richard II* (1857), and *Henry V* (1859). I will focus in this chapter on Kean's grand revivals of Shakespeare's history plays to show that an antiquarian approach to Shakespeare (the poetic narration of English history, the astonishing accuracy of his mise-en-scène, and the reenactment of famous events) reunited and resurrected "fragments" of the medieval past in order to construct a model of Englishness that could be shared by all segments of the audience. I believe, therefore, that Kean's antiquarian dramaturgy is not a naïve fascination with historical accuracy — not interior decoration with a vengeance — but historical consciousness in action: an attempt to make the past speak to the present; to make the past live again.

No other society had so rapidly and so completely embraced technological innovation, and yet no other society sought so desperately to reanimate its past. Not since the Renaissance had a people combined such "confidence in their own powers with so much antiquarian retrospection."[11] But the Victorians' aggressive identification with the future and the past could not conceal their discontent with the present. As Matthew Arnold knew, the nineteenth century was an age of self-conscious transition, "wandering between two worlds, one dead / the other powerless to be born." Out of the Victorians' fear of being lost within history — of being dispossessed — sprang the impulse to prescribe the future by restoring the past.

The obsession with restoring the medieval past, including in the theater, was driven by an antiquarian curiosity for reviving the past in all its detail, which was itself a fearful response to an overwhelming sense of loss and to an acute awareness of what Hayden White has called "the seriality of existence."[12] In other words, a people dispossessed by their own history — dememorialized in their own time — are always already struggling to repossess that history in its former totality and unity by rehabilitating the material things — fragments, artifacts, and relics — that are authorized to constitute a national heritage. History was a strategy of recuperation, a way of aesthetically recovering what has already passed away.[13] And so the artistic expression of nineteenth-century historical consciousness — and we see this most of all in theatrical representations of architecture — was an attempt to *reverse* the ruin: to ensure that representations of the past would evoke presence, not absence; wholeness, not fragmentation; and fulfillment, not loss. Thus, ruined buildings—medieval castles and cathedrals, notably—were depicted through painted scenery in their original intact state, as if they had never fallen into ruin in the first place.

Anxieties over the heterogeneity of historical discourses could be eased, then, through the recovery and display of historical objects, and the nineteenth century's effort to reground its own place in history took strength from the enduring, if obsessive, practices of antiquarians. Indeed, from the Renaissance onward, antiquarianism had always been a genealogical pursuit. Obsessed with establishing the pedigree and lineage of "our own" history, and thereby validating the present by reference to its ancestral past, the antiquarian was forever moving from disinheritance to reclamation. "My love for my national antiquities," Joseph Strutt wrote in 1774, "is greater than I can express . . . for it is not our least honor to be so nobly descended."[14] When Charles Kean, in his 1857 playbill for *Richard II*, referred to the Middle Ages as the "homestead of history," he invoked the classic antiquarian images of the past as dwelling place.

Charles Kean (1811–68) may have been the most determined actor-*historian* in the long history of the British theater, but he was hardly the first. His determination to turn the stage into a history book represents the full flowering of a century-long tradition of emerging historical consciousness among actors and scene designers, from David Garrick in the late-eighteenth century to John Philip Kemble at the turn of the century and to William Charles Macready in the 1830s and '40s. The emergence was gradual and slow.

Throughout the eighteenth century, and, indeed, for a good part of the nineteenth, British theaters recycled stocks of generic flats, wings, and borders that symbolized the conventional dramatic settings of palaces, chambers, prisons, gardens, and forests. Only infrequently would any play, and Shakespeare's least of all, be mounted with new and expensive scenery. Eighteenth-century audiences expected a logical coherence, a conforming generality, between scenery and dramatic action, to be sure; but they also expected that a given scenic ensemble would appear in productions of many different plays. "To the Georgian mind," argues Richard Southern, "any conception of scenery as factual background to action was wholly unmeaning and indeed alien."[15]

Since representing the past on stage initially meant *illustrating* the past, the emergence of historical consciousness in the theater depended entirely on advancements in scenery. When the great Georgian actor-manager David Garrick visited the Comédie Française in Paris in 1763, the British theater first recognized the powerful capacity of scenery, masterfully painted and adequately illuminated, to convey information and arouse an audience's emotions. As practiced by Philippe de Loutherbourg, the Alsatian painter whom Garrick engaged in 1771 to oversee the creation of scenery at Drury Lane, the Romantic picturesque style offered the Georgian theater a new range of subjects to be strikingly depicted and emotions to be intensely felt. Late-eighteenth-century scenography drew its inspiration less from historical research and the collection of source materials than from the robust traditions of painting.

De Loutherbourg established topographic scenery in the British theater and, indeed, the twelve scenes of *The Wonders of Derbyshire* (1779) were, as Sybil Rosenfeld rightly points out, "localised and painted from drawings made in the places themselves."[16] These scenes acquired a kind of authenticity because they were "localised," but that authenticity was more geographical than historical. The picturesque panorama, unpeopled and unspoiled, was the realm of nature (the *phusik* of de Loutherbourg's Eidophusikon) and not of historical events with their attendant demands of sources and authorities.

Even when architectural elements did appear in landscape scenes, as in the cult of the Gothic or classical ruin, those decaying structures stood outside the orbit of historical narrative and beyond the possibility of being located in chronology. And it was precisely the obsession with fixing an object's unique place in time that marked the advent of modern historical consciousness. Jean Starobinski, writing on the late-eighteenth-century transition from elegists to antiquaries, argues that "those who remained attached to their sentimental emotion considered that it was a sacrilege to *date* things which should impart a sense of the *immemorial*."[17]

Because de Loutherbourg felt what Starobinski calls the "sentimental emotion," or poeticization of ruins, the part he played in the rise of theatrical historicism was not to adopt antiquarian empiricism but to emancipate set design from the tedious nullity of the previous hundred years. The theater of David Garrick was, in effect, poised to become historical. The appearance of scene painters' names on playbills at the end of the eighteenth century bespeaks the new legitimacy and seriousness of purpose that theatrical scenery had won. Empowered by the example of de Loutherbourg, late-Georgian scenic artists followed the example of their more academic colleagues and profited from the increasing availability of historical source materials. Scene painters like William Capon (1757–1827), trained in drafting and architecture, could find inspiration in antiquarian handbooks and manuals and so convert themselves into antiquaries. In other words, representing the past *as* past and not just as milieu was the job not of the traditional landscape painter, but of the new artist-antiquary.

The first expressions of modern historical consciousness in the British theater were thus part of a larger shift in history painting away from the fantastic imprecisions of the Gothic picturesque.[18] The artist-antiquary, who collected historical engravings and pored over the works of historians such as the French Benedictine monk Bernard de Montfauçon, moved in a world not of sublime and imaginative fancy, but of scholarship, archaeology, and research. Such a world was amateur and gentlemanly, to be sure, but no less painstaking or demanding for that. Publications from groups such as the Society of Antiquaries transformed the picture galleries and playhouses of Georgian England inasmuch as the circulation of historically accurate images of the Middle Ages and classical antiquity created the pressure to translate those images into other media.

Beginning in the late eighteenth century, both easel painters and actor-managers began to read the same antiquarian manuals, and so their respective representations of the past drew from the same compilations of historical detail. In 1789, for example, the well-known painter Benjamin West consulted Joseph Strutt's *Regal and Ecclesiastical Antiquities of England* (1773) to obtain correct fourteenth-century detail for his *Edward III and the Burghers of Calais*. When similar illustrations from antiquarian manuals reappeared as painted scenery, the Georgian theater discovered not history—it had never been lost—but a *philosophy* of history. Decades later, when Charles Kean also turned to Strutt's illustrated histories of England as sources for his own revivals of Shakespeare, he was merely continuing a precedent set two generations earlier. And in asserting the authenticity of his theatricalized histories, Kean was only renewing the guarantee made by Strutt more than half a century earlier: that each instance or figure of historical recreation claimed a "proper authority," was faithfully copied "without the least unnecessary deviation," and could be independently verified by reference "to the original books themselves."[19]

The series of designs William Capon created for John Philip Kemble at both Drury Lane and Covent Garden between 1794 and 1809 represent the first sustained use of antiquarian scenery in a late-Georgian playhouse. As renovated by Henry Holland, the new Drury Lane opened in 1794 with a dramatically enlarged stage and auditorium: the theater now accommodated nearly 3,600 spectators, double its previous capacity; the actors, in turn, were compelled to project 100 feet out instead of the former 60, to reach the most distant member of the audience.[20] The greater scale also rendered the old stock scenery obsolete, and Kemble, as actor-manager and coproprietor, turned to the architectural draftsman William Capon to design new drops, borders, and wings. It was a time when "nearly everything, as to correctness, was [still] to be done," Kemble's biographer James Boaden recalled.[21] "The old scenery exhibited architecture of no period and excited little attention ... nothing could be less accurate or more dirty."

Capon's new scenery was not only picturesque but also antiquarian, for his specialty was the illustration of medieval architecture. Using drawings that he had made on site he reproduced onstage a series of medieval and Tudor buildings. On the reopening of Drury Lane,

Boaden remembered with pleasure that Capon, "cast in the mould of antiquity," was the ideal choice to "carry into effect the true and perfect decorations which [John Philip Kemble] meditated for the plays of Shakespeare."[22] Capon's designs were intended "to be records as well as decorations, and present with every other merit, that for which Kemble was born, — truth."

Boaden then recounts a visit to Capon's atelier where the artist's new scenery lay before its installation at the renovated playhouse. In impressive detail he describes the medieval architecture depicted in the painted wings and flats:

> a chapel of the pointed [Gothic] architecture, which occupied the whole stage . . . Six chamber wings, of the same order, for general use in our old English plays — very elaborately studied from actual remains. A view of the New Palace Yard, Westminster . . . The ancient palace of Westminster, as it was about 300 years back; from partial remains, and authentic sources of information — put together with the greatest diligence and accuracy . . . Two very large wings, containing portions of the old palace, which the artist made out from an ancient draught met with in looking over some records . . . It was but a pen and ink sketch originally, but though injured by time, exhibited what was true. Six wings representing ancient English streets; combinations of genuine remains, selected on account of their picturesque beauty. The tower of London, restored to its earlier state, for the play of King Richard III.[23]

These deceptively simple descriptions not only reveal which medieval scenes Capon painted but also claim a historical legitimacy for those scenes. Boaden's inventory of the contents of Capon's workshop is really the first interpretive guide to theatrical historicism. Indeed, many of the themes that this study explores with reference to Charles Kean are themselves suggested by Boaden: the fascination with the Middle Ages ("pointed architecture"), the theater's use of antiquarianism ("a scene painter . . . cast in the mould of antiquity"), the balancing of the historical and the picturesque ("records as well as decorations"), the nationalistic reading of dramatic literature ("our old English plays"), the interest in fragments ("actual remains," "genuine remains"), the appeal to the sanction of historical documents ("authentic sources of information," "looking over some records"), the synecdochic progression from part to whole ("restored to its earlier state"), and the equation between truth and stage setting ("true and perfect decorations," "exhibited what was true").

Capon's scenery was historically authentic because, like de Loutherbourg's landscapes, it was copied from actual sites; but such locational authenticity had nothing to do with the plays that the scenery would eventually illustrate. More to the point, he never actually designed a production in its entirety, but rather devised new scenery to be interspersed with whatever was drawn from stock. "Capon simply used actual Gothic buildings or remains," as Rosenfeld has remarked, "to produce scenes of a church or hall in no particular place."[24] The historical propriety of Capon's scenery — its new claim to represent "actual remains" verified by "authentic sources" — was not as important as its pictorial delights. Indeed, the surviving sketches of his medieval and Tudor scenery created for the 1809 reopening of Covent Garden mix pictorial fantasy with antiquarian exactness.

No archaeologist could object to the historical pedigree of the individual buildings that lined Capon's "ancient street," but that street existed only in the painter's mind. Capon was as much artist as antiquary because he not only selected "architectural remains in different parts of the kingdom," but also "brought [them] together in one point of view."[25] That singular, picturesque point of view — a wide avenue flanked by Gothic and Tudor buildings meeting at a market cross, with the spires of a Gothic church visible in the distance — was explicitly arranged and harmonized. Capon's impulse to historicize did not displace the impulse to pictorialize because there was, in fact, no contradiction between them. Boaden himself does not hesitate to call Capon's scenery for the new Drury Lane "decorations" and feels no need to apologize for the "picturesque beauty" of the six wing-sets of "ancient English streets."

John Philip Kemble was substantially the opposite of his antiquarian scenographer, for the rigors of modern historical research did not appeal to the actor's mind, despite his avowed bibliomania.[26] Even the most untutored classicist, recalling Caesar Augustus's boast that he found Rome clothed in brick and left her dressed in marble, would have recognized Kemble's error of depicting imperial marble structures — the Arch of Constantine, Trajan's Column, and the Coliseum — in *Coriolanus*, a play set in republican Rome. Indeed, when the eminent antiquary Francis Douce apprised Kemble of the necessity to depict unadorned brick buildings in stagings of Shakespeare's Roman plays, the horrified tragedian protested, "If I did . . . they would call me an antiquary."[27]

Kemble's revivals of *Coriolanus* are intriguing for what they reveal about the actor-manager's variable commitment to historical representation. As theater historians have long noted, the dress and composition of Kemble's staging appears to have been inspired by the famous neoclassical paintings of Nicolas Poussin (1594–1665). Moelwyn Merchant and Stephen Orgel, among others, have observed that the scene from *Coriolanus* illustrated in Ackerman's *Microcosm of London* (1809), of Volumnia imploring her son in the Volscian camp, is a version of an 1809 Rowlandson and Pugin engraving that itself adopted Poussin's horizontal composition. The origin, then, of the stage scene's *Romanitas* was "not history or archaeology," Orgel concludes, "but the presence of the artist."[28] That is, Kemble's production claimed a kind of historical legitimacy because it emulated familiar painterly images of Coriolanus. But that legitimacy was much weaker than the one his brother Charles would later claim for his 1823 revival of *King John*. For John Philip Kemble, artistic representations of historical subjects, though perhaps influenced by historical texts, were themselves appropriate and sufficient models for theatrical representations of the past.

In November 1820, three years after his retirement from the stage, John Philip Kemble transferred by deed of gift his entire one-sixth share of Covent Garden to his brother Charles. Upon receipt of the gift, the younger Kemble became manager of that theater, a post he held until 1833. Like other theater managers of the time, Charles Kemble was unable to "make Shakespeare pay" because of the popularity of burletta and melodrama at other London theaters. But try he did. And his most novel attempt to face down his competition was a revival of *King John* with costumes of unprecedented historical accuracy.

Charles Kemble's first production of *King John*, in March 1823, actually paid little attention to historical correctness. It was not a financial success, and the *Theatrical Observer* noted that by the second performance, the "house was not very well attended."[29] In that same year, the antiquarian and playwright J. R. Planché complained to Charles Kemble that while "a thousand pounds were frequently lavished on Christmas pantomime or an Easter spectacle . . . the plays of Shakespeare were put upon the stage with make-shift scenery, and, at best, a new dress or two for the principal characters."[30] According to the future Somerset herald, then aged all of twenty-seven, "lovers and patrons of the theatre" had long regretted that the plays of Shakespeare "should be decidedly the worst dressed and most *incorrectly* decorated of any productions, ancient or modern, exhibited upon our metropolitan stages."[31]

Historical incongruities in stage costumes were, for Planché, both intellectually absurd and morally indefensible. Since it "was not requisite to be an antiquary" to realize that people dressed differently throughout history, it was an affront to the audience's intelligence to have actors playing thirteenth-century soldiers at Angiers clothed "precisely the same as those fighting at Bosworth at the end of the 15th. If one style of dress was right, the other was wrong."[32] Such high-minded principles of intellectual integrity aside, Planché was also banking on the commercial value of historically accurate mise-en-scène; and it was equally on the basis of box-office potential that he pleaded his case to Charles Kemble. The beleaguered actor-manager, hoping that a spectacular staging of Shakespeare would result in a pecuniary advantage comparable to that of holiday extravaganzas, allowed Planché to restage Covent Garden's production of *King*

John and perform it the following season with costumes based upon thirteenth-century visual and material authorities.

The new *King John* premiered on November 28, 1823, featuring Kemble as Faulconbridge and William Charles Macready in the title role. If it is possible to judge from Planché's account, the historical consciousness of the opening night audience for *King John* was so highly developed that upon seeing appropriate medieval dress used in a Shakespearean production for the first time, the audience could scarcely contain its enthusiasm. When the spectators discovered Macready as "King John dressed as his effigy appears in Worcester Cathedral, surrounded by his barons sheathed in mail, with cylindrical helmets and correct armorial shields, and his courtiers in long tunics and mantles of the thirteenth century, there was a roar of approbation, accompanied by four distinct rounds of applause, so general and so hearty, that the actors were astonished . . . a complete reformation of dramatic costume became from that moment inevitable upon the English stage."[33]

Heir, and exemplar, of this tradition of historicist zeal, Charles Kean—the actor turned antiquary—"rummaged out old books," "turned over old prints," and "brushed the dirt off old music" in preparing historically correct revivals of Shakespeare in the 1850s.[34] As generations of theater students have been taught, Kean's antiquarian spectacles were famous for their sets, costumes, and properties of unprecedented historical precision; adherence to the descriptions and illustrations set forth in the works of historians; reenactment of events not dramatized by Shakespeare; historiographical playbill essays; and the publication of quasi-academic editions of the plays to commemorate their revivals at the Princess's Theatre.

Much of the scenery in Charles Kean's Shakespearean revivals continued the time-honored arrangement of wings and flats set into rows of grooves cut into the stage floor. These basic units of two-dimensional painted scenery could be shifted in four directions simultaneously: wings were easily slid onstage and off, while drops were set and removed through a "rise and sink." A backdrop was not a single piece of canvas but was actually composed of two pieces, an upper half and a lower half. In shifting a drop, the top portion was flown up — or raised — into the fly tower while the lower portion was pulled — or sunk — beneath the stage floor. This was not an especially elegant procedure, for no matter how "delicately painted" were the landscapes used in Kean's productions, as the *Art Journal* complained in 1853, they were still "divided by a cutting line, which is also frequently disfigured with dirt from the handling of the sceneshifters."[35]

Wing-and-drop sets, whether besmirched or pristine, were increasingly augmented by the use of three-dimensional set pieces such as platforms, furniture, or even practical doors, windows, steps, and bridges. Built scenery enhanced the perception of historical accuracy, as with the "room in Ely-House" from Kean's *Richard II* (2.1), in which the dying John of Gaunt speaks as a "prophet new-inspired." Sitting upright in a heavily decorated and canopied bed, and surrounded by tables and a footstool, the actor Walter Lacy does not so much appear in front of a two-dimensional scenic backdrop as he inhabits a three-dimensional historical environment.

While a flat scene could be shifted in front of the audience, "set scenes" (as these more complicated spatial arrangements were known) needed to be prearranged so that they were already fully in place when discovered by the audience. This was accomplished by the familiar practice of alternating full-stage set scenes with narrow "carpenter's scenes." If a scene were played in the shallow space in front of the most downstage drop (i.e., the ones placed in the first row of grooves), the backstage carpenters could, unbeknownst to the audience, put an elaborate historical set scene into place. Filling nearly the entire stage, the set scene would, in turn, be revealed all at once as the downstage wings and drop of the previous scene were removed. At the conclusion of the set scene the process was reversed, and another downstage drop was brought on. As the second carpenter's scene was played, the stagehands would strike the set scene and put yet another in its place. The alternations would continue in similar fashion throughout the performance.

If for no other reason than necessity, Kean adhered to this practice. The banquet scene in his *Macbeth* was clearly a set scene occupying most of the stage, from the *scops* or bards placed in the upstage gallery to the Keans playing downstage of the twin pillars. "The banquet was prepared on the upper half of the stage," the pseudonymous "Cuthbert Bede" recalled in 1889, "under a sloping timber roof, supported on either side by a row of Saxon pillars. At the back of the hall was an opening in the wall, half way up, admitting to a small minstrel's gallery, in which were seven bards with harps . . . Much of the business of the scene was done by the Keans between these pillars and the footlights."[36]

As confirmed by Bede's description, as well as by promptbook and journalistic illustrations, the banquet scene was sufficiently elaborate that it had to be preceded and followed by two carpenter's scenes: a "Glen near the Palace" and the "Distant View of Iona by Moonlight." As their pictorial captions suggest, those two scenes — or vistas, to be more precise — were obviously painted landscapes and so could easily have been placed well downstage of the banquet set.

Set scenes could themselves be enhanced by the use of gauzes and traps. Commonly featured in vision scenes and associated with otherworldly phenomena, gauzes were a staple item in Kean's repertoire of spectacular effects and were used to great effect in the witches' scenes from *Macbeth*. Sudden appearances of isolated figures such as Banquo's ghost or Ariel were achieved through the use of simple traps. In *The Tempest*, Ariel was repeatedly seen to "descend in a ball of fire."[37] This bit of fancy stage business required nothing more than a trap, a ground row, and focused limelight. As Prospero called "approach now my Ariel," a stagehand in the fly gallery shone a beam of red-tinted limelight onto a ground row painted as a bush. Behind the ground row, and thus masked from the audience's view, was an open trap through which Ariel emerged. As Kate Terry, the actress playing the part, was brought up through the trap, the red light was extinguished. The entire sequence thus created the impression that Ariel herself had emerged from within the flame — or, more exotically still — that she had metamorphosed from fire to matter.[38]

Since many of the locations represented in Shakespeare's history plays were themselves grandly expansive, and since the stage of the Princess's Theatre was disappointingly narrow, Kean was compelled to create the perception of unlimited offstage space. He accomplished this by using a "raking flat" set at a 45-degree angle to a backdrop and held in place, not by grooves, but by braces. This arrangement can be seen most clearly in the scene from *Henry VIII* of Wolsey's banquet in "the presence chamber at York Palace." The placement of the banqueting tables parallel to the diagonal raking flat enhances the illusion of interior space and, moreover, assists the spectator in imagining the "indefinite length" of the space that was presumed to lie beyond the proscenium arch.[39]

As Kean's antiquarian spectacles became increasingly lavish, changing the scenery became more and more of a problem. In *Henry VIII*, Kean was compelled to adopt "folding curtains, of magnificent velvet" to mask and muffle the activity of the sceneshifters.[40] During the run of *The Tempest*, only two years later, matters were so out of control that Kean apologized to his audience *in advance* for what he knew would be seemingly interminable delays in the performance while "Scenic Appliances" such as Juno descending in a peacock-drawn carriage were put in place. Beseeching the indulgence of his spectators even before the curtain rose was a shrewd thing to do, since, in the four and a half-hour performance on opening night, more than one hour was taken up by scene changes. "If the hundred and forty operatives cannot get through their work somewhat more quickly," the *Literary Gazette* cautioned, "the production will run a serious risk of meeting an untimely doom. The audience on the first night was willing to make all reasonable allowances, but they could not restrain their impatience between the acts." Nor could the frustrated spectators even converse amongst themselves during the intervals, because the men "working the machinery . . . although unseen, [were] never unheard."[41]

The lighting for Kean's productions was neither as extravagant nor as unmanageable as the scenic displays, and perhaps this is why it was generally admired. Kean really had no choice in the matter, since the lighting instruments available to the mid-Victorian theater were the familiar range of gas lamps that would remain unchanged until the end of the century: footlights, overhead borders or battens, ground rows or "lengths" (short battens placed on the stage floor to illuminate low pieces of scenery such as rocks or ocean waves), sidelights, and striplights ("trees" or vertical stands placed behind wings to illuminate upstage areas).[42] When displayed under a gas lamp, materials such as foil, tin, and armor would be, quite literally, dazzling; when lit by an oil lamp, those same surfaces appeared dull and flat.[43] So when John Ryder appeared as Bolingbroke in the "lists at Gosford Green," he did so as the proverbial knight in shining armor. That is but one example of how stage lighting enhanced the illustration of history.

The main innovation in stage lighting in the mid-nineteenth century was the introduction of limelight. A block of quicklime, when heated by a combined flame of oxygen and hydrogen, would produce a brilliant white light. The hand-operated oxy-hydrogen lamp threw a larger and more powerful beam of light over a greater distance than had ever been possible. The intense light could be used for a general "wash" or flood of white light, while focused limelight (i.e., filtered through a lens, which could itself be colored) functioned as a primitive follow-spot. Kean is generally credited for its first theatrical use in the vision scene from *Henry VIII*, in which a beam of light was focused on the host of angels who visited Queen Katharine as she slept.

So fastidious was Kean in his insistence on authentic stage accessories that his detractors at *Punch* dubbed him not the "Upholder" of Shakespeare, but the "Upholsterer."[44] What follows is a brief look at some of the exceptionally upholstered productions that gave Mr. Punch ample cause to complain.

KING JOHN

Kean's first antiquarian staging of Shakespeare, whose scenery was similar to that used in Macready's revival at Drury Lane a decade earlier, premiered on February 9, 1852, and received a total of only sixty performances. It was a modest production, although we might think otherwise, given that 15,000 square feet of painted scenery was used. In the spring of 1852, it was being presented on only one night a week while Dion Boucicault's cape-and-sword melodrama *The Corsican Brothers* — also starring Kean — was playing to capacity houses five times a week. While the *King John* playbill does not feature the actor-manager's trademark historical essay, it does cite the customary antiquarian authorities — Strutt's *Dresses and Habits of the English People*, Montfauçon's *Monarchie Française*, and even J. R. Planché's *Costume of Shakespeare's Historical Tragedy of "King John"* — that Kean had consulted in getting up the production. This antiquarian staging earned royal approbation, for Victoria commissioned drawings of the production from E. H. Corbould, history painter and tutor to her children. Kean himself recognized the power of antiquarian dramaturgy to animate historical exempla, and thus he wrote in the playbill for *King John* that "history ... combined with pictorial and correct embellishment, tends to promote the educational purposes for which the stage is so pre-eminently adapted." Just as the stage required the example of history for its own "educational purposes," history, in turn, required the "pictorial and correct embellishment" of antiquarian staging.

MACBETH

The first of Kean's productions to be accompanied by a lengthy playbill essay on the production's archaeological and antiquarian veracity, *Macbeth* opened on February 14, 1853, having been performed at Windsor Castle the week before. The play was repeated fifty-four times during the 1852–53 season and thirty-five additional times in the farewell season of 1858–59, when it alternated with *King John* in a retrospective of Kean's productions. To the dismay of many critics, Kean interpolated passages from Thomas Middleton's *The Witch* into Act 3 and retained the convention of having the witches, in Act 2, sing and dance. While critics generally found favor with the production's supernatural scenes, and especially with the appearance of Banquo's ghost, they were less satisfied by the rude Scandinavian costumes that the actor-manager had selected for the Scottish thanes.

In redressing, as it were, Macbeth, Kean was heeding the advice of Charles Hamilton Smith, his principal antiquarian researcher, who advised that "the costume applicable to Scottish chiefs of the Era of Macbeth must be sought in the Norwegian and Saxon dresses of the eleventh century."[45] Dispensing with anachronistic kilts, tartans, and ribboned bonnets (such as he himself had worn when playing Macbeth in the 1840s) and trusting, moreover, in the authority of Xiphilinus and Diodorus Siculus, Kean, committed to historical accuracy in costume, wore the "tunic, mantle, cross-gartering, and ringed byrne of the Danes and Anglo-Saxons," as he explained in the playbill. Mrs. Kean, for her part, wore parti-colored woolens decorated with quasi-runic figures on the authority of Strabo's description of the costume of Boadicea, Queen of the Iceni.

So unrecognizably Scottish was Kean's Macbeth (to say nothing of Ellen Kean's Lady Macbeth with a Victorian silhouette) that J. R. Planché, the godfather of theatrical historicism, featured a tableaux parodying Kean's antiquarian stage dress in *The Camp at the Olympic* (1853). The manager of the Olympic, Alfred Wigan, playing himself in Planché's comedy, located Kean's costume in a precise history and geography, but not the one that had been intended. Facetiously mistaking the Scandinavian tunic for a Roman toga, Wigan declared that this Celtic chieftain of the year "one thousand and fifty-three" looks "more like an antique Rum'un than a Scot."[46] It was an effective lampoon of historical accuracy in the theater: if the audience could not recognize an authentic costume, then what was the point?

HENRY VIII

Kean was on firmer historical ground two years later in this famed revival, in which he initiated the practice of publishing acting editions of Shakespeare to coincide with—indeed, to commemorate—his own revivals at the Princess's. His indulgence of antiquarian splendor in this production met with greater critical approbation, since *Henry*

VIII was itself regarded as inherently spectacular. Since Shakespeare himself wrote banquets, masques, processions, visions, and christenings into the text, Kean could not be blamed for bringing out the play's embedded spectacle and pictorialism. In fact, he was to be praised for his efforts. Capitalizing on the wider scope for visual effects afforded by *Henry VIII*, the actor-manager ventured to display a "Grand Moving Panorama Representing London in the Reign of Henry the Eighth" immediately before the scene of Princess Elizabeth's christening in the Church of the Grey Friars, on the grounds that the Lord Mayor would have "proceed[ed] to the Royal Ceremonial" in a state barge.[47]

One less frequently noted moment in the production — the trial of Queen Katharine — is especially instructive on the fervor with which Kean pursued antiquarian dramaturgy. In staging the trial scene, Kean was guided by historical accounts and biographies of Wolsey. Adopting, then, the conventions of a courtroom, Kean placed Cardinals Wolsey and Campeius, the adjudicators, on a dais upstage center overlooking all those present at the trial. On each side of the court, in the style of a consistory, were placed three banks of long tables reserved for bishops and other church officials. Henry, though sitting on a canopied throne, was nonetheless placed downstage right in the area reserved for plaintiffs. Katharine, as the defendant, entered when called and stood downstage left. Surrounded by her ladies in waiting, she points an accusatory finger at her husband.

For John Philip Kemble, the proceedings of Tudor ecclesiastical trials had no standing in Regency playhouses. Henry Harlow's 1817 painting of John Philip Kemble as Wolsey, Sarah Siddons as Queen Katharine, and Charles Kemble as Henry turns on a set of priorities quite different from those of Charles Kean. The portrait (and, presumably, the staging with which it surely had some relation) does not depict a historical event as meticulously recreated by famous actors but rather memorializes famous actors recreating a moment from Shakespeare's *Henry VIII*, a moment that just happens to be a matter of historical record. The painting is first and foremost a family portrait, and thus the head of the theatrical family, John Philip Kemble, assumes the most prominent position within it. If, to risk an anachronism, Kean's stage composition was the Victorian equivalent of a courtroom sketch, then Kemble's was a photo-op.

The facticity of the trial of Katharine of Aragon was, for John Philip Kemble, irrelevant and thus passed unacknowledged. But for Charles Kean, facticity was all. If the trial scene did not reenact the event as described by contemporary sources, then the scene accomplished nothing. And as J. W. Cole was quick to point out, the historical accuracy of the trial scene in Kean's *Henry VIII* was superior "even in a dramatic sense" to Kemble's version, since, presumably, the replication of a real trial room would only enhance the inherent drama of the narrative itself.[48]

RICHARD II

This chronicle play of monarchy in dereliction had not been a success on the London stage since the Restoration. And after Kean's 1857 revival there would not be another significant West End production until those mounted by Herbert Beerbohm Tree and Frank Benson in the early twentieth century. Anomalous, then, in the production history of *Richard II*, Kean's revival was both a critical and personal success. It ran a total of 111 performances between March 12, 1857, and January 8, 1858, and afforded the actor some of his most flattering press notices. Moreover, its archaeological exactness — from the tournament at Gosford Green in Coventry (complete with real horses) to the entrance of St. Stephen's Chapel — seems to have secured Kean's 1857 election to the Society of Antiquaries. The splendor of the costumes achieved such notoriety that Kean's *Richard II* became the first theatrical performance to be featured in the stereoscope photographs so popular in the middle and late nineteenth century.[49] Even the usually churlish *Literary Gazette* was compelled to admit that the production "leaves nothing to be desired. The costumes are in perfect taste, and [are] as accurate as the architecture and the heraldic blazonry."[50]

HENRY V

Shakespeare's most blatantly patriotic chronicle play was revived only at the end of Kean's tenure at the Princess's Theatre, when it held the stage for a modest eighty-four performances between March 28 and July 9, 1859. No doubt both the deferral of the play and its comparatively abbreviated run had something to do with the public distaste for military action in the years immediately following the Crimean War. Cultural aversions to warfare notwithstanding, *Henry V* had the advantage of being Shakespeare's only English history play that presents a largely, though not entirely, favorable model of monarchy. In Kean's pithy assessment, the play told the story of "England's favorite king." The two sensational moments in the production were the Siege of Harfleur and Henry's triumphal return to London after the victory at Agincourt, both of which featured literally hundreds of extras. In terms of the major themes of this work, the interpolation of Henry's royal entry (see fig. 20) deserves particular attention as it naturally raises questions about antiquarian verism, fidelity to the playwright, and theatrical effectiveness.

Henry's royal progress, as it occurred in 1415, would have taken him to multiple stopping points throughout London where various tableaux of historical, allegorical, and Biblical figures would have been presented to him. Since the theater was incapable of representing the spatial and temporal evolution of the entry, Kean had no choice but to select only the most "prominent" tableaux and place them "into one locality." What we have, then, is the simultaneous display of successive actions. The single "locality" chosen was old London Bridge, and the historical interlude was performed as a set piece between Acts 4 and 5. Royal coats of arms adorned the turrets of the bridge's towers, between which was hung a banner reading *Civitas Regis Justicie* (the city to the King's righteousness). Lodged in a balcony above the entrance to the bridge was a chorus of boys dressed as angels, who showered Henry with gold coins as he passed beneath them. A company of Biblical prophets, dressed in gold, stood on the right, and the twelve kings, martyrs, and confessors of England

Fig. 20. Historical Interlude from Charles Kean's production of *Henry V*, Princess's Theatre, 1859. The Charles Kean Collection, Victoria and Albert Picture Library.

were grouped on the left. A chorus of virgins stood in front of both groups. Pressing in on Henry were yet more singing angels, this time bearing tambourines. The Lord Mayor, aldermen, guards, standard bearers, and the joyous citizens of London filled the intermediary spaces, completing what must have been one of the most stunning images of the Victorian theater.[51]

The historical imprecision of Kean's mise-en-scène is no secret. Indeed, Kean himself readily admitted that the historical accuracy of his *Macbeth* was open to challenge. In the playbill essay for that production, Kean wrote that when he could not find any descriptions of Anglo-Saxon architecture or fashion, he turned to contemporaneous examples from the Danes on the mere presumption that Anglo-Saxon culture was a Danish knockoff.[52] The principle of historical fidelity was sometimes compromised for the sake of pragmatism. In 1858, Kean told George Godwin, his architectural advisor, that he wanted to place the forthcoming production of *King Lear* in the eighth century in order to recycle the scenery painted five years earlier for *Macbeth* and thus to save himself both "time and money."[53] In yet another instance of historical expediency, some of the props for *The Winter's Tale* (1856) — set in Sicily (Magna Grecia) and Bithynia — were used later that season for *A Midsummer Night's Dream* — set in Periclean Athens.[54] And most notorious of all historical inaccuracies were Ellen Kean's petticoats, whose ubiquitous presence proved that neither an Anglo-Saxon Lady Macbeth nor a Grecian Hermione had the strength to override Victorian moral imperatives.

But we should not let error and anachronism blind us to the real and powerful *effect* that staging the past had upon a Victorian audience. The historicizing performance is only a provisional totality or temporary unity because the performance itself is always already a fragment of the even larger history that unfolds beyond the margins of the dramatic text or the stage's proscenium arch. My repeated invocations of the fragment proceed not from poststructural piety but directly from mid-Victorian theatrical criticism. The *Examiner*, for example, described Kean's production of *King John* as a "solid fragment of our English history."[55] The oxymoronic "solid fragment," so readily apparent to the critic of 1852, is emblematic of the very synecdochic process which, I believe, can be claimed for the mid-Victorian theater: that performance was a way of simultaneously seeing history as whole ("solid") and history as part ("fragment"); of seeing the whole *in* and *through* the part.

In his 1857 revival of *Richard II*, the production that secured his election to the Society of Antiquaries — and led to widespread, though unfounded rumors of an imminent knighthood — Kean recreated a medieval interior to represent the bedroom of John of Gaunt. In the notes to his acting edition of the play, Kean explained that "in this scene . . . the walls are covered with paintings, selected from the very beautifully illuminated manuscripts in the British Museum, containing 120 miniature representations of scenes from the legendary lives of St. Edmond and St. Fremond."[56] The *Times* judged that "the second-act opens with a 'room in Ely-House' . . . not to be surpassed as a representation of a baronial interior . . . in archaeological accuracy."[57] And Kean's official biographer, J. W. Cole, contended that the setting and, indeed, the entire performance succeed in bringing "back the past to the eyes of the present, and bewildered the spectators with a mingled sensation of astonishment and admiration . . . The spell was rendered still more potent by the knowledge that we saw passing before us a resuscitation of a memorable passage from our own domestic chronicles."[58]

Despite the predictable hyperbole of commissioned biographies, Cole's interpretation of the *effect* of the performance reiterates a synecdochic process whereby spectators behold a reanimated version of the past and identify with it as their own. First, the historical fragment is put on display ("brought back the past to the eyes of the present"); next, the spectators are absorbed within the historical fragment, an experience of both pleasure and disorientation ("bewildered the spectators with a mingled sense of astonishment and admiration"); and finally, the spectators recognize that the fragment stands for the fullness of their own restored history ("a resuscitation of a memorable passage from our own domestic chronicles"). In his review of the same performance in the *Examiner*, Henry Morley described a similar process of display, absorption, and identification. Morley agreed that the text of *Richard II* "gives reasonable opportunity" for Kean's historical recreations (display).[59] He further attested that the reanimation of history "leave[s] the mind bewildered for a time," but that the spectacle would "ultimately settle on the memory" (absorption) as a "true picture . . . of a past state of society" (identification). The patriotic import of Kean's medievalizing productions was not lost on the critic of the *Illustrated London News*, who went so far in his praise of *Richard II* as to congratulate the audience for bestowing its patronage on Kean's revival of a "worthy drama, developing much of our national history, and comprehending a full political moral of the highest importance."[60]

Even more than his critics, Kean himself recognized the power of antiquarian dramaturgy to animate historical exempla, and thus he wrote in the playbill for *King John* that "history ... combined with pictorial and correct embellishment, tends to promote the educational purposes for which the stage is so pre-eminently adapted." Just as the stage required the example of history for its own "educational purposes," history, in turn, required the "pictorial and correct embellishment" of antiquarian staging. History needed performance because the integration of historical parts in theatrical mise-en-scène enhanced the power of the no-longer-isolated artifact to conjure up the fullness of the past that it betokened. History was "actualized to the senses," one reviewer of *Richard II* noted favorably, "by the picturesque artifacts and numerous stage expedients."[61] Referring to his own 1856 revivals of *The Winter's Tale* and *A Midsummer Night's Dream*, Kean wrote in the playbill for *Richard II* that in

> quitting the far-famed regions of classical antiquity, I now return to the homestead of history, and offer to the public one of those exciting dramas drawn from our own annals, in which our national poet has depicted the fierce and turbulent passions of our ancestors, and thus immortalised events of the deepest importance to every English mind ... In the present stage representation, I have endeavored to produce a true portrait of medieval history ... [The stage settings] are all either actually restored, or represented in conformity with contemporaneous authorities.

In 1857, while watching a private performance of Kean's *Richard II* at Windsor Castle, Queen Victoria experienced just such a bracing shock of recognition — a kind of genealogical flash-forward — when the final scene of Kean's production was set in St. George's Hall, the very room in which the performance itself was taking place. That uncanny historical coincidence — but was it really a coincidence? — was not lost on Victoria, who later reflected in her journal that "it was curious that a Play, in which all my ancestors figured, should just have been performed in St. George's Hall."[62] Though a highly personalized *coup de théâtre*, the reincarnation of Victoria's ancestral figures within her own home nonetheless exemplifies what the performance attempted to provide for its entire audience: an opportunity to review the personages and places of the nation's history and, more important still, to identify with that history.

This was precisely the opportunity afforded by Kean's 1859 revival of *Henry V*. Consider the *Leader*'s account of the final moment from Kean's spectacular staging of Henry's triumphal return to London. As the stage fills with the peals of "a full grown 'triple bob[,]' ... shouts of the commons, ... [and] a beautiful old carol," the victorious monarch appears from the Surrey side of London Bridge.[63] The crowd clears a path for "the monarch and his steed to near the archway," where a shower of gold coins falls about him. The stunning tableau is held for a rapturous moment, with "the limits of theatrical invention being here set for the present." Upon the fall of the drop scene, the audience immediately takes up the cries of stage mob and shouts for Kean to appear from behind the curtain. After "much boisterous invitation," the "dismounted sovereign ... comes simply forward to receive the frenzied applause of the modern Londoners." As the *Leader*'s commentary suggests, the ovation which the "dismounted sovereign" received at the hands of adoring "modern Londoners" was the moment of connection or recognition across time, the space where past and present touched. The clamorous spectators at the Princess's Theatre were, in that ecstatic moment, no less reground in the palpable reality of their own history than was Victoria in St. George's Hall when watching her theatrically resurrected ancestors in *Richard II*.

Charles Kean's revivals of Shakespeare's history plays authorized a model of "Englishness" anchored in the medieval fraternalism of free Englishmen. As Shakespeare's John of Gaunt proclaimed on his deathbed, Englishmen were a "happy breed," dwelling in an island fortress built by Nature herself to protect them from "infection and the hand of war" (2.1.43–44). This prescriptive model of a collective national identity—political superiority fortified by geographic insularity—traced its origins back to the Middle Ages. By going to the theater and seeing the history of England recalled to life, by reliving the moment when English culture and politics *became* English, the

Victorian middle class gained an increased sense of its own cultural rights at the moment when electoral reform was gradually expanding political rights. Indeed, cultural and political rights were inseparable. Shakespeare was the cultural equivalent of the franchise.[64]

Public opinion and majority rule, the animating principles of liberal democracy, were used by Kean himself to explain the attraction of his antiquarian stagings of Shakespeare. In reflecting on the unprecedented success of those productions, Kean concluded in the playbill for *Richard II* that the "course ... [he] adopted is supported by the irresistible force of public opinion, expressed in the suffrages of an overwhelming majority." This intersection of a historicizing dramaturgy, national identity, and political emancipation secures the position of mid-Victorian stagings of Shakespeare as acts of cultural and political "belonging" at a time when Britain's constitutional crisis was far from over.

But through the social inclusivity of performance, the self-indulgence of antiquarian retrospection could be transformed into a public encounter with the materiality of history. That is, the immediacy and community of public performance resurrects and reunites what would otherwise be a scattered array of inarticulate and fragmented facts.

Thus we find the assessment, in a review of Kean's 1857 production of *Richard II*, that "the exactness and the minuteness of the detail, the abundance of antiquarian resources" is subordinated to the performance as a whole, which the reviewer terms the "sentiment and action in every scene." Moreover, the subordination of fragment to whole allows for "this wealth of knowledge" to be "applied ... to the patriotic purpose of illustrating one of our national annuals and great dramatic histories."[65] In so assuming responsibility for historical recovery, performance began to articulate a shared genealogy, drawn from "our national annuals," which was strong enough to cut across the lines segregating the audience into the "gods" of the gallery, the pittites, and the holders of private boxes. Within the communal space of the Victorian playhouse—a space that constrained the hermetic excesses of antiquarianism but still accentuated its vitality—engaging history became a common pursuit with a "patriotic purpose."

This aesthetics of mid-Victorian historiography made the theater a privileged space for the antiquarian reanimation of the medieval past. But in performing a virtual history, Kean's productions not only preserved a reverent nostalgia for an imagined idyllic age, but they also inspired the formation of a shared cultural identity through the experience of collective spectatorship. The historicizing productions of Shakespeare's English chronicle plays in the 1850s constructed a model of Englishness rooted in the medieval past. This normative model of national origins (typically referred to as "our own" history) was then extended to the socially integrated audience of the mid-Victorian theater. The theater was an especially provocative site for the (invented) recovery of Britain's medieval heritage because it was already a self-consciously nationalistic form of social practice and cultural production. Much like the repeated visits of Queen Victoria and her subjects to the Crystal Palace to "wallow in the image of national greatness,"[66] theater going was an informal act of mass public patriotism, a chance to luxuriate in the display of English virtue.

During his tenure as lessee of the Princess's Theatre, Kean's audience was notable for the presence not only of "John Bull" in the gallery, but also of the respectable middle-class family, the aristocracy, and the sovereign herself. Queen Victoria's passion for the theater, although first criticized as a sign of youthful frivolity, became by midcentury the supreme example of the proper regard for "rational amusement." We ought not to underestimate the degree to which Victoria's unabated devotion to the drama precipitated the expansion of the theater-going public.[67] When she took her children to see Kean's productions — when her daughter, the Princess Royal, made sketches of those productions — the aristocracy could no longer hide out at Covent Garden (the London home of Italian opera) on the grounds that the national drama lacked royal patronage. In the antitheatrical camp, bourgeois moralists and low-church pamphleteers — who really did no more than ventriloquize Puritan and Augustinian prejudices — could no longer dismiss the playhouse as a pit of iniquity, seeing that it was good enough for the instruction of the monarch's children. And for the respectable middle-class family, which had by midcentury internalized Charles Lamb's dictum that Shakespeare was better read than performed, the high-profile visits of Victoria to the Princess's Theatre were a potent and unmistakable signal that the mental pleasures of the solitary reader could not compare to the physical delights awaiting the community of spectators. To those unwilling to set foot in a playhouse, Victoria's patronage of Charles Kean sounded a reassuring and encouraging "all clear."[68]

And thus for the first time since the late eighteenth century, a London theater audience achieved something resembling class integration. Even one of Kean's critics was compelled to admit, in the otherwise excoriating poem "The Celebrated Eton Boy," (1859) that at the Princess's Theatre, "Royalty sat in curtained state; / The Noble and the Gentle came (early or late), / The general Public thronged the Pit, / The Clergy of course in Stalls would sit." This diversity of the mid-Victorian theater audience, which continued the process of social cohesion begun at the Great Exhibition of 1851, suggests that theater was important to the development of British nationalism because it offered one of the few opportunities — perhaps the only opportunity — where a variety of citizens could learn together how to be English.

If, as John Ruskin proclaimed, "the Middle Ages are to me the only ages," then the theater was the best, if not the last, hope of Victorian medievalism.[69] For only through the perpetual present of theatrical performance could the medieval past be revived and embraced not as a cold and lifeless corpse, but as a living body with a steady pulse, flashing eyes, and warm touch. The Victorian theater's devotion to the past was not a disastrous form of unrequited love, but an affair to remember.

NOTES

1. *Blackwood's Magazine* 51 (1842): 278.
2. *National Review* (January–April 1856): 412.
3. *Blackwood's Magazine* 51 (1842): 426.

4. *Blackwood's Magazine* 51 (1842): 427. The terms "legitimate" and "illegitimate" refer to whether or not a particular theater was licensed by the Lord Chamberlain for the performance of scripted — i.e., "legitimate" — drama.

5. Charles Dunphy, letter to Charles Kean, March 17, 1857, Folger Y.c. 830 (2), Folger Shakespeare Library, Washington DC.

6. Alice Chandler, *A Dream of Order: The Medieval Ideal in Nineteenth-Century English Literature* (Lincoln: University of Nebraska Press, 1970); and Lee Patterson, *Negotiating the Past: The Historical Understanding of Medieval Literature* (Madison: University of Wisconsin Press, 1987).

7. While all "medievalisms" were collective national myths aimed at accommodating or smoothing over the disruptions wrought by material prosperity, they nonetheless offered competing diagnoses and prescriptions. The major proponents of nineteenth-century medievalism fall into three political camps: Tory neofeudalism (Disraeli and the Young England Movement), Whig liberalism (Macaulay), and Socialism (Morris).

8. "A Few Words in Defense of the Stage Addressed to Its Religious Objectors," *Tallis's Dramatic Magazine* (April 1851): 57.

9. Charles Kean, playbill essay, *Richard II*, Princess's Theatre, London, 1857, Victoria and Albert Museum, London.

10. For Victorian critics, the history of English drama and dramatic literature began with Shakespeare. Medieval dramatic texts fell outside the literary canon since liturgical tropes, morality plays, and the Corpus Christi cycles were regarded as morally bankrupt instruments of a Catholic social order.

11. David Lowenthal, *The Past Is a Foreign Country* (Cambridge: Cambridge University Press, 1985), 96.

12. Hayden White, *Tropics of Discourse* (Baltimore MD: The Johns Hopkins University Press, 1978), 235.

13. I am indebted to Stephen Bann's excellent discussions of Foucault in both *Romanticism and the Rise of History* (1995) and *The Clothing of Clio* (1984).

14. Joseph Strutt, *A Compleat View of the Manners, Customs, Arms, Habits &c of the Inhabitants of England* . . . , 3 vols. (London: T. Jones, 1774), 2:118.

15. Richard Southern, *Changeable Scenery* (London: Faber and Faber, 1952), 357.

16. Sibyl Rosenfeld, *Georgian Scene Painters and Scene Painting* (Cambridge: Cambridge University Press, 1991), 34.

17. Jean Starobinski, *The Invention of Liberty* (Cleveland: World, 1964), 181.

18. See Roy Strong, *And When Did You Last See Your Father?: The Victorian Painter and British History* (London: Thames and Hudson, 1978).

19. The quotes on "proper authority" and "unnecessary deviation" are from

Joseph Strutt, *Sports and Pastimes of the People of England*, ed., William Hone (London: Thomas Tegg and Son, 1838), lxvii. The "original books themselves" are mentioned in Strutt, *Compleat View*, 1:ii.

20. See Richard Leacroft, *The Development of the English Playhouse* (Ithaca NY: Cornell University Press, 1973).

21. Quoted in G. C. D. Odell, *Shakespeare from Betterton to Irving*, 2 vols. (New York: Charles Scribner's Sons, 1920), 2:86.

22. James Boaden, *Memoirs of the Life of John Philip Kemble* . . . , vol. 1 (Philadelphia, 1825), 440.

23. Boaden, *John Philip Kemble*, 1:441–43.

24. Rosenfeld, *Georgian Scene Painters*, 39.

25. William Lawrence, "The Pioneers of Modern Stage Design: William Capon," *The Magazine of Art* (1895): 289–92.

26. See Rosenfeld, *Georgian Scene Painters*, 46.

27. J. R. Planché, *Recollections and Reflections* (London: Sampson, Low, Marston & Co, Ltd, 1872), 37.

28. Stephen Orgel, "'Counterfeit Presentments': Shakespeare's Ekphrasis," in *England and the Continental Renaissance*, eds. Edward Chaney and Peter Mack (Woodbridge: The Boydell Press, 1990), 184.

29. *Theatrical Observer*, March 11, 1823.

30. Planché, *Recollections and Reflections*, 36.

31. J. R. Planché, *Costumes of Shakespeare's Historical Tragedy of "King John"* (London: John Miller, 1823), 2.

32. Planché, *Recollections and Reflections*, 36.

33. Planché, *Recollections and Reflections*, 56

34. Quoted phrases are from Review of *Henry VIII*, *Times*, May 16, 1855.

35. Quoted in Southern, *Changeable Scenery*, 328.

36. Cuthbert Bede [pseud.], "*Macbeth* on Stage," in *Notes and Queries* 8 (1889): 22. In a less appreciative view, *Fraser's Magazine* confessed that the banquet scene "was too much like a booth at an agricultural meeting, with the banners of the county militia hoisted over the Lord-Lieutenant's chair. It was doubtless correct, and as undoubtedly ugly." "Plays and their Providers," *Fraser's Magazine* 48 (September 1853): 348.

37. J. W. Cole, *Life and Theatrical Times of Charles Kean, F.S.A.*, 2 vols. (London: Bentley, 1859), 2:220.

38. Folger promptbook *The Tempest* 11, Folger Shakespeare Library, Washington DC.

39. Review of *Richard II*, *The Builder*, March 21, 1857.

40. *Illustrated London News*, May 19, 1855.
41. *Literary Gazette*, July 4, 1857.
42. See Frederick Penzel, *Theatre Lighting before Electricity* (Middletown CT: Wesleyan University Press, 1978) and Terence Rees, *Theatre Lighting in the Age of Gas* (London: Society for Theatre Research, 1978).
43. See Percy Fitzgerald, *The World behind the Scenes* (London, 1881).
44. In 1853, *Punch* facetiously announced that Charles Kean would shortly perform the title role in a new play, *The Carpenter on the Road to Ruin*. See *Punch* 25 (July–December 1853): 224.
45. Letter to Charles Kean, n.d., bound in Folger Art vol. d3, Folger Shakespeare Library, Washington DC.
46. J. R. Planché, *The Camp at the Olympic* (London, 1853), reprinted in *Plays by James Robinson Planché*, ed. Donald Roy (Cambridge: Cambridge University Press, 1986), 179.
47. The playbill described the panorama as "commencing at the Palace of Bridewell, and passing the Fleet Ditch — Blackfriars — St. Paul's — London Bridge — The Tower — Limehouse — the Celebrated Man-of-War — 'The Great Harry' (copied from the model in the Room of the Admiralty, Somerset House) — the Panorama terminating with the Greenwich Palace, Park, & c." The panorama was copied from a "drawing by Anthony Van Der Wynyrede AD 1543 (Sutherland Collection, Bodleian Library, Oxford)," which, according to Kean, was the "only authority we possess on the subject."
48. Cole, *Life and Theatrical Times of Charles Kean*, 2:145.
49. Six of the original sixteen Laroche stereoscope photographs of *Richard II* are held in the Princess's Theatre production file, Theatre Museum, Victoria and Albert Museum, London.
50. *Literary Gazette*, March 21, 1857.
51. The promptbook lists the following characters and supernumeraries required for the scene: "4 city trumpeters; 2 banner holders, 1 Mace bearer, 1 sword bearer, the Lord Mayor, 2 sheriffs, 6 aldermen, the King's trumpeters, 24 archers, 8 commoners, 7 standard bearers, bodyguards, King Henry, Westmoreland, Erpingham, Gloucester, Huntingdon, Warwick, 12 Glavemen, 20 boys for the chorus, 12 kings, 12 prophets, and 24 girl dancers," Folger promptbook *Henry V* 6, Folger Shakespeare Library, Washington DC.
52. Kean explains the course of his research in the playbill notes.
53. Folger Y.c. 393 (90). On March 5, 1858, Kean wrote Godwin, the editor of *The Builder*, that "for the sake of a date [for *King Lear*] I have fixed the eighth century of the Anglo-Saxons — May I use the chambers and castles of *Macbeth*?

If such an arrangement be admissible, it will save me time and *money*. Send me a line if you please and if you possibly can do so, say 'yes.'"

54. See the stage manager's (George Ellis) notes appended to the promptbook for *A Midsummer Night's Dream*. Folger promptbook, *Mid.* 9, Folger Shakespeare Library, Washington DC.

55. *Examiner*, February 14, 1852.

56. Charles Kean, *Shakespeare's Play of "King Richard II." Arranged for Representation at the Princess's Theatre* . . . (London: John K. Chapman, 1857).

57. *Times*, March 22, 1857.

58. Cole, *Life and Theatrical Times of Charles Kean*, 2:226.

59. Henry Morley, *The Journal of a London Playgoer from 1851 to 1866* (London: George Routledge & Sons, 1866), 166–67.

60. *Illustrated London News*, March 21, 1857.

61. *Illustrated London News*, March 21, 1857.

62. Queen Victoria's Journal, February 5, 1857, Royal Archives, Windsor Castle.

63. *The Leader*, April 2, 1859.

64. And thus it is no coincidence that the year 1832 saw not only the passage of the Great Reform Bill but also the establishment of the Parliamentary Select Committee on Dramatic Literature, chaired by the playwright and MP Edward Bulwer-Lytton. The Select Committee favored abolishing the long-standing monopoly of the two patent theaters in London (Covent Garden and Drury Lane) in order to establish "free trade" in drama — i.e., allowing anyone to produce Shakespeare at any licensed theater in the City of Westminster.

65. *Illustrated London News*, March 21, 1857.

66. David Morse, *High Victorian Culture* (New York: New York University Press, 1993), 33.

67. More quantifiable factors include the rise in London's population, stable ticket prices, railroad expansion, and gaslit streets.

68. On Queen Victoria's patronage of the theater, see Richard Schoch, *Queen Victoria and the Theatre of her Age* (Basingstoke: Palgrave Macmillan, 2004).

69. John Ruskin, *Collected Works*, ed. E. T. Cook and Alexander Wedderburn, 39 vols. (London: George Allen, 1903–12), vol. 37, qtd. in Lowenthal, *Past Is a Foreign Country*, 97.

5 Shops and Subjects

ANDREW BALLANTYNE

INTRODUCTION

This essay makes use of literary texts in order to show some ways in which people identify with their surroundings, or are portrayed by novelists as being interfused with their surroundings. The focus is on buildings, rather than natural surroundings, and for the most part on commercial buildings associated with retail transactions, moving from a shopping street in St. Petersburg, to an old curiosity shop in London, and ending in Paris with a department store and shopping arcades. The first part, however, presents two narratives that establish particularly strongly the more general idea of identifying a person with a place and in effect telling us about the person by actually telling us about the place. This is spelt out in Georges Rodenbach's *Bruges-la-morte*, and in Edgar Allan Poe's "The Fall of the House of Usher." I suggest that Dickens in *The Old Curiosity Shop* and Zola in *Au Bonheur des Dames* also do the same thing, but that is not what they claim to be doing, and given the more "naturalistic" tone of their novels, one might not notice it. By contrast "The Fall of the House of Usher" makes sense only if we identify the condition of the house with the condition of its inhabitants, which Poe explicitly invites us to do.

In *The Old Curiosity Shop* and *Au Bonheur des Dames* the shop in the title is used as the means to explain the character of one of the principal protagonists. The shop is described, and we come to know the proprietor through the description. The two novels make use of the idea of the shop in very different ways, in order to construct very different characters. The first is a failing enterprise that limps along gathering old curios. The other is a dynamic and exhilarating department store that generates a fantastic income. Moreover, it is not just that the characters are different from one another: they seem to operate with entirely different psychologies, as if their authors have completely different conceptions about what it is to be human.

The idea of actual buildings as symptoms of the state of the city's unconscious is taken up with reference to a Parisian arcade — a precursor of the department store — as described by Louis Aragon, who inspired Walter Benjamin to start work on his great enterprise that we know as "The Arcades Project." The line between the conscious and unconscious, real and imaginary, here becomes blurred, and we begin to realize that we do not need to dwell on the pages of fictional works to find buildings that are haunted by the presence of characters who are part of the scene; the relationship between buildings and characters inhabits even the modern world, in advertisements and ephemeral journalism, not just in the worlds created by accomplished novelists.

PERSON AND PLACE

In nineteenth-century literature the "pathetic fallacy" comes into its own. If there is an emotional crisis, then the weather becomes stormy, and the relation between cause and effect is so interfused that one can no longer tell whether it is the storm that has caused the emotional crisis, or the emotional crisis that has caused the storm. There is a sympathy between the characters and their environment that makes them inseparable in the fiction. We are made to feel the inner life of the characters, not so much by being told what they are thinking, as by being told about the details of their environment, which in turn helps to build the mood. The details of a person's dress, of the wallpaper, or the rocking of a boat, can take on dimensions of psychological significance. Where buildings are concerned, perhaps the most explicitly programmatic attempt to fuse the identity of a place with those of its characters is Georges Rodenbach's *Bruges-la-morte* of 1892, which very deliberately suggests that the town is controlling the actions of its inhabitants. Here is his foreword:

> In this study of passion I have tried first and foremost to evoke a city as one of the principal characters. This city, associated as it is with states of the soul, can advise, dissuade and persuade people to act in certain ways.
> Bruges, our elected city, is portrayed, in fact, as almost human ... All those who live there for any time fall under its spell.
> And they are moulded by the city according to its historical sites and its bells.
> What I wish to imply is this: that it is the town which directs all that occurs there; that its urban landscapes are not mere backdrops, settings selected almost haphazardly, but are fundamentally linked to the main action of the novel.
> It is because of this essential connection between these scenes of Bruges and the events described in the story that the photographic reproductions of the former have been inserted in the text — the quays, deserted streets, old dwellings, canals, the *béguinage*, churches, goldsmiths' shops where sacred objects are made, belfries — so that all those who read this work may themselves feel the presence and the influence of the city, experience the contagiousness of the waters, and be conscious of the long shadows of the high towers as they fall across the text.[1]

While parts of this are plainly fanciful, his project is nevertheless clear. The humans and the buildings will be portrayed as inseparable, caught up in one another. The photographs that illustrate his text are in fact quite unsensational, and one might take them to be quite conventionally picturesque, had Rodenbach not indicated that we should be projecting contagion into the waters and feel the gloom of shadows. There are towers in some of the pictures, but we see no shadows actually cast by towers there. Rodenbach invites us to be influenced by the photographs in ways that we certainly would not have been without his direction. Bruges now is a pleasant place, with charming old buildings and a thriving commercial center, but in the nineteenth century it was a dead place. It had been a prosperous medieval port, but it had silted up and was all but abandoned. It was reconnected to the sea not long after Rodenbach was writing, but the modern revival in prosperity followed the development of the port at Zeebrugge for container traffic after 1970. The abandoned qualities of the place had a real foundation, and they were relished by Rodenbach's protagonist, Hugh Viane — a morbidly sensitive widower, obsessively mourning his wife and taking up residence in Bruges in order to find an apt setting for his lugubrious feelings. "Bruges was desperately depressing at this time of day. That was the reason Hugh liked it so much.... [A] sense of the isolation of his existence weighed heavily upon him. From the windows of the funereal dwellings that stretched in spectral fashion along the margins of the canals, with their gable-ends reflected like skeletons of crepe in the waters, a mortuary impression was conveyed that seemed like the foreshadowing of a speedy dissolution."[2]

The rapport between the person and the place is overplayed with a sustained intensity that borders on the comical, and which depends on the reader's general familiarity with the mode of writing that externalizes the character's state of mind in this way. The intensity is unusual, as is the use of photographs to pin the states of mind to actual scenes and real buildings, which can hardly fail to have less of an effect on us, the readers, than they evidently do on the character Hugh Viane. He has a literary relative and precursor in Roderick Usher, although the building that is evoked in the comparison is purely fictional. The time and place of the action that takes place in "The Fall of the House of Usher" (1839) remain unspecified. The connection between the house and its inhabitants, however, is very strong, and the "House of Usher" means both the dwelling of Roderick and Madeline Usher, brother and sister, and their ancestral lineage, which ends when they die without issue. The house is bleak and somber. The description is built over the course of several paragraphs that make clear that the house has no redeeming or inspiring features. The very possibility of hope has been drained from it, and despite its size and the apparent drama of its location, there is nothing of the sublime about it:

> Its principal feature seemed to be that of an excessive antiquity. The discoloration of ages had been great. Minute fungi overspread the whole exterior, hanging in a fine tangled web-work from the eaves. Yet all this was apart from any extraordinary dilapidation. No portion of the masonry had fallen; and there appeared to be a wild inconsistency between its still perfect adaptation of parts, and the crumbling condition of the individual stones. In this there was much that reminded me of the specious totality of old wood-work which has rotted for long years in some neglected vault, with no disturbance from the breath of the external air. Beyond this indication of extensive decay, however, the fabric gave little token of instability. Perhaps the eye of a scrutinising observer might have discovered a barely perceptible fissure, which, extending from the roof of the building in front, made its way down the wall in a zig-zag direction, until it became lost in the sullen waters of the tarn.[3]

The architectural style of the house remains substantially unspecified, but such details as are mentioned are Gothic. The hall has a Gothic arch, and the room in which the narrator meets Usher is very long and lofty, with long, narrow pointed windows that admit "encrimsoned" light, which suggests that they had stained glass in them.[4] The story is, indeed, a classic of the "Gothic horror" genre, which made use of the old idea of Gothic as the product of the ignorance and superstition of the Middle Ages. This would change, at about the time that Poe was writing, under the influence of Pugin's *Contrasts* (1836), which redescribed Gothic as "Christian or pointed architecture" and promoted it as the product of piety and moral integrity, so that it became the preferred style, not only for the new churches that were being built, but also for such monuments as the new Palace of Westminster (1837–60), on which Pugin worked as a consultant. Poe's protagonist is as ruined as his dwelling, his physiognomy unheroic:

> Surely, man had never before so terribly altered, in so brief a period, as had Roderick Usher! . . . A cadaverousness of complexion; an eye large, liquid and luminous beyond comparison; lips somewhat thin and very pallid, but of a surpassingly beautiful curve; a nose of a delicate Hebrew model, but with a breadth of nostril unusual in similar formations; a finely moulded chin, speaking in its want of prominence, of a want of moral energy; hair of a more than web-like softness and tenuity; these features, with an inordinate expansion above the regions of the temple, made up altogether a countenance not easily to be forgotten. And now in the mere exaggeration of the prevailing character of these features, and of the expression they were wont to convey, lay so much of change that I doubted to whom I spoke.[5]

By the end of Poe's tale Usher, now demented, confuses the narrator with Ethelred, the hero of a medievalist romance (the "Mad Trist" of Sir Launcelot Canning). The Ushers, brother and sister, fall to the floor dead, and the narrator flees aghast, escaping the house in time to see it struck by lightning. The house's inner rot somehow catches up with it, now that the family's faltering life force no longer flickers within, and the whole edifice crumbles away and disappears silently beneath the waters of the tarn.[6] Of course there is nothing naturalistic about the story or the events that it portrays. The building's condition and its fate make sense only as the depiction of the state of the other House of Usher, the ancestral line, which seems to have been harboring problems for some generations, but which reaches its melodramatic end that night, by the light of the blood-red moon.

In this story, and in others, Poe reveals his personal fear of being buried alive, and the link between him and Rodenbach is sustained in Rodenbach's tomb in the Pere Lachaise cemetery in Paris. Rodenbach lived from 1855 to 1898, and his tomb is modeled as a huge stone block.

One corner of it is raised as if broken off by pressure from within, and at that corner Rodenbach is presented at full size, climbing out of the tomb, holding up a rose in his right hand. It is a fitting monument: as lurid as his prose. But the main point to be made here is that Poe and Rodenbach both, in an absolutely unequivocal way, present buildings as their way of showing the protagonists' characters and states of mind.

NEVSKY PROSPEKT

It is more common for texts to be more naturalistic, and for the symbolism to slip in quietly to accompany a description that seems to serve some other purpose. There is, for example, a double description of the street Nevsky Prospekt in Nikolai Gogol's story of that name. In architecture the most rigorously geometric forms are always taken to be expressive of rationality, because there seems to be something ideal and high-minded about them, and if sometimes they seem ill-adapted to particular circumstances, then they seem to be overcoming the mediocrity of the muddle that surrounds them. They seem utopian: better than their surroundings, more high-minded and ideal. The circle and the square define areas of rationality and civilization, while the straight line projects order indefinitely toward the horizon, as an axis or a grid. We find geometric figures deployed in various ways in the monumental architecture of all ages, from the pyramids to the Mall in Washington DC, but one of the most extreme examples, which was seen from the outset as an exercise in both reason and geometry, was the setting out of St. Petersburg on flat land, reclaimed from swamps, under the direction of Peter the Great, from 1703 onwards. It was established as "a window to Europe," a place in which to realize Enlightenment ideas, which were seen as advanced and "European," as opposed to traditional and "Russian" like Moscow.[7] St. Petersburg's geometry was laid out across the swamp at the beginning of the eighteenth century, and it became, along with London, Paris, Berlin, and Vienna, one of the great European capital cities of the nineteenth century. The spine of its geometric layout was a long

Fig. 21. Karl Karlovich Bulla, "Nevsky Prospekt, during the coronation of Nicholas II," 1896. Photo, Galitzine Library, St. Petersburg.

straight line, Nevsky Prospekt, a road that ran from the Admiralty and various palaces at one end to the Winter Provisions Market at the other. Gogol made this street the setting for, and virtually the hero of, one of his short stories, describing it in his opening from the point of view of the state's officials (see fig. 21):

> Nothing could be finer than Nevsky Prospekt, at least not in St. Petersburg; it is the be-all and the end-all. It positively gleams and sparkles — it is the jewel of our capital. I know that not one of the city's pallid civil servants would exchange Nevsky Prospekt for all the riches of the world. By this I mean not only the young fellow of twenty-five, sporting splendid moustaches and a remarkably well-cut frock coat, but also the old gentleman with white hairs jutting from his chin, and a pate as smooth as a silver dish — he too is in raptures about Nevsky Prospekt. And as for the ladies! — The ladies are even more enamoured of Nevsky Prospekt. Mind you, who wouldn't be enamoured of it?[8]

Already, something has gone awry. The officials' praise of Nevsky Prospekt might be reasonable, but their praise gives way to a more general enthusiasm, and it is an enthusiasm of an irrational kind, a rapture that made everyone fall in love with Nevsky Prospekt. The street worked a kind of enchantment, which entranced even the efficient and businesslike citizen as he went about his routine (see fig. 22).

> No sooner do you step out onto Nevsky Prospekt than you are swept up in its endless promenade. You may have some pressing business to attend to, but the moment you step onto Nevsky you will forget all your commitments. This is the only place where you will find people going without any special reason, where they are driven by neither mundane need nor by the mercantile interest which pervades all St. Petersburg. The person you meet on Nevsky Prospekt is likely to be less of an egoist than his counterpart on ... other streets, where you can read avarice, cupidity and opportunism on the faces of the passers-by and those flying along in carriages

Fig. 22. Karl Karlovich Bulla, "Religious procession on Nevsky Prospekt," 1907. Photo, Galitzine Library, St. Petersburg.

and droshkys. Nevsky Prospekt is St. Petersburg's main artery. Here the resident of the Petersburgskaya or Vyborgskaya districts, who has not visited his friend in Pesky or by the Moskovsky Gate for some time, may be sure of meeting him. No directory or inquiry bureau will furnish such accurate information as Nevsky Prospekt. Nevsky Prospekt is omnipotent![9]

Gogol saw that this street had everyone in its thrall. It brought people into contact, which made the city work as a social organism, and so in a manner of speaking, Gogol's manner of speaking, the street could be said effectively to run the city. It was omnipotent, but its main attraction was not the rationality expressed by the long straight line, which recommended it to the designers and to the Tsar, but the sociability that somehow had grown up on it. The citizens were drawn to it because they met their friends there.

It provides the one entertainment in a city starved of relaxation. Where else will you see such cleanly-swept pavements, bearing the imprint of so many feet? The muddy, clumsy boot of the retired soldier whose impact seems to splinter the very granite, and the tiny slipper, as light as a puff of smoke, of the young mademoiselle, who turns her pretty head to the sparkling shop windows as a sunflower to the sun, and the clashing sabre of the ambitious ensign, which leaves a distinct scratch on its surface — once on Nevsky they are able to give vent to their particular strength, be it that of brute force or that or subtle weakness. It is like a dizzying magic-lantern show, played out every single day and going through countless variations.[10]

The things that register in this description are not the things that were considered by the designers who laid out the city. The street's grandeur and its European manners are not mentioned at all. The fine architecture might have helped to establish the importance of the street and its fashionability, but once established, it was self-perpetuating and relied more assuredly on the presence of other people than it did on the quality of the architecture. The architectural elements that register most strongly in Gogol's description are the illuminated shop window displays, and the artificial light, gaslight, along with the general bustle of the street; and they play a still stronger role in his conclusion, after the events of the story have unfolded, when the street reappears in a villainous light, no longer the sparkling jewel, but a traitor:

> Oh, have no faith in this Nevsky Prospekt! I always wrap my cloak tighter around me when I walk along it and endeavour not to look at the objects I pass. It is all deception, a dream, not what it seems! ... Try to keep your eyes away from the shop windows: the knick-knacks displayed in them are fine to look at but they are redolent of large sums of money ... Keep your distance, I implore you, from the streetlamps! and hurry past them quickly, as quickly as possible ... everything, not only the streetlamp, exudes deceit. Nevsky Prospekt deceives at all hours of day, but the worst time of all is at night, when darkness spreads over it like a blanket and only the white and beige walls of the buildings can be discerned, when the entire city becomes a bedlam of noise and flashing lights, when myriads of carriages rattle down from the bridges, the postilions cry out and prance on their horses and when the devil himself is abroad, kindling the streetlamps with the sole purpose of showing everything in a false light![11]

This is a remarkable vision of any city to find in writing dating from 1834, and most of the elements seem familiar enough: artificial light, dangerous traffic, and shop windows luring us to part with more than we can afford. It is clearly an image of modernity, even though the technologies have now been superseded — electrified, motorized — and have often been separated so as to make the pedestrian safer if less stimulated. People interact with one another in the street, but also they interact with the street itself, and even the most rationally planned street can take on a demonic aspect. It is not necessarily that one arrives at Nevsky Prospekt in this frame of mind. It is something that can develop once one is there, on account of the various stimuli. It is vital and thriving, but one must be on one's guard.

THE OLD CURIOSITY SHOP

Charles Dickens (1812–70) published *The Old Curiosity Shop* in 1841, his fourth novel—quite an early one. Part of his project was certainly to give an impression of the state of the nation. Times were changing rapidly, and the characters encounter both survivals of tradition and the bracingly inhumane novelty of industrial production. The reader is drawn through the narrative by means of a sentimental story, which is not the focus of attention in this essay, but here is a very quick synopsis.

The Old Curiosity Shop is run by an old man (who will be the center of my attention). He is the character who sets everything in motion, and whose secrets are uncovered as the novel reaches its conclusion, but he is not the main focus of Dickens's attention through most of the narrative. He lives in London with his granddaughter, the saintly Little Nell, who is a child but behaves like an older, wiser person than her grandfather. She looks after him, both at home in the shop and, after it is repossessed by a villainous creditor, on their travels while they wander with no clear direction in search of a place of comfort, which they eventually find. They are surrounded by a mixture of kind people and grotesques in rural and urban environments, eventually returning to London where the plot is resolved, but where Little Nell dies, exhausted by her peregrinations and the extreme demands that have been made on her. Her death caused a sensation when the scene was published, and moved its audiences to tears.

Dickens did not name the particular street where the shop was supposed to be located, but it was within the warren of streets of the City of London, not in the more polished and genteel West End, which is better known to modern visitors. The shop was within walking distance of the river, and Limehouse, where there were wharves and commercial wheeling and dealing, and which was notorious for criminal activity, represented in the novel especially by the character of Mr. Quilp, the demonic creditor. Dickens's novel was published with illustrations, which help to give a concrete impression of what he

Fig. 23. George Cattermole, "The Shop," illustration for Charles Dickens, *The Old Curiosity Shop* (London: 1841).

had in mind. He had two illustrators, but the images with an "architectural" character are by George Cattermole, who gave an effective rendering of the place described in the text. The overall impression in the shop is of clutter (see fig. 23).

There are too many objects in the space, and they have little to do with one another. It is not a designed interior but something assembled from elements that have arrived there haphazardly. Cattermole's frontispiece shows a girl, Nell, and two old men — her grandfather, holding a candle, and relieved to see her, and the person who narrates the opening three chapters of the novel, and who then bids us farewell and disappears completely, leaving the characters "to speak and act for themselves."[12]

Here is that narrator's first impression of the shop. It was: "one of those receptacles for old and curious things which seem to crouch in odd corners of this town, and to hide their musty treasures from the public eye in jealousy and distrust. There were suits of mail standing like ghosts in armour, here and there; fantastic carvings brought from monkish cloisters; rusty weapons of various kinds; distorted figures in china, and wood, and iron, and ivory; tapestry, and strange furniture that might have been designed in dreams."[13]

The oneiric — dream space — is here explicitly conjured into the scene, without unsettling the sense that this could indeed be a real place that Dickens could have known. Cattermole precisely followed the text's instructions, and all the elements that are mentioned can be found there. The rapport between the old man and the place is made absolutely explicit in the text: "The haggard aspect of the little old man was wonderfully suited to the place; he might have groped among old churches, and tombs, and deserted houses, and gathered all the spoils with his own hands. There was nothing in the whole collection but was in keeping with himself; nothing that looked older or more worn than he."[14]

Here Dickens, like Poe, was making use of the sense of the Gothic that pervaded eighteenth-century culture. It is gloomy, damp, and miserable. If Dickens was out of step with Pugin and the artistic vanguard, he was in touch with his popular audience. The narrator contrasts the gloom of the shop with the comfort of his own home:

> A cheerful fire was blazing on the hearth, the lamp burnt brightly, my clock received me with its old familiar welcome; everything was quiet, warm, and cheering, and in happy contrast to the gloom and darkness I had quitted.
>
> I sat down in my easy-chair, and falling back upon its ample cushions, pictured to myself the child in her bed: alone, unwatched, uncared for (save by angels) yet sleeping peacefully. So very young, so spiritual, so slight and fairy-like a creature passing the long dull nights in such an uncongenial place! I could not dismiss it from my thoughts.[15]

And he goes on:

We are so much in the habit of allowing impressions to be made upon us by external objects, which should be produced by reflection alone, but which, without such visible aids, often escape us, that I am not sure I should have been so thoroughly possessed by this one subject, but for the heaps of fantastic things I had seen huddled together in the curiosity-dealer's warehouse. These, crowding on my mind, in connection with the child, and gathering round her, as it were, brought her condition palpably before me. I had her image, without any effort of imagination, surrounded and beset by everything that was foreign to its nature, and farthest removed from the sympathies of her sex and age. If these helps to my fancy had all been wanting, and I had been forced to imagine her in a common chamber, with nothing unusual or uncouth in its appearance, it is very probable that I should have been less impressed with her strange and solitary state. As it was, she seemed to exist in a kind of allegory; and having these shapes about her, claimed my interest so strongly, that (as I have already remarked) I could not dismiss her from my recollections, do what I would.

"It would be a curious speculation," said I, after some restless turns across and across the room, "to imagine her in her future life, holding her solitary way among a crowd of wild grotesque companions; the only pure, fresh, youthful object in the throng."[16]

This of course is a premonition of what is going to happen in the remainder of the novel. An illustration (see fig. 24) at this point shows Nell in bed, surrounded by a clutter of old and bizarre objects — none of them making any sense as furnishings for a child's room.

Note the panel of stained glass hung at the window, the breast-plate of a suit of armor on the floor, and statuary fragments. Remember also that this depiction is not a direct observation of Little Nell asleep in her bed, but a depiction of the reverie of the narrator, who is the inventor of this scene, based on what he has seen in the shop. The word that I would want to reach for in making a description of such a scene would be "surreal," as the juxtaposition is bizarre and seems to

Fig. 24. George Cattermole, "Little Nell Asleep," illustration for Charles Dickens, *The Old Curiosity Shop* (London: 1841).

have no internal logic — and that is what makes it memorable, as the narrator analyzed correctly. The idea of the surreal was not available to Dickens, and nor was psychoanalysis — they were invented later — but he is exploring territory here that connects with both, using everyday language and reflecting on where his imagination is taking him. The reference to the fact that "she seemed to exist in a kind of allegory" might be inviting us to see her story as allegorical, and to unpack its hidden meaning, but it is more likely in this context that Dickens is referring us to allegorical pictures, where the images do not make sense as ordinary events. The best comparison is with Albrecht Durer's famous illustration of Melancholy, where a brooding figure, an angel with wings, is surrounded by various objects — an hour glass, a bell, a magic square of numbers, a balance, solid geometric figures, tools, and instruments, while a rainbow stretches across the sky. Or take the small paintings by Giovanni Bellini — a set of "allegories" that he painted about 1490. We no longer know what they were intended to mean, and if we enjoy them now it is for their dreamy air of the surreal. "All that night," says Dickens's narrator, "waking or in my sleep, the same thoughts recurred, and the same images retained possession of my brain. I had, ever before me, the old dark murky rooms — the gaunt suits of mail with their ghostly silent air — the faces all awry, grinning from wood and stone — the dust, and rust, and worm that lives in wood — and alone in the midst of all this lumber and decay and ugly age, the beautiful child in her gentle slumber, smiling through her light and sunny dreams."[17]

The image of the child growing up innocently, surrounded by the accretions of the past her grandfather has selected, is a powerful one. The claustrophobic space turns out to be evocative of the grandfather's debilitating presence, as it becomes increasingly apparent to the reader what a liability he is to the child. She is held in the grip of his past. Already in the opening chapters the old man has mortgaged the shop to the gargoyle-like Mr. Quilp. We do not at that stage realize quite what is going on, but — and here I should issue a "spoiler warning" if you want to be surprised and delighted by the twists in the plot — what we learn a good deal later is that the old man is gambling everything he has, convinced that with the next game he will recover his fortune and all will be right for the child. In fact, of course what happens is that he sinks ever deeper into debt, and into criminality, but his character is in place from the outset of the novel, and from the start we are given clues about what is going on. He is inescapably in the grip of obsessions that have accumulated in his troubled past, from long before the beginning of the novel, and as the story unwinds, they are brought to light. The objects in his shop have two salient characteristics. First, nothing in the shop is useful. It is a curiosity shop, which sells curios, which are evocative things, but they are bought for their fascination. No one needs a suit of armor these days, and no one needs an odd-shaped figurine, in porcelain, in ivory, or in brass. If the things here have any value at all it is as aids to reflection, to prompt trains of thought that might be pleasant and amusing, but which in this instance would appear to be melancholic and gloomy. The second thing about the shop is that we do not witness any sale being made. The narrator calls its stock a "collection," and it has more of the character of a hoard than a stock of merchandise for sale. Once a thing arrives in the shop, it stays there. In fact, we see no acquisition of new stock for the shop. Everything is already in place, and everything will stay in place. When, early on in the novel, the shop is repossessed by Mr. Quilp, Nell and her grandfather leave the place and start traveling, so they spend only a very short part of the time of the plot actually in the shop. However, as the place is so strongly identified with the grandfather, it seems to be traveling with them, inescapably dogging their steps. The book's title does not seem inappropriate, despite the fact that they leave the old curiosity shop behind. The narrative continues to be branded with the shop's title, in the same way that the old man brings his Gothic attributes with him as his psyche, and blights Nell's various heroic attempts to find an honest niche in a world of travelers and charlatans, a world of indifference, tempered by occasional cruelty and more frequent kindness — and awakened by the pathetic sight of the resolute child and the increasingly burdensome old man. The world on the whole treats Nell fairly and even kindly. It is always her grandfather who does her the most harm, despite the fact that he wants to look after her.

What I want to do here is to point out the similarity between Dickens's use of the old curiosity shop as a concrete image of the old man's soul, with Freud's use of the city of Rome as an image of the psyche. In *Civilization and Its Discontents*, which dates from 1930, long after Dickens's narrative, Freud gave a detailed evocation of Rome as it had grown up over the ages, starting as a fenced settlement on the Palatine hill and overtaken by various waves of building under different regimes in different periods, during the Republic, under the emperors, and all that overlaid with the medieval and modern city. "It is hardly necessary to remark," he said, "that all these remains of ancient Rome are found dovetailed into the jumble of a great metropolis which has grown up in the last few centuries since the renaissance. There is certainly not a little that is ancient still buried in the soil of the city or beneath its modern buildings."[18] There is no difficulty here in seeing a parallel with the jumble of objects from various ages that is chaotically sedimenting in the old curiosity shop. Moreover, what Freud invites us to do is to see this laying down of archaeological strata as a mechanism that is at work in ourselves:

> Now let us, by a flight of imagination, suppose that Rome is not a human habitation but a psychical entity with a similarly long and copious past — an entity, that is to say, in which nothing that has once come into existence will have passed away and all the earlier phases of development continue to exist alongside the latest one. This would mean that in Rome, the palaces of the Caesars, the Septizonium of Septimus Severus would still be rising to their old height on the Palatine, and the castle of S. Angelo would still be carrying on its battlements the beautiful statues, which graced it until the siege by the Goths, and so on. But more than this. In the place occupied by the Palazzo Caffarelli would once more stand — without the Palazzo having to be removed — the Temple of Jupiter Capitolinus, and this not only in its latest shape, as the Romans of the Empire saw it, but also in its earliest one, when it still showed Etruscan forms and was ornamented with terracotta antefixes.[19]

And he continues in this vein at some length, building up an impression of a fantastically dense, impossibly overdeveloped clutter — impossible because the buildings are not only adjacent to one another but also overlaid in the same place.

Freud's image is more sophisticated in its application than was Dickens's, because what Freud wants us to infer is that somewhere buried within us there are primitive instinctual behaviors that do not normally find expression, but which are nevertheless well preserved behind the veneer of modern manners and forms of politeness. We have all learnt Freud's lessons well enough by now not to be surprised to learn that the most sophisticated people can, in the right circumstances, behave like wild animals. The newspapers that sell the most copies are those that are the least high-minded: they appeal to our baser instincts, and collectively, we humans seem to be in their thrall. As educated people, we learn to deal with these things in socially accomplished ways, but if we deal with our instincts only by denying that we have them, then we find ourselves in trouble, under arrest, or in rehab. Freud's vision reaches much further back into our collective past than did Dickens's, but the basic outlook and the basic image is the same. The old man is at one with his jumbled surroundings. They are an image of him. Dickens is explicit about that. There are reasons why he behaves oddly, why he is desperate, why he dotes on his granddaughter, and they lie in his past — the past that is buried around him, and that he carries with him. His wife and her early death, his daughter, his grief, his gambling, are unearthed by degrees before the book reaches its end. He is set on his course by his past, and however benevolent or challenging are his varied circumstances, he is always working out the agonies that are working on him from within as undercurrents that might never have come to the surface had the plot not demanded that they do so for the readers' satisfaction.

AU BONHEUR DES DAMES

Emile Zola (1840–1902) published *Au Bonheur des Dames* in 1883, but the action in the novel is set some time earlier, under the Second Empire (which lasted from 1851 to 1870). It was written as the eleventh of the twenty novels that make up the "Rougon Macquart" cycle. The works in the cycle make use of characters who are more or less closely related to one another, to explore a wide variety of themes across the set, and a number of them are importantly concerned with buildings, notably *Pot-bouille*, which is the story of the comings and goings in an apartment block, and *La curée*, which revolves around the character of a property developer. Zola was particularly well informed about architecture because of his long and close friendship with Frantz Jourdain (1847–1935), whose best-known building would be the Samaritaine department store, which he worked on between

1903 and 1907, well after Zola's novel was written.[20] Zola's information about the workings of a department store came from Au Bon Marché, the first department store, which grew from a smaller establishment and was operating as a department store by about 1850. In 1852, its sales totaled 450,000 francs, but by 1869, they had risen to 21 million.[21] Zola's notebooks include sketched plans working out how the building was organized.

As in *The Old Curiosity Shop*, the reader is drawn through the novel by a sentimental plot, which is not the actual focus of interest. The plot of *Au Bonheur des Dames* sounds very conventional indeed. A young woman, Denise Baudu, comes to Paris from the country, to stay with relatives who have a small tailor's shop. Nearby there is a department store, Au Bonheur des Dames, which is owned by a young widower, Octave Mouret. As the small family business limps along and fails, the department store grows, and Denise finds employment there. Life is not easy for her as the family loyalties pull against the glamour and dash of the department store and its proprietor. However, she can see the commercial sense of the operation and recognizes it as a harbinger of the future. Her good sense eventually attracts Mouret's attention, and they end up marrying one another. Zola presents Denise as the focus of attention, and it is her story that guides us through the narrative, but in the present essay, I am going to be looking at his handling of the character of Mouret.

In *The Old Curiosity Shop*, the old man seems to be encumbered by aspects of his past that he has taken on board and that he carries with him, unhelpfully, wherever he goes. His psychology is antiquarian: built up from the layers of the past, which are more or less unexcavated. This contrasts with the mechanism that is at work in Octave Mouret, who is not only a character of a very different temperament; he seems also to belong to another species, with a different order of psychology. He is young, vigorous, and successful, which of course puts him at some psychological distance from Nell's grandfather, but he too is completely identified with his shop. Here it is, in its first appearance in the novel, on the opening page. Denise Baudu, naïve, twenty years old, has just arrived in Paris with her younger brothers. They are making their way to find their uncle, and enter the Place Gaillon, where the sight of a building takes her breath away: "There's a shop for you!" she says.

> They were at the corner of the Rue de la Michodière and the Rue Neuve-Saint-Augustin, in front of a drapery shop, the windows of which, on that mild, pale October day, were bursting with bright colours. Eight o'clock was striking at the church of Saint-Roch, and the streets were deserted except for early risers, office workers hurrying to their desks and housewives scurrying to the shops. Two shop assistants, standing on a step-ladder outside the door, had just finished hanging up some woollen goods, while in the window in the Rue Neuve-Saint-Augustin another assistant, on hands and knees and with his back turned, was delicately folding a piece of blue silk. The shop, still waiting for its customers — the staff themselves had only just arrived — was buzzing inside like a beehive coming to life.[22]

The building's decoration is extravagant and theatrical, bringing explicit sensuality into play. The location for the building is real, close to the Garnier Opéra, whose architecture this fictional commercial building seems to reflect. The Place Gaillon is a tiny *place* that is more than a crossroads where five streets meet, only because one corner is set back and carries a splendid masonry fountain on the wall. It has become the location for La Fontaine Gaillon (a restaurant owned by Gérard Depardieu, the French film star), and the Théâtre Michodière is in the block where the fictional department store is located. But the building that was actually constructed on that particular corner falls a long way short of the glamour of the department store in the fiction (see fig. 25).

It is an area that underwent great change under the influence of Haussmann at a time that was recent if not still current when the novel was set. Property development under Haussmann's influence was the subject of the second novel in Zola's Rougon-Macquart cycle, *La curée*

Fig. 25. The corner of the Rue de la Michodière and the Rue Neuve-Saint-Augustin, Paris. Photo: Andrew Ballantyne.

(The Kill), where the developers were portrayed as utterly dissolute, morally bankrupt in their pursuit of both money and pleasure. In fact, if we had been reading the series of novels from the beginning, we would already have encountered the proprietor of this shop in the apartment block that is the subject of *Pot-bouille*. "Pot-bouille" could be translated as "stockpot," but with the social connotations it would have in the expression "melting pot," which is now only ever used as an expression to suggest cultural assimilation, but unlike the stockpot, a melting pot was never a piece of ordinary kitchen equipment (it was a crucible). In *Pot-bouille* Mouret is a good-looking bachelor whose amorous pursuits sit alongside his ambitions in business, so his dalliances cease when he finds more serious satisfaction with the widow Hédouin, who owns her own business.[23] Au Bonheur des Dames is that same business some time later, after Mouret has married the widow, and after her death. Mouret has taken the business to new heights. The idea of pleasure and seduction lies at its heart. Going back to Denise:

> This shop, which had suddenly appeared before her, this building that seemed so enormous, brought a lump to her throat and held her rooted to the spot, excited, fascinated, oblivious to everything else. The high plate-glass door, facing the Place Gaillon, reached the mezzanine floor and was surrounded by elaborate decorations covered with gilding. Two allegorical figures, two laughing women with bare breasts thrust forward, were unrolling a scroll bearing the inscription: *The Ladies' Paradise* [Au Bonheur des Dames]. The shop windows stretched along the Rue de la Michodière and the Rue Neuve-Saint-Augustin, where, apart from the corner house, they occupied another four houses which had recently been bought and converted.[24]

The description of the store's allure is continued at some length. There are amazingly inexpensive goods piled up around the main entrance, luring the customers in, and there are elaborate window displays showing a level of luxury and refinement that Denise has never seen before. Denise's uncle's shop, which is called Au Vieil Elbeuf, is in the same street, the Rue de la Michodière, and looks out across the road to these displays, but it is a very different sort of establishment:

> A green signboard, its yellow letters discoloured by the rain: *Au Vieil Elbeuf, drapery and flannels, Baudu (formerly Hauchecorne)*. The house, coated with ancient, mildewed whitewash, looked very squat next to the tall Louis XIV mansions, and had only three front windows; and these windows, square and without shutters, were decorated merely with an iron railing, two crossed bars. But what Denise found most striking among all this bareness, her eyes still full of the bright displays at *Au Bonheur des Dames*, was the shop on the ground floor, crushed by a low ceiling, topped by a very low mezzanine floor, with prison-like, half-moon shaped windows. To the right and left, woodwork of the same colour as the signboard — bottle green, shaded by time with ochre and

Fig. 26. Félix Vallotton (1865–1925), "Le bon marché," 1893, woodcut on velin, 20.2 x 26.1 cm. © 2010 Kunsthaus Zürich. All rights reserved.

pitch — surrounded two deep-set windows, black and dusty, in which the heaped-up goods could hardly be seen. The door, which was ajar, seemed to lead into the dank gloom of a cellar.[25]

The signs of poverty and neglect evident here become more pronounced as the novel progresses, and it is hardly a surprise to learn that the business does not thrive. Denise is embarrassed to find that her family loyalties oblige her to affiliate herself with this failing enterprise, when she can see that it is doomed — as can all the world, except the long-established shopkeepers, who feel that because they have been there for a long time, they have a right to continue to be there into the future, and an ill-founded conviction that their loyal customers will keep them afloat, even if they could buy the goods cheaper and in more pleasant surroundings across the road. I will not dwell on Au Vieil Elbeuf, which is in as desperate a state as the old curiosity shop, but which does not have its evocative power. It is fusty and it is not working, but its hold on the character we care about, Denise, is not so firm as to be inescapable, and she is inevitably drawn into the ambit of the shop across the road that manifestly is working.

Zola continually uses the language of machines in his descriptions of *Au Bonheur des Dames*, and these machines encompass not only the more-or-less mechanical operations of the shop, such as the production and delivery of the goods to be sold there, but also the organization of the people who make the whole operation function (see fig. 26). People are treated like machines, and they connect together to make a machine. The building is part of the machine that comprises also the customers and the operatives. The machine produces desire, and to some extent satisfies desire by turning it into money.

> Denise felt that she was watching a machine working at high pressure; its dynamism seemed to reach the display windows themselves. They were no longer the cold windows she had seen in the morning; now they seemed to be warm and vibrating with the activity within. A crowd was looking at them, groups of women were crushing each other in front of them, a real mob, made brutal by covetousness. And these passions in the street were giving life to the materials: the laces shivered, then dropped again, concealing the depths of the shop with an exciting air of mystery; even the lengths of cloth, thick and square, were breathing, exuding a tempting odour, while the overcoats were throwing back their shoulders still more on the dummies, which were acquiring souls, and the huge velvet coat was billowing out, supple and warm, as if on shoulders of flesh and blood, with a heaving breast and quivering hips. But the furnace-like heat with which the shop was ablaze came above all from the selling, from the bustle at the counters, which could be felt behind the walls. There was the continuous roar of the machine at work, of customers crowding into the departments, dazzled by the merchandise, then propelled towards the cash-desk. And it was all regulated and organized with the remorselessness of a

machine: the vast horde of women were as if caught in the wheels of an inevitable force.[26]

So the idea of the shop as a machine is very clearly established, and notice that already here — this is still the same day as the opening of the book — there is a blurring of boundaries between the mechanical and the living. The living people are of course part of the machine, but equally, the machine itself seems to be alive and to breathe life into the goods. (It need hardly be pointed out that nothing remotely similar is going on across the road at Au Vieil Elbeuf. There is little sign of life there, even among the people who live in the building, and it does not seem to be working as any sort of machine. It seems to be a place where life can just soak away, drawn into the depths of darkness.) Elsewhere it is remarked that the people who run Au Bonheur des Dames are "just machines for exploiting people," and later, Denise, when she is working there, "felt ashamed at being treated like a machine which they were freely examining and joking about."[27] The shop Au Bonheur des Dames is repeatedly said to be a machine. Denise is "inside the machine ... terrified that she would be caught up in its motion"; she is utterly forlorn at feeling herself so insignificant in that huge machine, which would crush her with its calm indifference."[28] The women who work there are all "nothing but cogs, caught up in the workings of the machine, surrendering their personalities."[29] The machine was constructed and is regulated by Mouret, who "breathed fire into his customers with the calm grace of someone operating a machine"; "I must show you my machine in action," he says to a visitor; and it is seen as a "machine for devouring women."[30] It is driven by desire, not only Mouret's desire for women, but also by the women's desires, which are made to compete with one another.

> Upstairs in the mezzanine departments the havoc was the same: furs littered the floor, ready-made clothes were heaped up like the greatcoats of disabled soldiers, the lace and underclothes, unfolded, crumpled, thrown about everywhere, gave the impression that an army of women had undressed there haphazardly in a wave of desire;

while downstairs, in the depths of the shop, the dispatch department, operating at full stretch, was still disgorging the parcels with which it was bursting, and these were being carried away by the delivery vans in a final movement of the overheated machine. But it was in the silk department that the customers had been at their most voracious. There they had made a clean sweep . . . [T]he hall was bare, the whole colossal stock of Paris-Paradise had just been torn to pieces and carried away, as if by a swarm of ravenous locusts.[31]

And among the staff there was a "struggle of appetites, this pressure of one against another, [. . . making] the machine run smoothly, stimulating business and igniting the blaze of success which was astonishing Paris."[32] Mouret is made rich by his machine, but he is consistently presented as debonair and charming rather than avaricious. It seems to be almost incidental that the flow of goods through the shop brings in a flow of money in which he revels and takes delight; the delight seems to be in seeing the flow rather than in acquisition, just as he relishes the steady stream of pretty shopgirls that he beds, without him being presented as overly lustful or predatory. Denise, of course, will change all that, but for the duration of the novel's main action, everything is in a state of emotional flux that corresponds with the motion of goods through the shop—from the factory to the delivery bay, from there to the stock rooms and the shop floor, to be packaged for dispatch and on the way to the homes of the customers. Nothing hangs around. If things aren't moving, then their price is dropped. The important thing is to keep everything in motion, so that the profit margins can be low but the turnover high; the customers find amazing bargains, and Mouret finds himself growing richer every hour.

This way of operating is of course utterly unlike that of Denise's uncle's shop, or the old curiosity shop, where the goods seem to arrive and stay, just as in Freud's image of the unconscious as an ancient Rome in which the old monuments build up and accumulate in a multilayered proximity. Mouret's shop is closely identified with him, but Freud's image does not suit him. He has a past, but it is not what matters about him. He belongs in the present, and has his eye on the future. "All the joy of action, all the gaiety of existence resounded in his words. He repeated that he was a man of his own time. Really, people would have to be deformed, they must have something wrong with their brains and limbs to refuse to work in an age which offered so many possibilities, when the whole century was pressing forward into the future."[33]

The unconscious of which Mouret stands in need is that offered by Gilles Deleuze and Felix Guattari. Their book, *Anti-Oedipus,* opens with a chapter entitled "The Desiring-Machines," in which they set out a description of their "machinic unconscious":

> What a mistake to have ever said *the* id [singular]. Everywhere it is machines — real ones not figurative ones: machines driving other machines, machines being driven by other machines, with all the necessary couplings and connections. An organ-machine is plugged into an energy-source-machine: the one produces a flow that the other interrupts. The breast is a machine that produces milk, and the mouth a machine coupled to it. . . . [H]ence we are all handymen [*bricoleurs*]: each with our little machines. For every organ-machine, an energy-machine: all the time, flows and interruptions.[34]

The ramifications of this idea spread out in many directions in the text, and involve not only the issue of the making of identity, but also politics, economics, physics, and much else besides. The important thing here is that these machines are composed of all sorts of things, conscious and unconscious, that come together to produce our conscious states of mind — our desires, which we then take deliberate steps to satisfy. So various bodily and mental states are produced by the actions of the world on our bodies and minds, and the mind and body are inseparable also. There are machines such as the internal organs that provide the body with the things that it needs — the lungs that supply oxygen for the rest of the body, the heart that distributes it around the body by way of the blood, et cetera. There are machines that incorporate conscious mental operations. If I start to feel hungry, then my body is informing me that I need food, which I experience as a desire for food, and which I take deliberate steps to satisfy. In a more architectural context I might desire warmth, so I might move closer to the fire, or turn up the thermostat, or put on another layer of clothes. Of course eating or making myself warm are more or less mechanical operations, but what is making me feel the desire for food or warmth? These desires are produced by mechanisms in my body, or rather, they're produced by mechanisms that include parts of my body and parts of the world outside, and they're both mechanisms that can go wrong—with anorexia or hypothermia for example, the signals from outside do not get translated in the way that the body needs if it is to function properly. The body is always in touch with its surroundings and is inseparably part of its *milieu*, but the particular machines that are at work are not things that occupy our conscious deliberations. The body deals with a great many things without troubling us for a decision about the action that it will take.

We have seen that Zola continually thinks of the department store as a machine, and identifies his protagonist Mouret with the store. The whole operation is portrayed programmatically as a machinic production of desire, which is well understood by Mouret, and less consciously assimilated by his customers, who know that they want to buy the products but are not altogether clear why they would need them.

One thing that should be mentioned in passing, because it would be a shame to miss it (although a mistake to make too much of it), is that the department store in the novel was founded by the Deleuze family. Zola tells us that it was founded originally in 1822 by the Deleuze brothers, and that Mouret married the elder's daughter Caroline, *née* Deleuze, so there is a coincidence that looks like a premonition of the store's Deleuzean characteristics.[35] It can also be noted (with regret) that Gilles Deleuze does not make reference to this particular book, *Au Bonheur des Dames*, in his writing, although he did write an essay on Zola that discusses another of his novels, *La bête humaine*.[36] In that novel there is a sustained mood of mechanical determinism, as the various characters make unwise decisions that are informed by instinct and desire rather than by reason or even common-sense self-interest. The machines that dominate the story are railway locomotives, which become as animal-like to the people who tend them, while the humans become mechanical as they drive themselves to their destinies. However, the point to make here is that where Dickens was finding his way intuitively toward a view of human nature that was in some respects like Freud's, Zola sets out something quite different, something mechanical, that seems equally like a premonition of Deleuze and Guattari's idea of the machinic unconscious.

PASSAGES

Parisian shops reappear in connection with the unconscious in another remarkable text, dating from 1924, in which Louis Aragon wrote about the Passage de l'Opéra. It was seedy and scheduled for demolition when he wrote about it, but its heyday was during the time when *Au Bonheur des Dames* was set. It was constructed in 1822–23, not far from the Opéra Garnier and the Place Gaillon. It might have survived and been refurbished had it not been in the path of the Boulevard Haussmann, which in 1924 ran up to the Rue Lafitte, two blocks west of the Passage de l'Opéra, but it was steadily progressing so as to connect through to the east, and this *passage* was in its way.[37] Smart department stores — Au Printemps, and the Galeries Lafayette — had opened on the Boulevard Haussmann, while the life drained away from this *passage*, their precursor.[38] The fashionable life had long gone, and Aragon describes the Passage de l'Opéra as a demimonde of twilight and disrepute. It belonged to a dream state, which did not sit easily alongside the rational geometries of the waking world, and it was on the point of being demolished, largely, according to Aragon, on that account:

> The whole fauna of human fantasies, their marine vegetation, drifts and luxuriates in the dimly lit zones of human activity, as though plaiting thick tresses of darkness . . . Wherever the living pursue

particularly ambiguous activities, the inanimate may sometimes assume the reflection of their most secret motives: and thus our cities are peopled with unrecognized sphinxes . . . Henceforth, it is the modern light radiating from the unusual that will rivet his attention.

How oddly this light suffuses the covered arcades which abound in Paris in the vicinity of the main boulevards and which are rather disturbingly named *passages*, as though no one had the right to linger for more than an instant in those sunless corridors . . . The great American passion for city planning, imported into Paris by a prefect of police during the Second Empire and now being applied to the task of redrawing the map of our capital in straight lines, will soon spell the doom of these human aquariums. Although the life that originally quickened them has drained away, they deserve, nevertheless, to be regarded as the secret repositories of several modern myths: it is only today, when the pickaxe menaces them, that they have at last become the true sanctuaries of a cult of the ephemeral, the ghostly landscape of damnable pleasures and professions. Places that were incomprehensible yesterday, and that tomorrow will never know.[39]

It is these neglected parts of the city that contain its secret memories, its unconscious, where the city's "unofficial" culture, bizarre and unrespectable, could flourish away from the glare of reason and commerce. In Aragon's mind these places therefore took on a religious aspect:

Man no longer worships the gods on their heights. Solomon's temple has slid into a world of metaphor where it harbours swallows' nests and corpse-white lizards. The spirit of religions, coming down to dwell in the dust, has abandoned the sacred places. But there are other places which flourish among mankind, places where men go calmly about their mysterious lives and in which a profound religion is very gradually taking shape. These sites are not yet inhabited by a divinity. It is forming there, a new godhead precipitating in these recreations of Ephesus like acid-gnawing metal at the bottom of a glass.

Life itself has summoned into being this poetic deity which thousands will pass blindly by, but which suddenly becomes palpable and terribly haunting for those who have at last caught a confused glimpse of it. It is you, metaphysical entity of places, who lull children to sleep, it is you who people their dreams. These shores of the unknown, sands shivering with anguish or anticipation, are fringed by the very substance of our minds. A single step into the past is enough for me to rediscover this sensation of strangeness which filled me when I was still a creature of pure wonder, in a setting where I first became aware of the presence of a coherence for which I could not account but which sent its roots into my heart.[40]

We can see here a preoccupation with city's unconscious, a desire to analyze it, and also an exposure to Freud's ideas that had been unavailable to Dickens, so there are more references to Greek mythology, and dreaminess is pervasively present. Aragon alludes to unrecognized sphinxes, which must, as a logical consequence, turn us into unrecognized Oedipuses, neglecting to answer their questions. Aragon was one of the founders of the Surrealist movement, along with Philippe Soupault and André Breton. From 1919 they and their friends would meet at a café in the Passage de l'Opéra, which led Walter Benjamin to say that an arcade was the mother of Surrealism.[41] The Surrealists were fascinated by Freud's writings, but Freud for his part famously wanted nothing to do with the Surrealists. This is completely understandable, as Freud was trying to identify his studies with science and medicine, whereas the Surrealists' colorful behavior could only have brought his work into disrepute had their names been linked with his. In Freud's essay on the uncanny, though, he seems to be investigating something very close to the surreal;[42] and no one was more determined than the Surrealists to see the return of the repressed: it is programmatic in their work. "The simplest Surrealist act," Breton said, in the *Second Manifesto of Surrealism*, "consists of dashing down into the street, pistol in hand, and firing blindly, as fast as you can pull the trigger, into the crowd."[43] The whole point is that established categories of sense are violated and destabilized. What is remarkable is that this technique, which on the face of it is so easily dismissed as adolescent nonsense, should have proved to be so memorable and enduring. It has not only influenced the avant-garde art of the twentieth century but is now completely recuperated within the commercial culture to which it once seemed to pose a challenge. It is the norm in advertising, as a way to make products memorable. In architecture, as Anthony Vidler has noticed, the uncanny has a way of erupting "in empty parking lots around abandoned or run-down shopping malls,"[44] and it is undoubtedly this sense of the uncanny that Aragon was trying to capture in his account of the *passage*. The arcades themselves did not start out uncanny. In 1840 a German visitor noted: "Rainshowers annoy me, so I gave one the slip in an arcade. There are a great many of these glass-covered walkways, which often cross through the blocks of buildings and make several branchings, thus affording welcome shortcuts. Here and there they are constructed with great elegance, and in bad weather or after dark, when they are lit up bright as day, they offer promenades—and very popular they are—past rows of glittering shops."[45]

It is after the original activities that took place in them have fled that the arcades take on the state that is aestheticized and valued by Aragon, in just the same way that Heidegger would notice that the ancient Greek temples turned into works of art at the moment when their gods fled.[46] It makes better sense, perhaps, to join Walter Benjamin in seeing the arcades as having been temples in their earlier manifestation, "temples of commodity capital," or a "nave with side chapels," which have become objects of aesthetic interest now that their gods have fled[47]—just as Bruges becomes aesthetically compelling in its deathly condition, and the old curiosity shop's goods become evocative memorabilia once they have been taken out of the circuit of usefulness, or the anticipation of usefulness. That is not the case for the arcades in their heyday, or the fully active department store Au Bonheur des Dames. It was never the most useful of objects that the fashionable crowd sought out in such places, but luxury goods, maybe for low prices, but always things that were not strictly

Shops and Subjects 187

necessary. These stores produced the desire for what they sold, and that sustained them for as long as it lasted—there was actually a Passage du Désir.[48] As a conclusion we might suppose that the arcades introduced, and the department store intensified, the characteristic condition for life in the modern commercial city. Zola's *Au Bonheur des Dames* is absolutely his most optimistic novel. He can see where the future is going, and is excited to be able to do so. Nevertheless, it is in this realist novel that we see the value of the commodities on sale becoming something like a collective hallucination. It is not an absolute change, just an intensification of a process that had been developing for as long as affluence, but for Zola it is the very motor that drives the store, the city, and his novel. Aragon inspired Benjamin to think about the Parisian arcades, and Benjamin came to see them as having cultural significance. They became a preoccupation for him and a frustration for years, as he assembled his archive without being able to settle to giving it form. However, he could see that he had to go beyond what Aragon had been able to say. He sounds as if he wanted to shake Aragon. There is impatience alongside the admiration, knowing that what Aragon glimpsed must be brought out from the realm of dreams and mythology into a waking world of reason and analysis. He proposed to write about the hallucinatory function of architecture, and on dream images that rise up into the waking world.[49] The world of our fictions comes to take over our waking lives.

NOTES

1. Georges Rodenbach, *Bruges-la-morte* (Paris: Flammarion, 1892); all page references are to *Bruges-la-morte*, trans. Thomas Duncan, rev. Terry Hale (London: Atlas, 1993), 15.

2. Rodenbach, *Bruges-la-morte*, 21, 22.

3. Edgar Allan Poe, "The Fall of the House of Usher" (1839). This is available in many editions; all page references are to Edgar Allan Poe, *Selected Writings* (Harmondsworth: Penguin, 1967), 140–41.

4. Poe, "Fall of the House of Usher," 141–42.

5. Poe, "Fall of the House of Usher," 142.

6. Poe, "Fall of the House of Usher," 156–57.

7. Marshall Berman, *All That Is Solid Melts into Air: The Experience of Modernity* (London: Verso, 1983), 176–77.
8. Nikolai Gogol, "Nevsky Prospekt," in *Nikolai Gogol: A Selection*, 2 vols., trans. Christopher English (Moscow: Progress, 1980), 1:114.
9. Gogol, "Nevsky Prospekt," 1:114–15.
10. Gogol, "Nevsky Prospekt," 1:115.
11. Gogol, "Nevsky Prospekt," 1:145–46.
12. Charles Dickens, *The Old Curiosity Shop* (London: 1841). Page references are to the Everyman's Library edition (New York and London: Alfred A. Knopf, 1995), 28.
13. Dickens, *Old Curiosity Shop*, 4–5.
14. Dickens, *Old Curiosity Shop*, 5.
15. Dickens, *Old Curiosity Shop*, 13.
16. Dickens, *Old Curiosity Shop*, 13.
17. Dickens, *Old Curiosity Shop*, 13–14.
18. Sigmund Freud, "Civilization and Its Discontents," in *The Standard Edition of the Complete Psychological Works of Sigmund Freud*, trans. James Strachey, The Penguin Freud Library (Harmondsworth: Penguin, 1991), 12:256–58; also quoted in Andrew Ballantyne, *Architecture Theory* (New York: Continuum, 2005), 119.
19. Qtd. in Ballantyne, *Architecture Theory*, 119.
20. Meredith L. Clausen, *Franz Jourdain and the Samaritaine* (Leiden: Brill, 1987).
21. Gisela Freund, *La photographie du point de vue sociologique* (MS, 85–86), citing Ernest Lavisse, *Histoire de France*; quoted by Walter Benjamin, *Das Passagen-Werk*, ed. Rolf Tiedemann (Frankfurt am Main: Suhrkamp Verlag, 1982); page references are to Walter Benjamin, *The Arcades Project*, trans. Howard Eiland and Kevin McLaughlin (Cambridge MA: Belknap/Harvard University Press, 1999), 46.
22. Emile Zola, *Au Bonheur des Dames* (Paris: Librarie Charpentier, 1883). Page references are to Emile Zola, *The Ladies' Paradise*, trans. Brian Nelson (Oxford: Oxford University Press, 1995), 3.
23. Emile Zola, *La curée* (Paris: Librairie Charpentier, 1872); Emile Zola, *Pot-Bouille* (Paris: Librarie Charpentier, 1882).
24. Zola, *Au Bonheur des Dames*, 4.
25. Zola, *Au Bonheur des Dames*, 7.
26. Zola, *Au Bonheur des Dames*, 16.
27. Zola, *Au Bonheur des Dames*, 18, 114.
28. Zola, *Au Bonheur des Dames*, 49, 155.

29. Zola, *Au Bonheur des Dames*, 134.
30. Zola, *Au Bonheur des Dames*, 254, 67–68, 77.
31. Zola, *Au Bonheur des Dames*, 117.
32. Zola, *Au Bonheur des Dames*, 161.
33. Zola, *Au Bonheur des Dames*, 67.
34. Gilles Deleuze and Félix Guattari, *L'anti-Oedipe* (Paris: Minuit, 1972); page references are to Gilles Deleuze and Félix Guattari, *Anti-Oedipus: Capitalism and Schizophrenia*, trans. R. Hurley, M. Seem, and H. R. Lane (New York: Viking, 1977), 1–2.
35. Zola, *Au Bonheur des Dames*, 22.
36. Gilles Deleuze, "Zola and The Crack-Up," in *Logique du sens* (Paris: Minuit, 1969); page references are to Gilles Deleuze, *The Logic of Sense*, trans. Mark Lester and Charles Stivale (New York: Columbia University Press, 1990) 321–33.
37. Louis Aragon, *Le paysan de Paris* (Paris: Gallimard, 1926); page references are to Louis Aragon, *Paris Peasant*, trans. Simon Watson Taylor (Boston MA: Exact Change, 1994), 14.
38. Susan Buck-Morss, *The Dialectics of Seeing: Walter Benjamin and the Arcades Project* (Cambridge MA: MIT Press, 1989), 83.
39. Aragon, *Le paysan de Paris*, 13–14.
40. Aragon, *Le paysan de Paris*, 12–13.
41. Benjamin, *The Arcades Project*, 82.
42. Sigmund Freud, "The 'Uncanny'" (1919), in *The Standard Edition of the Complete Psychological Works of Sigmund Freud*, trans. James Strachey, The Penguin Freud Library (Harmondsworth: Penguin, 1985), 14:335–76.
43. André Breton, "Second Manifesto of Surrealism" ["Second manifeste du surréalisme"], in *Manifestoes of Surrealism*, trans. Richard Seaver and Helen R. Lane (Ann Arbor: University of Michigan Press, 1969), 125.
44. Anthony Vidler, *The Architectural Uncanny* (Cambridge MA: MIT Press, 1992), 3.
45. Eduard Devrient, *Briefe aus Paris* (Berlin: 1840), 34, qtd. in Benjamin, *The Arcades Project*, 42.
46. Martin Heidegger, "The Origin of the Work of Art" [*Der Ursprung des Kunstwerkes*, 1935], in *Basic Writings, Martin Heidegger*, ed. David Farrell Krell, trans. Albert Hofstadter (London: Routledge, 1993), 168.
47. Benjamin, *The Arcades Project*, 37.
48. Benjamin, *The Arcades Project*, 48.
49. Benjamin, *The Arcades Project*, 908, 909.

6 Pride and Prejudice

Establishing Historical Connections among the Arts

JOSH SILVERS AND TOBY D. OLSEN

INTRODUCTION

Jane Austen's *Pride and Prejudice* was first published on January 28, 1813. Originally titled *First Impressions*, the novel was written between October 1796 and August 1797.[1] It initially was rejected for publication, but after the publication of *Sense and Sensibility* in 1811, Austen revised the manuscript, initially titled *First Impressions*, probably between 1811 and 1812, and renamed it. *Pride and Prejudice* demonstrates a unique ability to transcend time because at its core lies the human search for connections: to people, places, and through establishing a particular niche in the economic sphere. The characters' efforts to make and maintain connections, whether they are young women trying to find and attract marriageable men (Elizabeth Bennet and her sisters), or social climbers attempting to sustain or improve their place in the social sphere (Mr. Collins with Lady de Bourgh), appear as relevant to modern readers as they did to those in the early nineteenth century.

Another subtle device in Austen's novel is the intertwining of architecture and social hierarchy. Because Austen favors the use of dialogue over description to move the story forward, she uses very little symbolism — with the exception of architectural setting, which is used as a means of identifying, depicting, and symbolically representing significant characters in the novel as they seemingly take on the attributes of their homes. In *Pride and Prejudice*, as in England during the early nineteenth century, the country house is a familiar setting for both pleasure and business. The surrounding land could be used for hunting or walking, while the homes' interiors hosted large, formal dinners as well as balls, parties, and receptions for important dignitaries. Far more than merriment and amusement took place during these occasions, however; the act of entertaining was an essential element in aristocratic society because it offered opportunities for entertaining business prospects, fostering economic connections, and impressing fellow members of the aristocracy. Thus, despite its connotation of leisure and relaxation, the country house was both proof of prosperity and necessary to its continuation.

Repeatedly, Austen places her characters in a setting that appropriately reflects just their economic, social, or intellectual conditions; this is especially true in the cases of Lady Catherine de Bourgh and her nephew Fitzwilliam Darcy, with whom Elizabeth Bennet eventually falls in love.[2] Early in the novel, we see how Austen uses the pretentiousness of Rosings, Lady Catherine's country house, to reveal her character. Elizabeth's impression of the older woman upon meeting her at Rosings is captured in this quote: "Lady Catherine was a tall, large woman, with strongly-marked features, which might once have been handsome. Her air was not conciliating, nor was her manner of receiving them such as to make her visitors forget their inferior rank. She was not rendered formidable by silence; but whatever she said was spoken in so authoritative a tone, as marked her self-importance" (chap. 29, para. 11).[3] Although it rapidly becomes clear that a more thorough understanding of Lady Catherine's character will not make Elizabeth more eager to spend time with her, this is not true of everyone in the novel she initially dislikes.

From an early perception of Darcy—that is, "not all his large estate in Derbyshire could then save him from having a most forbidding, disagreeable countenance" (chap. 3, para. 5)—we are provided an opportunity to imagine what Pemberley may be like. But this hint leaves the reader uncertain about Pemberley and, by extension, Darcy. The reader is given additional clues to Darcy's character when we read: "'His pride,' said Miss Lucas, 'does not offend me so much as pride often does, because there is an excuse for it. One cannot wonder that so very fine a young man, with family, fortune, everything in his favour, should think highly of himself. If I may so express it, he has a right to be proud'" (chap. 5, para. 18). However, do these comments give a thorough understanding of Darcy and Pemberley? The reader's desire to know Pemberley so we may better know Darcy is not satisfied until much later in the story (chap. 43).[4]

The joining of architectural setting and characterization lends itself well to screen adaptations of *Pride and Prejudice*. The built environment is used to enhance the films, which are visually stunning, and the story, which is rooted deeply within the stratified society of eighteenth- and nineteenth-century England. Architecture allows the audience a glimpse into an historical world, one that is entrenched in the confines of class, money, and connections as well as the limitations felt by those sheltered—and confined—by the gilded walls of the aristocracy. Austen's novel arguably paints a picture of only the upper echelons of English society. As this is indeed largely true, one can gain a better understanding of how this class of people interacted with one another and with people of a lower rank through an examination of the depictions of important estates in *Pride and Prejudice*. Further, the actual buildings selected for filming offer a unique opportunity to understand the working residences of English countryside society.

Pride and Prejudice has spawned numerous adaptations. Some notable film versions include Fay Weldon's 1979 screenplay for the BBC, featuring Elizabeth Garvie and David Rintoul; a 1995 adaptation by Andrew Davies for the BBC in collaboration with A&E, starring Jennifer Ehle and Colin Firth and directed by Simon Langton; and the most recent 2005 production adapted by Deborah Moggach (assisted by Emma Thompson) and directed by Joe Wright for Working Title Films with Keira Knightley and Matthew Macfadyen in the lead roles.⁵ In addition, there was a 1936 stage version by Helen Jerome, starring Celia Johnson and Hugh Williams, which played at the St. James's Theatre in London; and a 1959 Broadway musical version, *First Impressions* (the original name for *Pride and Prejudice*), starring Polly Bergen, Farley Granger, and Hermione Gingold.

The following discussion is a comparative analysis of two specific country homes that play major roles in *Pride and Prejudice* — Rosings, the residence of Lady Catherine de Bourgh, and Pemberley, the home of Fitzwilliam Darcy — as they are portrayed in Austen's text and the film versions of the 1995 BBC miniseries and the 2005 Working Title Films production. For the 2005 film, the art direction staff chose especially grand-looking structures to showcase the formality, wealth, and strength of the rich people Elizabeth Bennet encounters. The grand houses selected for the immensely popular 1995 miniseries are less visually stunning, but the estates are arguably of a more proper scale and may be more appropriate with regard to the estimated fortunes of the principal characters in Austen's novel.

ROSINGS AS PORTRAYED IN THE 1995 BBC MINISERIES

The house chosen for Rosings in the BBC production is the Belton House in York, which Sir John Brownlow constructed for his family in the late seventeenth century. The architect thought to have been responsible for the initial design is William Winde, although the house also has been attributed to Sir Christopher Wren, while others believe the design to be so similar to Roger Pratt's Clarendon House in London that it could have been the work of any talented draftsman.⁶ The original house was modest compared to today's form, which was remodeled by Sir Jeffrey Wyatville in the early nineteenth century.⁷ Belton House is presently considered a perfect example of a Carolean style country house.⁸

Clearly, this example of English country architecture won over the director, Simon Langton, of the BBC miniseries to be the location for the scenes set at Rosings because Rosings is known as one of the premier houses in Austen's work, although not as symbolically important as Pemberley. Belton House is not only a grand country house; it also has wonderful formal gardens to the front and grand rising parkland to the side.[9] As with most large country estates, the site past the main building envelope is made up of many different gardens that surround the property. Little is left of the original baroque garden that was created by Brownlow, but today it still offers grand formal gardens and an impressive array of sculptures, water features, and parterres.

The grandeur of Rosings is expressed in Austen's text through William Collins (first cousin once removed of Elizabeth Bennet), and the air of Rosings is rendered beautifully in this quote from the novel: "But of all the views which his garden, or which the country or kingdom could boast, none were to be compared with the prospect of Rosings, afforded by an opening in the trees that bordered the park nearly opposite the front of his house. It was a handsome modern building, well situated on rising ground" (chap. 28, para. 4). Further, Mr. Collins's admiring enumeration of the windows in front of the house, and his relation of what the glazing altogether had originally cost Sir Lewis de Bourgh (chap. 29, para. 8), reminds us that one of the functions of the country house was to display a family's inherited wealth and their continued prosperity.

There are five key times the audience sees Rosings in the 1995 BBC version of *Pride and Prejudice*. The first two scenes and the last are helpful in providing to the viewer a better understanding of the character of Lady Catherine de Bourgh, whereas the other two scenes focus much more on Elizabeth Bennet and Mr. Darcy. We initially are introduced to Rosings with Mr. Collins prattling on about the number of windows in the house and their cost as he leads the group of Charlotte (his wife), Elizabeth Bennet, Sir William Lucas (Charlotte's father), and Maria Lucas (a younger sister of Charlotte's) up the wide path to the main entrance of the house (see fig. 27).

Along each side of the path are evenly spaced urns and perfectly trimmed formal shrubbery. Belton House has four floors, one partially below grade and one as part of the roof, and is in the shape of

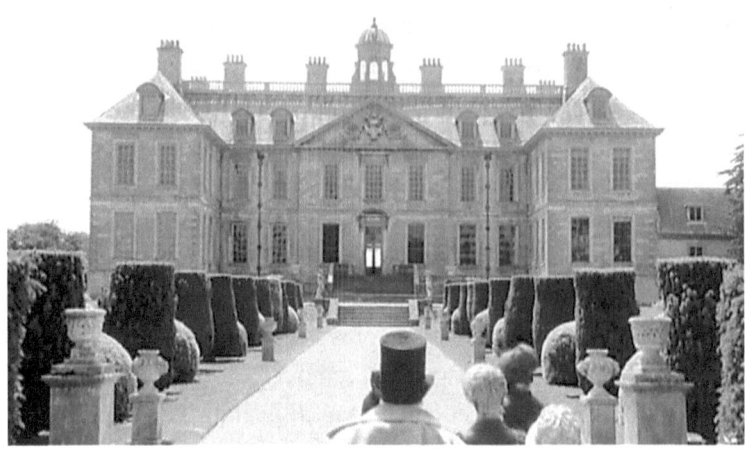

Fig. 27. Belton House, York, exterior as Rosings, *Pride and Prejudice*, BBC miniseries, directed by Simon Langton (UK, 1995).

an H, with the family housed on the west side, the public spaces in the center, and the guest rooms on the east side.[10] The north façade of the house is quite symmetrical because of the use of double room design, which allowed rooms to be back to back and made the home much more compact. The west façade of the building has many windows; interestingly, many of them are false to provide a greater sense of symmetry.

Another visually important aspect of Belton House is the roof, which is embellished with a balustrade, cupola, and many chimneys. The cupola was introduced by the English architect Roger Pratt. Inside the cupola, a staircase gives access to a viewing platform that provides a sweeping vista of the perfect symmetry and avenues of the gardens. Although the view is impressive, its perfection is intimidating because it lacks warmth and natural charm.

In the next scene, we see Mr. Collins and the group uncomfortably crammed onto two stiff-backed couches in front of and to each side of Lady Catherine, who is providing various lessons on life and conduct (see fig. 28). The room is dark green, and Lady Catherine, dressed in black and wearing a lace mantilla, is seated on a large

Fig. 28. Belton House interior as Rosings, *Pride and Prejudice*, BBC miniseries, directed by Simon Langton (UK, 1995).

throne-like chair. Behind her is a huge painting, nearly as large as the wall, in deep, rich colors depicting a pastoral scene with birds of many kinds. Lady Catherine queries Elizabeth about her age and whether her sisters have "come out." Elizabeth seems unfazed by Lady Catherine's questions and answers in her own unaffected, forthright way. Lady Catherine is taken aback, as people rarely contradict her, and she does not take kindly to Elizabeth. The last scene at Rosings is similar to this one in that it is in the same room, and Lady Catherine once again is holding forth on her throne. This time, she is trying to persuade Elizabeth to stay on at Rosings for another month, but Elizabeth will not be cowed by her and says she must return to her home because her father needs her. Lady Catherine's response is "I'm quite put out."

Gerry Scott, the production designer, tells us that she reserved rich, strong colors for where they were needed to make an enormous impact, such as the deep-jade green of Rosings. She felt that if anyone would dare to have a powerful color, it would be Lady Catherine.[11] In other words, the production designer uses the setting to reinforce Austen's characterization of Lady Catherine and her need to maintain

Fig. 29. Burghley House, near Stamford in Lincolnshire, exterior as Rosings, *Pride and Prejudice*, Working Title Films, directed by Joe Wright (USA, 2005).

her superiority through the chair in which she sits, the powerful color of the room, and the pastoral backdrop that frames her actions. Yet despite Lady Catherine's attempts to use displays of wealth to intimidate those around her, Elizabeth, at least, refuses to be cowed.

ROSINGS AS PORTRAYED IN THE 2005
WORKING TITLE FILMS PRODUCTION

In the 2005 adaptation of *Pride and Prejudice* directed by Joe Wright and starring Keira Knightley and Matthew Macfadyen, Wright had an agenda of social realism that was not a concern in Andrew Davies's 1995 BBC adaptation.[12] Because the Wright production places greater emphasis on class differences between characters, the country homes of the aristocrats are more luxurious. In this adaptation, Rosings is represented by Burghley House, which is located near the town of Stamford in Lincolnshire (see fig. 29). It is one of the largest houses of the Elizabethan Age and is much grander than Belton House. Built and designed by William Cecil, Lord High Treasurer to Queen Elizabeth I, between 1555 and 1587, the main part of Burghley House has thirty-five major rooms on the ground and first floors.[13] There are more than eighty lesser rooms and numerous halls and corridors that house an extensive collection of art and the possessions a family of great wealth would collect over the generations.

Fig. 30. Burghley House interior as Rosings, *Pride and Prejudice*, Working Title Films, directed by Joe Wright (USA, 2005).

Burghley House exudes pretentiousness, is grandiose in size, and appears to be an attempt at expressing quintessential aristocratic wealth; these qualities make it highly appropriate for depicting the overpowering personality of its owner in the film, Lady Catherine de Bourgh. The visual presence and scale of Burghley House create a dynamic experience for the viewer. When we first encounter the building, we see Mr. Collins rushing across a large expanse of grass with Charlotte and Elizabeth in tow. He is coaxing them along as he extols the wonders of Rosings, such as the many windows whose cost was in excess of £200,000. When we first behold the four-story structure, with its numerous cupolas and spires on the roof, splendorous late-afternoon sunlight is hitting the upper stories and the lower ones are in shade. Clearly, the dynamic effect produced when one first sees Burghley House is one of the key reasons the home was chosen to stand in for Rosings.

In the following scene, Mr. Collins, Charlotte, and Elizabeth are being ushered into an ornately decorated room with deep, richly colored Persian carpets on the floors and lush historical murals covering all of the visible wall surfaces (see fig. 30). The same warm, late-afternoon sunlight we saw in the exterior scene streams into the room from the left. Lady Catherine and her daughter are seated on an ornately carved, high-back upholstered couch with their backs to the camera and the entering guests. Mr. Collins, Charlotte, and Elizabeth enter and face Lady Catherine, who does not turn her head or acknowledge them until they have bowed and curtsied before her. They remain standing as Lady Catherine asks them various questions and introduces Mr. Darcy and Colonel Fitzwilliam (cousin of Mr. Darcy). The sumptuous setting and Lady Catherine's imperious behavior indicate clearly her expectation of superiority and control.

The following scene takes place the same evening. All of the guests are standing at a huge table with servants in full formal attire prepared to push forward their chairs as they are seated for a formal dinner. Our view is down the length of the table with Lady Catherine at the head and her guests on each side. The table is laden with an overwhelming number of exquisite dishes. The room is dark with deep shadows around the edges; the available light comes from the warm glow of candles in finely wrought candelabras. Austen captures the splendor of Rosings in her novel through the following description of this scene: "The dinner was exceedingly handsome, and there were all the servants, and all the articles of plate which Mr. Collins had promised; and, as he had likewise foretold, he took his seat at the bottom of the table, by her ladyship's desire, and looked as if he felt that life could furnish nothing greater" (chap. 29, para. 14).

The scene proceeds with Lady Catherine asking Elizabeth whether she or her sisters play the pianoforte or draw. Upon learning that Elizabeth and her sisters did not have a governess, Lady Catherine cannot believe it. She continues by asking whether Elizabeth's sisters have "come out" yet and is astonished by Elizabeth's willingness to give her opinion despite her youth. The scene and setting reinforce our perception of Lady Catherine as snobbish, intimidating, and utterly overwhelming in her efforts to maintain control of everything in her purview.

Later in the novel Lady Catherine comes to visit Elizabeth at Longbourne, the home of the Bennets. Accustomed to the enormous size of her own home and parks, she condescendingly remarks to Mrs. Bennet when she arrives, "You have a very small park here madam" (chap.

56, para. 9), and after a brief response of excuse from Mrs. Bennet, adds, "This must be a most inconvenient sitting room for the evening in summer; the windows face full west" (chap. 56, para. 11). Clearly, the ability to craft subtle social barbs that mean far more than what is literally said comes easily for Lady Catherine when addressing those of a lower rank than herself. Her home is of a much grander style, and although our introduction to the exterior and the first interior scene are caught in the late-afternoon sunlight, lending them some warmth, generally the scenes are cinematically portrayed as dark, looming, stuffy, and dead. Again, architecture is used symbolically to represent its owner, and Burghley House was quite an appropriate, suitable, and visually powerful symbol in the 2005 film.

PEMBERLEY AS PORTRAYED IN THE 1995 BBC MINISERIES

Pemberley, perhaps the most symbolically significant building in the entirety of the novel, is the country residence of Mr. Darcy, who at first repulses but eventually attracts Elizabeth Bennet. As Austen clearly tells us early in the novel, Mr. Darcy is very well off, with a large estate in Derbyshire. Describing Pemberley as one of the most exquisite houses of the land is a way of giving concrete form to the wealth and power of Mr. Darcy, as illustrated in the following excerpt, which describes Elizabeth's perceptions when she, along with her aunt and uncle, sees the estate for the first time:

> Elizabeth's mind was too full for conversation, but she saw and admired every remarkable spot and point of view. They gradually ascended for half-a-mile, and then found themselves at the top of a considerable eminence, where the wood ceased, and the eye was instantly caught by Pemberley House, situated on the opposite side of a valley, into which the road with some abruptness wound. It was a large, handsome stone building, standing well on rising ground, and backed by a ridge of high woody hills; and in front, a stream of some natural importance was swelled into greater, but without any artificial appearance. Its banks were neither formal nor falsely

adorned. Elizabeth was delighted. She had never seen a place for which nature had done more, or where natural beauty had been so little counteracted by an awkward taste. They were all of them warm in their admiration; and at that moment, she felt that to be mistress of Pemberley might be something! (chap. 43, para. 3)

The large, sweeping views of the vast parkland around Pemberley and the long, winding approach were indeed a luxury in the days of the Regency period and served as signifiers to the reader of the importance of the owner. Austen is setting the stage in this excerpt from the novel, as has Simon Langton, the director of the 1995 miniseries, in his choice of filming locations.

The 1995 BBC miniseries used two locations for Pemberley (Lyme Park and Sudbury Hall) to portray this extravagant home.[14] Sam Breckman, the location manager, in discussion with the production designer, director, and producer, suggested Pemberley should project the image, "I am powerful, I am wealthy, but I have taste."[15] Lyme Park was their original choice for Pemberley; however, because of a change in the estate's management during filming, the filmmakers were allowed only to film the exterior of Lyme Hall and the gardens. The need to change locations caused continuity and production problems because the production team then had to find interiors that would match in another location. Fortunately, Sudbury Hall was not far from Lyme Park, and they were able to use it for the interior scenes, which are striking.

Lyme Park is an estate and park near Disley, in the county of Cheshire, England, which includes Lyme Hall, an Elizabethan manor house resembling an Italianate palazzo.[16] The estate was given to the first Piers Legh and his wife Margaret by Richard II in 1398 for battle heroics. The Leghs made it their main home in 1514 and through the next few centuries; the rebuilding and renovation of the estate continued with subsequent generations. During the 1720s, the architect Giacomo Leoni altered one of the buildings to make it appear like an Italianate palazzo, and in the nineteenth century, Lewis Wyatt

Fig. 31. Lyme Park, near Disley, exterior as Pemberley, *Pride and Prejudice*, BBC miniseries, directed by Simon Langton (UK, 1995).

renovated every room in the building.[17] Lyme Park has a seventeen-acre Victorian garden that includes a sunken parterre, an Edwardian rose garden, a lake, and a ravine garden. This garden is enclosed by a medieval deer park that covers nearly 1,400 acres of parkland, moorland, and woodland and includes herds of red and fallow deer. By the twentieth century, the upkeep and maintenance of Lyme Park had become difficult for the family, and in 1942 1,400 acres of land was given to the National Trust in order to secure its future.[18]

The vastness of the parkland and gardens was an important indicator of wealth in the time of Austen, as it is today. As described in the novel, the gardens were used quite often for walks around the estate, and the pond was used for some fishing by Mr. Darcy and his guests (chap. 43, para. 60). In the miniseries, our first view of Pemberley is from a luxurious carriage in which Elizabeth and her uncle and aunt, Mr. and Mrs. Gardiner, have been riding on a seemingly endless journey through the parkland surrounding the house. Finally, Pemberley is revealed; our view of the house is framed by the trees and we see the house reflected in the water (see fig. 31).

The party is awestruck by the sight of the house, which is truly magnificent. Lyme Park is a good match for Austen's description of Pemberley, and the director emphasizes the same thing about it that Austen does—namely, its natural beauty. The long shot of the house, as viewed from across the lake as if it were part of an organic landscape, is truly memorable and serves as a way for the director to begin to reshape our view of Mr. Darcy's character.[19]

Sudbury Hall, in Derbyshire, was built during the reign of Charles II and also is a most impressive building. In the 1660s, George Vernon decided to rebuild the old manor house, and as its squire for forty-two years, he did so without the help of an architect. Thus, the structure was a particularly individualistic one. The house continued to be the property of the Vernons until 1967, when it was gifted to the National Trust, which has owned and maintained it since the ninth Lord Vernon passed away. Much of the building has stayed the same since it was built with the exception of the addition of the east wing in 1873, which served as a servant's block. The addition makes the house appear colossal, but does break the classical symmetry of the home.[20] Nonetheless, Sudbury Hall contains many fine rooms that captured the location manager's attention and were featured in the BBC miniseries. The production designer, Gerry Scott, said, "Pemberley had to be in exquisite taste. Though the grandest house [of the film] I wanted it to have a sense of natural elegance. Darcy's family has been secure in its place at the top of the social hierarchy for many generations, so there is no need to impress."[21] She ends by saying that at Sudbury Hall the rooms were already painted in very soft colors—pale pink, oyster, and cream—that were ideal for indicating both wealth and good taste.

Guests entering Sudbury Hall are greeted with the entrance passage's original stone paving, which was laid in the late 1600s. The viewer sees this space more than once in the miniseries. Initially, the viewer sees it as Elizabeth and the Gardiners arrive at Pemberley in their carriage to tour the house. The other time is when they are leaving after having spent an enjoyable evening of dinner, conversation, and listening to Elizabeth and Georgiana, Mr. Darcy's younger sister and ward, play the pianoforte and sing. The latter scene is significant as it shows Mr. Darcy, Georgiana, and Mr. Bingley standing in front of the arched entry passage wishing their guests goodnight. It is a dark night so there is light streaming out from the passage behind them, which is flanked by large iron lamps on standards burning brightly. Mr. Bingley takes Georgiana's arm and escorts her back into the house while Mr. Darcy, with firelight reflecting on his face, gazes at the retreating carriage. It is a poignant moment, and the setting helps to reinforce our perception of Mr. Darcy as one who is deeply in love.

Internally, the splendor of Sudbury Hall can be somewhat overwhelming, especially the Caroline ceilings, which take on the appearance of the baroque: "Already very decorative, they were enhanced with ceiling paintings by Laguerre in the 1690s to make them even more elaborate. Possibly the most impressive ceiling of any house in England, however, is in the Long Gallery, which runs the entire length of the house (over 138 feet). Its plasterwork detail ranges from heads of Emperors, to shells, to palm fronds and seedpods, all created around a central rosette. This work is considered by many to be the most magnificent feature of the house, closely followed by the lavishly decorated staircase balustrade designed by Edward Pearce."[22]

In the BBC miniseries, the viewer has the pleasure of seeing both the Long Gallery and the staircase. After the housekeeper has shown Elizabeth and the Gardiners Mrs. Darcy's (Mr. Darcy's late mother) favorite room and the music room, they arrive at the room containing the elaborately carved staircase. The staircase's oaken balustrade is painted white but looks as if it could be intricately carved stone or plaster. The room has yellow-ochre walls with ornate white trim around the doorways and is brightly lit by sunlight streaming in the tall windows. On an elegantly carved wooden table at the base of the stairs are two miniature pictures, one of Mr. Wickham and the other of Mr. Darcy. The group stops to view the pictures, and, after mentioning that Mr. Wickham has turned out very wild, the housekeeper goes on to extol Mr. Darcy's virtues: "'He is the best landlord, and the best master,' said she, 'that ever lived; not like the wild young

Fig. 32. Sudbury Hall interior as Pemberley, *Pride and Prejudice*, BBC miniseries, directed by Simon Langton (UK, 1995).

men nowadays, who think of nothing but themselves. There is not one of his tenants or servants but will give him a good name. Some people call him proud; but I am sure I never saw anything of it. To my fancy, it is only because he does not rattle away like other young men'" (chap. 43, para. 38). If we are to believe the housekeeper, Mr. Darcy is quite different than Elizabeth has been led to believe by her own experiences with him and by Mr. Wickham's account. What should she believe?

The group then proceeds up the gracious stairs to the opulent Long Gallery. It was unusual to find a long gallery in a house of this time period, but it is an excellent setting in which to exhibit the portraits that date back to the seventeenth century (as well as the fortune it took to purchase such a collection).[23] Portraits were significant to tourists like the members of Elizabeth's group because the people in them spoke to the power of the family and its place in British society.[24] In the miniseries, the housekeeper ushers Elizabeth and the Gardiners down nearly the length of the gallery to a portrait of Mr. Darcy. The Gardiners seem overwhelmed by the splendor of the long room and under their breaths utter numerous expressions of awe (see fig. 32).

Elizabeth appears transfixed by the picture of Mr. Darcy, which makes him seem "comparatively warm and approachable" as he "stands outside Pemberley in the landscape, set against a pool of light and framed by wispy Gainsborough-like branches; [he smiles] at the viewer and [strikes] a casual pose."[25] It is during the tour of Pemberley that we begin to feel a shift taking place in Elizabeth. Has she misjudged Mr. Darcy? This quote from Austen regarding Elizabeth's impression of Pemberley's interior, and by extension Mr. Darcy, is particularly apropos the BBC miniseries: "The rooms were lofty and handsome, and their furniture suitable to the fortune of its proprietor; but Elizabeth saw, with admiration of his taste, that it was neither gaudy nor uselessly fine; with less of splendor, and more real elegance, than the furniture of Rosings" (chap.43, para. 5).

One other space important to our discussion is the music room. Our first view of this room is of Mr. Darcy sitting comfortably, seeming very pleased as he listens to Elizabeth play a beautiful pianoforte and sing while Georgiana assists her. Mr. Gardiner is seated on the couch with Mr. Darcy. As the camera pans the scene, we see Mr. Bingley and Mrs. Gardiner, seated in comfortable cream-colored gold brocade chairs, also listening attentively. Then, after some protestation, Georgiana also plays the pianoforte but declines to sing. While Elizabeth assists Georgiana, Mr. Darcy continues to gaze at Elizabeth with a smile on his face and a look that feels like an embrace. The director has used the music room of Sudbury Hall, which is the epitome of restrained elegance — oyster-colored walls with gold detail and many gilt candelabra casting a warm glow on the guests — to help the viewer better understand Mr. Darcy's character and his feelings for Elizabeth.

Later that night after everyone is in bed, Mr. Darcy walks through the long room with his two hounds. There is no light except for a candle in a holder in his hand and the light cast from the moon. He returns to the music room and stands at the fireplace, a pensive look on his face. He gazes at the place where Elizabeth stood while Georgiana played the pianoforte and sees her in his mind's eye. Because it has been said that Mr. Darcy is sensitive to setting and character, and because we have seen him be affable at Pemberley in the company of friends but unapproachable or forbidding in other venues with those he does not know well, setting is extremely important in helping to reveal his character.[26] Each of the scenes we have described is used by the director to help the viewer gain some insight into who and what Mr. Darcy is. Their color, decoration, furnishings, and lighting help these settings to reinforce Darcy's feelings toward Elizabeth.

PEMBERLEY AS PORTRAYED IN THE 2005
WORKING TITLE FILMS PRODUCTION

Because Austen clearly indicates that Darcy's estate is the physical manifestation of the man who owns it, choosing a real estate to represent Pemberley on film is an important decision. It is believed the director Joe Wright chose the Chatsworth estate because of Chatsworth House itself and its sprawling grounds, complete with famous features.[27] Chatsworth also is where it is thought that Jane Austen first gathered inspiration for the Darcy estate.[28] The original structure on this site was constructed in the mid 1550s by "Bess of Hardwick" and her second husband Sir William Cavendish,[29] and the current building stands in the exact footprint of the original home. The site is of great historical importance because it was where Elizabeth I imprisoned her cousin Mary, Queen of Scots at various times between 1569 and 1573.[30] The house's current façades all were erected during the first two decades of the 1700s along with the great water cascade and Spring House from where the waterway originates. The great Canal Pond, the water feature that Mr. Darcy and Elizabeth Bennet gaze upon from the drawing room at the fictional Pemberley, was created in 1702. Chatsworth House visually feels light, airy, and comfortable, all elements that would appeal to Elizabeth Bennet.

During the Regency period, the Chatsworth gardens were remade into their current configuration by the sixth Duke of Devonshire and the garden designer Joseph Paxton. Paxton also created the extensive greenhouse and conservatory, which covered over three quarters of an acre. The historically accurate gardens and visual follies on the

Fig. 33. Chatsworth House as Pemberley, *Pride and Prejudice*, Working Title Films, directed by Joe Wright (USA, 2005).

property allowed the director an opportunity to create a cinematic experience without the labor of constructing expensive sets. Further, the gardens seem to provide an almost cleansing element for the characters in the film. Indoors the rules of society are constrained, but outdoors it seems people begin to let down their guards and are more natural.

Elizabeth's visit to Pemberley marks the point in the novel where she becomes charmed by Mr. Darcy. Elizabeth and the Gardiners arrive at Pemberley via an open carriage traveling on a road with a row of immense trees on each side. The sun is low in the sky to our left, casting long shadows. Finally, Pemberley is revealed from behind the trees and across a pond of water (see fig. 33). The structure is bathed in warm late-afternoon sunlight; the sky is a crystalline blue with billowy white clouds. We hear the sounds of the horses pulling the carriage and of ducks in the background. When the travelers stop the carriage to take in the magnificence of the sight, Elizabeth is wide-eyed and gives out a stifled laugh, and the Gardiners are awed by what they see. Because the director has introduced us to Pemberley in its best light and from a spectacular angle, we are likewise impressed.

After their initial view of the grounds and Pemberley's exterior, Elizabeth and the Gardiners speak to Mr. Darcy's housekeeper, and she takes them on a tour of the house. In this cinematic version, the director shows Elizabeth falling behind the others and eventually wandering off by herself. The scene begins with an Olympian view from above of the housekeeper leading the group across a black and white checkered marble floor to ascend a grand staircase. Enthralled by the stunning ceiling mural depicting a Biblical story in rich reds, oranges, and blues, Elizabeth begins to trail behind the group. As the camera pans down from the ceiling we see the full extent of the staircase with a balustrade of highly decorative metal tendrils. The enormous door at the head of the staircase has a stone frieze of ornate intertwining vines that frames the doorway. The director has made sure the group and the viewer are duly impressed by their first encounter with the splendor of Pemberley's interior.

In the next scene, we first see Elizabeth gazing at a classical sculpture of a woman clothed in a flowing robe with a shroud around her head and a sheer veil covering her face. She seems quite taken by this statue. She then turns and continues to wander among these life-size sculptures, many of which are nudes of men and women and appear quite sensual. The housekeeper and the Gardiners are in the background talking in muffled tones. The room is of a beautiful creamy marble, and we sense daylight shining down through a skylight, providing exquisite lighting for the sculptures. Finally, Elizabeth arrives at a bust of Mr. Darcy in formal attire. This representation of Mr. Darcy shows him as vulnerable and approachable, with tousled hair and a quiet smile, and the contrast between the prim attire of the bust and the gallery of nudes reflects Darcy's inhibitions and restraint.[31] Elizabeth's subsequent dialogue with the housekeeper marks the catalyst for the shift in her feelings for the master of this great estate. The verbal exchange seems inconsequential, but the subtext is powerful. As Elizabeth admires the bust, Mrs. Gardiner walks up behind her and asks, "Is it a true likeness?" The housekeeper asks, "Does the young lady know Mr. Darcy?" Elizabeth replies, "Only a little." The housekeeper continues, "Don't you think him a handsome man?" Her reply, "Yes. Yes, I dare say." Throughout this exchange Elizabeth admires the bust of Mr. Darcy, and she continues to stare at the sculpture, seemingly mesmerized, as the others move away. Only after some time does she finally pull herself away from it.

One additional scene is worth presenting to provide a better understanding of Mr. Darcy's character. Elizabeth wanders into a beautifully appointed study with a richly inlaid wood desk and bookshelves to the ceiling. She goes to the window and looks out on a formal garden with fountains splashing. Behind her she hears the sound of music coming from the adjacent room. As she peers through the partially open door, she views Georgiana's reflection in a mirror as she plays the pianoforte. A moment later Mr. Darcy arrives; his sister is thrilled to see him, and he sweeps her up in his arms and swings her around. When he stops, he happens to see Elizabeth through the slightly open door, and their eyes momentarily lock. Immediately, Elizabeth bolts, but before she does, it seems clear to the viewer that she now thinks Darcy a loving, caring man with whom she is falling in love. In each of the scenes discussed earlier, the director has used the grounds of the estate, the splendid house, and its contents to help unravel the character of Mr. Darcy.

CONCLUSION

Jane Austen's *Pride and Prejudice* offers her audience an opportunity to escape into a romantic past. However, the novel also carries with it a sense of contemporaneity in that at its core abides the human desire for connection with others. The ability of the novel to be molded, shaped, and readapted has enabled Austen's work to maintain popularity over the past two hundred years. Perhaps this notion of connection carries even more poignancy today in an age of increasing isolation. Connection can be made through architecture, art, film, literature, and theater because they enable the past to breathe once again. Architecture, in the case of *Pride and Prejudice*, serves as a portal to visually, physically, and mentally connect us with the past as it truly was in Austen's time.

Architecture is a tangible link to the past, a functional art that serves as the framework for human action. Austen uses this notion as a means to accentuate the personalities of the primary characters in her novel as well as to reinforce aspects of the society's rigid formal hierarchies. The audience draws meaning from this in conjunction with her text. Likewise, in the analysis of the two film versions of the novel — the 1995 BBC miniseries and the 2005 Working Title Films production — we see how the directors have used physical settings to establish, reinforce, or refine the viewers' understanding of Lady Catherine de Bourgh and Mr. Darcy. Their country homes become an extension of who they are, an expression of their characters. In the case of Mr. Darcy, Pemberley also is where he feels most comfortable being himself. The directors' choice of country houses and the settings in which to present the characters, in addition to how they present them, provide the viewer a clearer insight into the snobbish, domineering personality of Lady Catherine and the true nature of Mr. Darcy, which is generous, kind, and wise.[32]

Clearly, the link between literature, film, and architecture is strong because they work together in both adaptations to tell a compelling story. Interestingly, this interplay between the humanities enables future readers and audiences to reinvent or rediscover the meanings behind Austen's work. The meanings discussed here (social hierarchy, architecture, deep literary study) were not necessarily at the forefront of Austen's mind when she wrote her novel, but readers' ability to connect themselves to the greater world around, whatever and however that may be, is indeed why we study historical fiction and the connections it reveals.

NOTES

1. Deirdre Le Faye, *Jane Austen: The World of Her Novels* (New York: Harry N. Abrams, 2002), 178.

2. Charles McCann, "Setting and Character in *Pride and Prejudice*," *Nineteenth-Century Fiction* 19, no. 1 (1964): 66–75, see 73.

3. All chapter and paragraph designations for Jane Austen's *Pride and Prejudice* are from the Project Gutenberg E-Book, http://www.gutenberg.org/etext/1342. The standard terms of agreement for the E-Book are as follows: "This eBook is for the use of anyone anywhere at no cost and with almost no restrictions

whatsoever. You may copy it, give it away or re-use it under the terms of the Project Gutenberg License included with this eBook or online at www.gutenberg.org. Last Updated: March 12, 2009; Release Date: August 26, 2008 [EBook #1342]."

4. See McCann, "Setting and Character in *Pride and Prejudice*," 66.

5. See Linda V. Troost, "Filming Tourism, Portraying Pemberley," *Eighteenth-Century Fiction* 18, no. 4 (2006): 477–88, 477.

6. Nigel Nicolson, *Great Houses of Britain* (London: Hamlyn Publishing Group, 1965), 149.

7. National Trust, "Belton House," http://www.nationaltrust.org.uk/main/w-vh/w-visits/w-findaplace/w-beltonhouse (accessed November 24, 2007). The National Trust maintains a Web site at http://www.nationaltrust.org.uk.

8. *Academic Dictionaries and Encyclopedias*, "Belton House," http://en.academic.ru/dic.nsf/enwki/100922.

9. See Sue Birtwistle and Susie Conklin, *The Making of Pride and Prejudice*, (London: Penguin Books, 1995), 25.

10. National Trust, "Belton House."

11. See Birtwistle and Conklin, *Making of Pride and Prejudice*, 42.

12. Troost, "Filming Tourism, Portraying Pemberley," 480.

13. Burghley House Preservation Trust Limited, "Burghley," Burghley House official Web site, http://www.burghley.co.uk (accessed November 10, 2007).

14. BBC UK, "Pride and Prejudice," http://www.bbc.co.uk/drama/prideandprejudice (accessed September 29, 2007).

15. Birtwistle and Conklin, *Making of Pride and Prejudice*, 24.

16. National Trust, "Lyme Park," http://www.nationaltrust.org.uk/main/w-vh/w-visits/w-findaplace/w-lymepark (accessed September 10, 2008).

17. National Trust, "Lyme Park."

18. Heritage Trail, "Lyme Park, Cheshire." To view this page, go to the Heritage Trail Web site (http://www.theheritagetrail.co.uk) and type "Lyme Park" in the Property Search field.

19. Troost, "Filming Tourism, Portraying Pemberley," 477–98.

20. Derbyshire UK, "Sudbury Hall," http://www.derbyshireuk.net/sudbury_hall.html (accessed September 18, 2008).

21. Qtd. in Birtwistle and Conklin, *Making of Pride and Prejudice*, 42.

22. Heritage Trail, "Sudbury Hall, Derbyshire." To view this page, go to the Heritage Trail Web site (http://www.theheritagetrail.co.uk) and type "Sudbury Hall" in the Property Search field.

23. On the Long Gallery and portraits, see National Trust, "Sudbury Hall and the National Trust Museum of Childhood," http://www.nationaltrust.org.uk/main/w-vh/w-visits/w-findaplace/w-sudburyhall (accessed November 24, 2007).

24. Adrian Tinniswood, *The Polite Tourist: A History of Country-House Visiting* (London: National Trust, 1998), 42–44.

25. Troost, "Filming Tourism, Portraying Pemberley," 491.

26. McCann, "Setting and Character in *Pride and Prejudice*," 71.

27. See "Filming and Photography" at the Chatsworth House official Web site (http://www.chatsworth.org, accessed July 17, 2010): click on "Media Centre" and then "Filming and Photography."

28. East Midlands Tourism, "Chatsworth — Pride and Prejudice" (accessed September 22, 2008). To access this source, go to the East Midlands Tourism Web site (http://www.discovereastmidlands.us/) and type "Chatsworth — Pride and Prejudice" into the Search Site field.

29. Chatsworth Settlement Trustees, Chatsworth House official Web site, http://www.chatsworth.org (accessed November 10, 2007).

30. "Chatsworth House," Peak District Information Web site (http://www.peakdistrictinformation.com, accessed July 12, 2010). From the "Tourist Attractions" menu, choose "Chatsworth House."

31. Troost, "Filming Tourism, Portraying Pemberley," 494.

32. McCann, "Setting and Character in *Pride and Prejudice*," 70–72.

CONTRIBUTORS

MICHAEL ALEXANDER held the Chair of English Literature at the University of St. Andrews, Scotland, where he is now Emeritus Professor. Among his extensive publications are *Beowulf: A Verse Translation* (1973, 2001), *The Canterbury Tales: The First Fragment* (1996), *The Earliest English Poems* (1966, 1991), and *A History of English Literature* (2000, 2007). Professor Alexander's most recent publication is *Medievalism: The Middle Ages in Modern England* (2007).

ANDREW BALLANTYNE is a professor of architecture at Newcastle University, UK. He has recently chaired the Society of Architectural Historians of Great Britain and is a board member of the European Architectural History Network. He worked as an architect, and then with an archaeologist, Gill Ince, on the survey and analysis of a Byzantine settlement, published as *Paliochora on Kythera* (2007). His interest in history and philosophy has drawn him into wide-ranging studies that include *Tudoresque: Histories of a Popular Architecture* (2011), with Andrew Law; *Deleuze and Guattari for Architects* (2007); *Architecture Theory: A Reader in Philosophy and Culture* (2005); *Architecture as Experience* (2004), with Dana Arnold; *Architectures: Modernism and After* (2003); *What Is Architecture?* (2002); and *Architecture: Landscape and Liberty* (1997). His *Architecture: A Very Short Introduction* (2003) has been translated into many languages, including Chinese and Kurdish, and has been republished with additional illustrations as *Brief Insight: Architecture* (2010).

STEPHEN BANN, a Fellow of the British Academy, is Emeritus Professor of art history at the University of Bristol. Between 2000 and 2004 he served as president of the Comité international d'histoire de l'art, a consortium of thirty-three national committees of art history. Professor Bann's research interests include museum history and theory, historical representation in painting and other visual media, the twentieth-century avant-garde movement, postmodern media and installation art, and land art and landscape theory. His *Parallel Lines: Printmakers, Painters and Photographers in Nineteenth Century France* (2001) was awarded the R. H. Gapper Prize for French Studies in 2002. The interest of Professor Bann's work can be assessed by the publication of *About Stephen Bann* (2006), a collection of essays written by a group of eminent scholars.

IAN CHRISTIE, a Fellow of the British Academy, is a professor of film and media history in the School of History of Art, Film, and Visual Media, Birkbeck College, University of London. He has written extensively on Russian and British cinema, especially on the work of Eisenstein, Powell, and Pressburger, and is also coeditor of the regularly updated *Scorsese on Scorsese*. He has also contributed to many exhibitions, including *Spellbound: Art and Film* (1996) and *Modernism: Designing a New World* (2006). A frequent broadcaster and DVD commentator, he coproduced a series for BBC Television in 1994, *The Last Machine: Early Cinema and the Birth of the Modern World*, presented by Terry Gilliam. In 2006 he was Slade Professor of Fine Art at Cambridge University, with a series of lectures entitled "The Cinema Has Not Yet Been Invented." His book *The Art of Film: John Box and Production Design* (2009) deals in more detail with some of the films discussed in his chapter in the present work, especially *Oliver!* He is currently working on the early history of British cinema and on the challenge of the digital revolution.

RUMIKO HANDA is a professor of architecture and serves as the graduate committee chair of the architecture program at the University of Nebraska–Lincoln. She holds a bachelor of architecture degree from the University of Tokyo and a master of architecture, a master of science in architecture, and a PhD in architecture from the University of Pennsylvania. A licensed architect, she practiced in Tokyo and Philadelphia. She taught at the University of Michigan and Texas Tech

University and was a guest lecturer/critic at a number of institutions in Japan, Ireland, and the United States. She is the recipient of the 2002 National Educator Honor Award from the American Institute of Architecture Students. Professor Handa's research grants and fellowships include those from the Graham Foundation for Advanced Studies in the Fine Arts, the Huntington Library, the Association for Asian Studies, and the Newberry Library Consortium. Her writings have appeared in the *Encyclopedia of Twentieth-Century Architecture*, *Architectura: Elements of Architectural Style*, and *Transportable Environments: Theory, Context, Design and Technology*; the journals of the Society of Architectural Historians and the Design Research Society; and in *Nexus: Architecture and Mathematics*, as well as elsewhere.

TOBY D. OLSEN is a graduate of the University of Nebraska–Lincoln's College of Architecture where he received a bachelor of science degree in design and architectural studies with a minor in community and regional planning in 2007 and his master of architecture degree in 2009. During his undergraduate studies at UNL Toby participated in the UNL Chancellor's Leadership Class, the University Honors Program, Phi Delta Theta Fraternity, and Phi Sigma Pi Honor Society; received an Ak-Sar-Ben Ike Friedman Student Leadership Award; was a Peter Kiewit Distinguished Scholar; and studied at the Dublin Institute of Technology in Ireland. During his graduate studies, Mr. Olsen participated in a National AIA Regional Urban Design Assistance Team in New York City, completed his thesis, entitled "Phasic Edge," and received the Harry F. Cunningham Bronze Medal for excellence in academic and design achievement. In 2009 he participated in a National AIA Sustainable Design Assistance Team in Orange, Massachusetts. He currently works at OPN Architects in Cedar Rapids, Iowa.

JAMES POTTER is a former Douglass Professor (1994–98, 2000–2004) and has served as chair of the board of directors for the Environmental Design Research Association (1991–92) and as the chair of the University of Nebraska–Lincoln's Department of Architecture (1986–90). He is a former Fulbright Senior Scholar (1983–84) and is the recipient of a 1974 Progressive Architecture Award. He is involved in environmental design research, presenting numerous papers at professional conferences, including the Environmental Design Research Association and the International Association of Person-environment Studies, and publishing a variety of research in scholarly journals, including the *Journal of Architecture & Planning Research* and *Environment & Behavior*. His basic research goal has been to understand the impact of rapid development on people's quality of life. More recently, he has turned his interest to the relationship between buildings and other humanistic endeavors, such as literature, film, theater, and art. He and Rumiko Handa are developing an interdisciplinary, multimedia, relational database that focuses on architecture appearing in historical novels, films, plays, and paintings. The database is available to interested teachers and students worldwide at http://aith.unl.edu.

RICHARD SCHOCH is a professor of the history of culture and the director of the Graduate School for Humanities and Social Sciences at Queen Mary, University of London. His publications include *Shakespeare's Victorian Stage: Performing History in the Theatre of Charles Kean* (1998) and *Not Shakespeare: Bardolatry and Burlesque in the Nineteenth Century* (2002). Professor Schoch is the recipient of fellowships from the American Society for Theatre Research, the Folger Shakespeare Library, the University of Texas at Austin's Harry Ransom Humanities Research Center, the Leverhulme Trust, the Stanford Humanities Center, and the Whiting Foundation. His books have been short-listed for the Theatre Book Prize and the Barnard Hewitt Award.

JOSH SILVERS is an architect working at Miller & Associates in Kearney, Nebraska. He has also worked in Tianjin, China, for an international architecture and planning firm. Mr. Silvers graduated from the University of Nebraska–Lincoln in 2009 with a master of architecture degree.

www.ingramcontent.com/pod-product-compliance
Lightning Source LLC
Chambersburg PA
CBHW030342240426
43661CB00052B/1717